Contents

40005728

Preface

The purpose of this Handbook continues to be the presentation of an elementary statement of the law of contract. It is intended particularly for those who are preparing for professional examinations in banking, accountancy, insurance, etc., 'A' level candidates and first year law students may find the work useful as a pocket summary of contract law.

This eighth edition deals with several important areas of change and development in the law of contract. In particular, the effects of the Law of Property (Miscellaneous Provisions) Act 1989, are far reaching with regard to the need for writing and other formalities in the formation of contracts. Other areas which have been revised in this edition include illegality, damages, frustration and consideration.

My thanks are due to my daughter, Alison, who did a great deal of secretarial and the editorial work in the preparation of the original manuscript. In doing this work she cheerfully gave much of her time when she really had little to spare. I am grateful also to Andrew Harvey who, as Reviser, did the responsible work of updating.

Extracts from the Unfair Contract Terms Act 1977 are reproduced in Appendix 2 by kind permission of Her Majesty's Stationery Office.

I should like to thank David Palfreman who supplied Appendix 1 on examination technique.

1992   WTM

Table of cases

Table of statutes

To Bridget, William, Katie and Thomas

1
Introduction

1. Simple contracts

A contract is made where parties have reached agreement, or where they are deemed to have reached agreement, and the law recognizes rights and obligations arising from the agreement. Almost all contracts are simple contracts, as distinguished from specialty contracts, i.e. contracts made under seal. Any general study of the law of contract must be concerned almost entirely with simple contracts.

2. Essential elements

There are three fundamental elements in any simple contract. They are:

(a) *Agreement*. The parties must have reached, or be deemed to have reached, agreement.
(b) *Intention*. The parties must have intended, or be deemed to have intended, to create legal relations.
(c) *Consideration*. According to the terms of the agreement, some advantage moves from each party to the other. The giving of mutual advantages by the parties is the essence of a bargain. Any advantage or benefit moving from one party to another is known as consideration.

In any transaction where one of these elements is missing there is no contract.

3. Manner of agreement

An agreement may be made in any manner whatsoever, provided the parties are in communication. An agreement may be made:

(a) in writing, or

(b) by word of mouth, or

(c) by inference from the conduct of the parties and the circumstances of the case, or

(d) by any combination of the above modes.

4. The test of agreement

Adequate tests are necessary to enable the court to decide cases involving dispute:

(a) as to whether agreement was reached at all, or

(b) as to the extent of the agreement, i.e. the terms of the agreement.

In both issues the intention of the parties is paramount. The function of contract law is, largely, to develop principles which may be used towards the settlement of such disputes.

It is very important to understand that the question of terms of contract does not arise unless and until it is established that agreement has been reached.

5. Intention and agreement

The intention of the parties is gathered from the express terms of contract. Also, where necessary, the conduct of the parties is taken into account, for much can be inferred from conduct. The court is not concerned with the inward mental intent of the parties, but rather with what a reasonable man would say was the intention of the parties, having regard to all the circumstances. Where it is necessary to give a contract business efficacy, the court will imply terms to give effect to the presumed intentions of the parties. The presumed intention may or may not be the same as the actual intention. It must follow that when we speak of 'agreement' in contract, we include the notional agreement which the parties may be deemed to have reached.

It has been held by the House of Lords that in construing the written terms of a contract, evidence of the preceding negotiations is not admissible, nor is evidence of the parties' intentions during negotiations: *Prenn* v. *Simmonds* (1971).

6. Offer and acceptance

In order to discover whether agreement was reached between

the parties, it is usual to analyse the negotiations into offer and acceptance. Many negotiations are too complicated to lend themselves to an easy analysis of this kind, but the courts will try to discover whether, at any time, one party can be said to have accepted the firm offer of the other.

Sometimes analysis will show a unilateral contract, i.e. that the offeror has included in his offer an express provision that performance by the offeree in a manner stipulated in the offer will conclude a binding contract. A common example would be the offer to pay a reward to the finder of a lost valuable.

7. Rights and obligations

Where parties have made a binding contract, they have created rights and obligations between themselves. The contractual rights and obligations are correlative, e.g. X agrees with Y to sell his car for £500 to Y. In this example, the following rights and obligations have been created:

(a) X is under an obligation to deliver his car to Y: Y has a correlative right to receive the car.

(b) Y is under an obligation to pay £500 to X: X has a correlative right to receive the £500.

8. Breach of contract

Where a party neglects or refuses to honour a contractual obligation, there is a breach of contract. A breach by one party causes a right of action to accrue to the other party.

The usual remedy for breach of contract is damages, i.e. the award of a sum of money to put the aggrieved party in the position he would have enjoyed had the contract not been broken. The sum is paid, of course, by the contract-breaker following the award of the court. In certain special circumstances, the court may order the contract-breaker to carry out his contractual promise specifically. This is known as the equitable remedy of specific performance. Specific performance is never awarded where damages will suffice.

9. Form

In English law there is no general requirement of form in the making of a valid contract. By statute, however, certain specified kinds of contract must have been made in writing or, in some cases, be evidenced by writing. Where the parties have agreed on written terms of contract it is less likely that a dispute will occur. The written terms will also be useful where one of the parties wishes to claim against the other for breach of contract. Finally, form is sometimes required in order to safeguard the position of a vulnerable party, for instance the hirer in a hire-purchase agreement.

(a) *Contracts under seal.* The most formal contract known to English law was the contract under seal. Contracts under seal are sometimes known as specialties. Any contract which was not made under seal is classed as a simple contract. The vast majority of contracts are simple contracts, whether made in writing or not.

By the Law of Property (Miscellaneous Provisions) Act 1989, s. 1(1)(b), any rule of law which requires a seal for the valid execution of an instrument as a deed by an individual is abolished. By the Companies Act 1989, s. 130(1), there is no longer the requirement of sealing for the execution of deeds by companies incorporated under the Companies Acts. Companies which were not incorporated under the Acts remain subject to the common law requirement of sealing for the execution of a deed.

(b) *Contracts which must be in writing.* The following are examples of contracts which are required by the statute to be in writing:- bills of exchange and promissory notes (Bills of Exchange 1882), hire-purchase agreements (Consumer Credit Act 1974) and the sale of land or other disposition of an interest in land (Law of Property (Miscellaneous Provisions) Act 1989, s. 2).

(c) *Contracts which must be in writing or evidenced by writing.* By section 4 of the Statute of Frauds 1677, certain kinds of contract were unenforceable unless the claimant could show either that the contract was in writing or that there was sufficient written evidence of the existence of the contract. Section 4 now governs contracts of guarantee only (See Chapter 13).

Progress test 1

1. What are the three fundamental elements of a valid simple contract? **(2)**

2. 'An agreement may be made in any manner whatsoever, provided the parties are in communication.' Explain this statement. **(3)**

3. How do the courts discover the 'intention' of the parties? **(5)**

4. Do you think it possible that contracting parties might be deemed to have reached an agreement which is different from the one they thought they reached? **(5)**

5. Make up an example to illustrate the correlative nature of rights and obligations arising from a contract. **(7)**

6. What do you understand by the expression 'breach of contract'? **(8)**

7. Outline and explain the provisions of the Law of Property (Miscellaneous Provisions) Act 1989. **(9)**

2
Agreement

The offer must be definite

1. The terms must be certain

The offer is an undertaking by the offeror to be contractually bound in the event of a proper acceptance being made. Upon acceptance, the terms of the offer become the terms of the contract made by that acceptance. The offer must, therefore, be clear, complete and final. Any statement falling short of this requirement is not an offer: in this case, a purported acceptance will not result in a contract.

> *White* v. *Bluett* (1853): A father promised to release his son from an obligation to pay on a promissory note if the son would cease from complaining. HELD: There was no enforceable contract because the son's promise was too vague.

> *Guthing* v. *Lynn* (1831): L bought a horse from G on the terms that 'if the horse was lucky to him he would give five pounds more'. HELD: Too vague to be binding.

> *Scammell and Nephew* v. *Ouston* (1941): O ordered a motor van from S 'on the understanding that the balance of the purchase price can be had on hire purchase terms over a period of two years'. HELD by the House of Lords: The order (i.e. the offer) was so vague that it had no definite meaning. Further negotiations would be required before agreement could be reached.

2. Bilateral and unilateral contracts

An offer may be regarded as a proposal to make a contract.

There are two kinds of offer. First, the proposal may call for an acceptance in the form of an unqualified promise to perform according to the terms contained in the offer. The acceptance of this kind of offer leads to the most usual kind of contract, generally known as the bilateral contract. Secondly, the offeror's proposal may be in terms which call for an act to be performed, e.g. the return of specific lost property. A unilateral or 'if' contract is made upon performance according to the terms of the offer. *See Carlill* v. *Carbolic Smoke Ball Co.* (1892); *Errington* v. *Errington and Woods* (1952) and *Harvela Investments Ltd* v. *Royal Trust Co. of Canada* (1895).

3.   An invitation to treat is not an offer

An offer must be distinguished from a mere invitation to treat. An invitation to treat is a first step in negotiations which may, or may not, be a prelude to a firm offer by one of the parties. It usually takes the form of an invitation to make an offer.

Harris v. *Nickerson* (1873): N, an auctioneer, advertised that he would sell certain goods, including office furniture, on a specified date. H attended the sale with the intention of buying some office furniture. N withdrew the office furniture from the sale. H claimed damages for breach of contract, contending that the advertisement was an offer which he had accepted by attending the sale. HELD: The advertisement was a mere statement of intention amounting to an invitation to treat.

Fisher v. *Bell* (1960), an appeal by way of case stated: B displayed in his shop window a flick-knife behind which was a ticket bearing the words 'Ejector knife - 4s'. He was charged with offering for sale a flick-knife, contrary to the provisions of the Restriction of Offensive Weapons Act 1959. HELD: The displaying of the flick-knife was merely an invitation to treat.

Pharmaceutical Society, etc. v. *Boots, etc.* (1953): the B company operated a self-service shop in which certain drugs specified under the Pharmacy and Poisons Act 1933 were displayed with prices attached. The P society contended that the sales of the listed poisons took place when the customers took the goods from the shelves and put them in the wire baskets provided, and that, accordingly, the sales took place otherwise than 'under the supervision of a registered pharmacist' as required by the Pharmacy and Poisons Act. HELD by the Court of Appeal: the display of goods on the shelves was an invitation to treat. An offer was made by the customer when he presented the goods at the cash desk. The customer's offer could be accepted or rejected by the pharmacist whose duty it was to supervise transactions at the cash desk.

Partridge v. *Crittenden* (1968): A notice 'Bramblefinch cocks and hens, 25s each' was placed in the classified advertisements page of a periodical. On the question whether this was an offer, HELD: the notice was an invitation to treat.

Gibson v. *Manchester City Council* (1979): The City Treasurer wrote to a tenant saying that the council 'may be prepared to sell the house to you at the purchase price of £2,725 less 20 per cent = £2,180 (freehold)'. The letter went on: 'If you would like to make formal application to buy your council house please complete the form and return it to me as soon as possible.' The tenant completed and returned the form. Subsequently, the council changed its policy on council houses and, accordingly, the tenant was advised that the council was unable to proceed with his application. The tenant brought this action claiming that the council's letter was an offer which he had accepted by returning the application form. HELD by the House of Lords: There was no binding contract because there never was an offer made by the council. The council's letter stating that the council 'may be prepared to sell' was merely an invitation to treat.

4. Offers to sell land

In the early stages of negotiations for the sale of land, before detailed conditions have been agreed, it sometimes happens that the vendor makes in writing what appears to be an offer to sell for a stated price. Although there is nothing to prevent a vendor from selling on the basis of the most informal description of the property or the most unfavourable terms, the courts will approach the construction of such statements as to price being preliminary only and not intended to be fully binding. In *Clifton* v. *Palumbo* (1944), before the parties had agreed to any detailed conditions of contract, the plaintiff wrote to the defendant saying, 'I am prepared to offer you or your nominee my Lytham estate for £600,000.' It was held by the Court of Appeal that this could not be construed as an offer.

> *Harvey* v. *Facey* (1893): The following telegraph messages passed between the parties:
>
> H: 'Will you sell us Bumper Hall Pen? Telegraph lowest cash price.'
>
> F: 'Lowest cash price for Bumper Hall Pen £900.'
>
> H: 'We agree to buy Bumper Hall Pen for £900 asked by you.'
>
> There was no reply to the last message. H claimed that there was a contract. HELD by the Privy Council: 'Lowest cash price for Bumper Hall Pen £900' was not an offer: it was merely a statement of the lowest price in the event of a decision to sell. The last message could not, therefore, be regarded as an acceptance.

Although an agreement on price alone does not constitute an agreement for sale and purchase, nevertheless, such an agreement may constitute an element in a contract subsequently to be concluded.

> *Bigg* v. *Boyd Gibbins* (1971) CA: The parties were negotiating for the sale of certain freehold property. During the course of dealings the plaintiffs wrote to the defendants saying, 'As you are aware that I paid £25,000 for this property, your offer of £20,000 would appear to be at least a little optimistic. For a quick sale I would accept £26,000 . . .' The defendants replied, 'I accept your offer'. In their reply, the defendants asked the plaintiffs to contact their (the defendants') solicitors. The plaintiffs then wrote: 'I am putting the matter in the hands of my solicitors. My wife and I are both pleased that you are purchasing the property.' On the question whether a contract had been formed, HELD: the plaintiffs' first letter constituted an offer which was accepted by the defendants, thus making a binding contract.

5.   Referential bids

A prospective vendor may choose to invite bids from two or more prospective purchasers. A referential bid is one which is framed in reference to the other bids and whose price cannot be ascertained except by reference to those other bids. Where fixed bids are invited, referential bids are invalid as being inconsistent with the purpose of fixed bidding. The purpose of fixed bidding is to provoke the best price from prospective purchasers regardless of what rival bidders are prepared to pay.

> *Harvela Investments Ltd* v. *Royal Trust Co. of Canada* (1985): The first defendants held a parcel of shares for which the plaintiff and the second defendant were rival offerors. The parcel of shares would give to either purchaser control of the company. The defendants invited the prospective purchasers to submit by sealed offer or confidential telex a 'single offer' for the whole parcel by a stipulated date. The defendants stated that 'we bind ourselves to accept the highest offer' which complied with the terms of the invitation. The plaintiff tendered a bid of $2,175,000. The second defendant tendered a bid of $2,100,000 or $101,000 in excess of any other offer expressed as a fixed money amount, 'whichever is the higher'. The defendants accepted the second defendant's bid as being a bid of $2,276,000 and entered into a contract for the sale of a parcel of shares. The plaintiff contended that there was a binding contract between the defendant vendors and the plaintiff for the sale of the shares for the price of $2,175,000. After succeeding in the first instance and failing in the Court of Appeal, the plaintiff appealed to the House of Lords where it was HELD that the appeal would be allowed because the referential bid was invalid as being inconsistent with the purpose of fixed bidding. Whether an invitation from a vendor was to be construed as an invitation to participate in a fixed bidding sale or in an auction sale depended on the presumed intention of the vendor as deduced from the provisions of the invitation to bid. The facts (a) that the vendors had undertaken to accept the highest offer, (b) that the same invitation was extended to both parties, and (c) that they had insisted that offers were to be confidential, were only

consistent with the intention to sell by fixed bidding. The facts were inconsistent with the intention to create an auction sale by referential bids.

In the *Harvela* case Lord Diplock explained carefully the nature of 'the invitation' sent by the vendor to the two parties wishing to make bids. He explained that the invitation was not a mere invitation to negotiate for the sake of the shares. Its legal nature was that of a unilateral or 'if' contract, or rather two unilateral contracts in identical terms. In each case the vendor was promisor and the bidders were, respectively, the promisees. Each unilateral contract was made at the time when the invitation was made to the promisee to whom it was addressed. At this point, the promisees were under no obligation to the vendor. The vendor, on the other hand, did assume a legal obligation under each contract. This obligation was conditional on the happening, after the unilateral contracts had been made, of an event which was specified in the invitation. The obligation was to enter into a synallagamatic contract with one of the promisees, i.e. whichever made the higher fixed bid in accordance with the terms of the invitation.

Special rules apply to the formation of contracts for the sale of land (*see* 13:**7**).

An invitation to tender may give rise to a binding contract if the facts establish a clear intention to create contractual obligations: *Blackpool and Fylde Aero Club* v. *Blackpool Borough Council* (1990).

Communication of the offer

6. Manner of communication
An offer may be communicated in any manner whatsoever. Express words may be used, orally or in writing, or an offer may be implied from conduct. An offer may be partly expressed and partly implied.

7. Necessity of communication
An offer has no validity unless and until it is communicated to the offeree so as to give the opportunity to accept or reject.

Taylor v. *Laird* (1856): T threw up the command of L's ship during the course of a voyage. T then helped to work the ship home. He claimed to be paid for this work. HELD: Since T had not communicated his offer to do the work so as to give L the opportunity to accept or reject the offer, there was no contract.

8.   Communication may be particular or general

An offer may be communicated to a particular person or group of persons; or it may be communicated generally to the whole world.

(a) Where an offer is made to a particular person or group of persons, no valid acceptance may be made by a person who is not an offeree.

Boulton v. *Jones* (1857): The plaintiff had been manager for one Brocklehurst, with whom the defendant had a running account. The plaintiff bought and paid for Brocklehurst's business and, immediately afterwards, a written order was received from the defendants, addressed to Brocklehurst. The goods were supplied to the defendant and the plaintiff's bookkeeper struck out Brocklehurst's name on the order, inserting the plaintiff's. When the plaintiff sent an invoice to the defendant, he said that he knew nothing of him and refused to pay him. The plaintiff brought this action for the price of goods sold. HELD: There was no contract because the offer made by the defendant was not addressed to the plaintiff who, therefore, could not accept it. Per Pollock CB: 'The point raised is, whether the facts proved did not show an intention on the part of the defendants to deal with Brocklehurst. The plaintiff, who succeeded Brocklehurst in business, executed the order without any intimation of the change that had taken place, and brought this action to recover the price of the goods supplied. It is a rule of law, that if a person intends to contract with A, B cannot give himself any right under it. Here the order in writing was given to Brocklehurst. Possibly Brocklehurst might have adopted the act of the plaintiff in supplying the goods, and maintained an action for their price. But since the plaintiff has chosen to sue, the only course the defendants could take was to plea that there was no contract with him.'

Powell v. *Lee* (1908): P had applied to a committee of school managers for the post of headmaster of a school. The committee decided to appoint P, but did not inform him of the decision. One of their number, without authorization, informed P that he had been selected. The committee then had a change of mind and selected another person. P contended that there was a breach of contract. HELD: There was no contract because the committee had not communicated an acceptance of P's offer to take the post. The purported acceptance made without authority was not binding on the committee.

(b) Where an offer is made generally to the world at large, a valid acceptance may be made by any person with notice of the offer: *Carlill* v. *Carbolic Smoke Ball Co.* (1892). It seems that an acceptance is valid even though made for a motive which is quite unconnected with the terms of the offer: *Williams* v. *Carwardine* (1833). But it is essential that the person purporting to accept the offer had notice of that offer.

Acceptance must be unqualified

9. Unreserved assent

Acceptance must be unqualified and must correspond exactly with the terms of the offer. Not all transactions lend themselves to an easy analysis into 'offer' and 'acceptance', yet the court will always examine the communications between the parties to discover whether, at any one time, one party may be deemed to have assented to all the terms, express and implied, of a firm offer by the other party. *See*, for example, *Brogden* v. *Metropolitan Rail Co.* (1877). An assent which is qualified in any way does not take effect as an acceptance. For example, where goods are offered at a certain price, an assent coupled with a promise to pay by instalments is not an acceptance.

10. A counter-offer operates as a rejection

Where an offeree makes a counter-offer, the original offer is deemed to have been rejected and cannot be subsequently accepted.

> *Hyde* v. *Wrench* (1840): On 6 June, W offered H a farm for £1,000; H made a counter-offer of £950. On 27 June, W rejected the counter-offer. On 29 June, H made a purported acceptance of the offer of 6 June. HELD: The counter-offer operated as a rejection of the original offer. No contract.

If, on receipt of an offer, the offeree requests the offeror to inform him whether he would be prepared to add a term to the offer, the offeree's request may be construed as a request for further information. In this event, since there has been no counter-off, the original offer remains open.

> *Stevenson* v. *McLean* (1880): One Saturday the defendant offered to sell to the plaintiffs 3,800 tons of iron 'at 40*s* nett cash per ton, open till Monday'. On Monday morning the plaintiffs telegraphed: 'Please wire whether you would accept 40 for delivery over two months, or if not longest limit you would give.' Having received no reply at 1.34 p.m., the plaintiffs despatched a telegram accepting the original offer. At 1.25 p.m., the defendant despatched a telegram to say that he had sold the iron to a third party. This telegram did not reach the plaintiffs until some time after they had sent their telegram at 1.34 p.m. The plaintiffs brought this action for breach of contract, contending that the defendant's offer was still open when he sent the telegram of acceptance. The defendant argued that the Monday morning telegram constituted a counter-offer. HELD: The plaintiffs had not made a counter-offer but had made a mere enquiry which did not reject the offer: a binding contract had been made when the plaintiffs sent the telegram accepting the offer.

Where a counter-offer is accepted then its terms and not the terms of the original offer become the terms of the contract. *See*, for example, *Davies & Co.* v. *William Old* (1969) and *Butler Machine Tool Co.* v. *Ex-cell-o Corporation* (1979).

Davies & Co. v. *William Old* (1969): In April the defendants
entered into a building contract with employers (not parties
to this action) in the RIBA standard form of contract. In
May 1965 the architect, as agent for the employers, invited
the plaintiffs to tender for certain subcontract worked and
the plaintiffs tendered. The architect, as agent for the
employers, gave written instructions to the defendants to
enter into a subcontract with the nominated subcontractors,
i.e. the plaintiffs, for the shop-fitting work.

The defendants thereupon sent to the plaintiffs their own
standard form of order, instructing them to carry out the
subcontract works according to their tender. At the bottom
of the order form, it was stated that the order was subject to
the conditions overleaf. On the other side of the form were
certain conditions, number 8 of which provided that the
contractor (i.e. the defendants) should from time to time
apply under the main contract for certificates of payment to
include the amount for the subcontract work, but that the
main contractor would be under no liability to pay the
subcontractor for his work until it had been approved and
paid for by the employers under the main contract.

The plaintiffs accepted the order by letter dated 15 June
and work was done for which the plaintiff received
payments. On 2 November the architect certified £307 8*s* to
be due but the defendants failed to pay this sum to the
plaintiffs. The plaintiffs brought this action against the
main contractor contending that the failure to pay the sum
certified was a breach of the subcontract.

HELD: The conditions on the back of the order form were
binding and the main contractor was under no liability to
pay the subcontractor until he (the main contractor) was
paid by the employers, Per Blain J: 'The problem is to
define the subcontract itself. The architect was not the
agent of the defendant in nominating the subcontractors.
The tender when received by the architect constituted an
offer by the plaintiffs. The defendants had done what was
reasonable to bring the conditions or the existence of the
conditions to the notice of the plaintiffs. The general
principle is that in case of doubt and where words of a
contract are in conflict, greater force is to be given to words

selected by the parties to express their intent than to
general words of a pro forma nature, but for that doctrine
to apply the words selected by the parties had to be selected
to show a mutual intent. The conditions in the order varied
or modified the terms of the tender, and so the order was
not an unqualified acceptance of the offer comprised in the
tender but was a counter-offer. That was accepted by the
plaintiffs' letter dated 15 June either by itself or together
with the carrying out of the work. The conditions were
incorporated in the subcontract, and since the defendants
had not received from the employer the sums claimed, they
were not liable to pay them to the plaintiffs.'

11. 'Subject to contract'

The expression 'subject to contract' creates a strong inference
that the parties do not intend to be bound until the execution of a
formal contract. In *Chillingworth* v. *Esche* (1924) Sargent LJ said:
'The words "subject to contract" or "subject to formal contract"
have by this time acquired a definite ascertained legal meaning.
The phrase is a perfectly familiar one in the mouths of estate
agents and other persons accustomed to deal with land; and I can
quite understand a solicitor saying to a client: "Be sure that to
protect yourself you introduce into any preliminary contract you
may think of making the words *subject to contract*". I do not say that
the phrase makes the contract containing it necessarily and
whatever the context a conditional contract. But they are words
appropriate for introducing a condition, and it would require a
very strong and exceptional case for the clear prima facie meaning
to be displaced.' *Chillingworth* v. *Esche* and *Eccles* v. *Bryant and Pollock*
are cases where the prima facie meaning of 'subject to contract'
took effect. These cases should be compared with *Alpenstow* v.
Regalian Properties (1985), in which there was a sufficiently strong
and exceptional case for the rejection of the prima facie meaning.

Acceptance 'subject to contract', prima facie, is not binding. In
sale of land, it is usual to express tentative preliminary agreements
to be 'subject to contract', so as to give the parties an opportunity
to reflect or to seek legal or other advice before entering a binding
contract. The expression 'subject to contract' has received judicial
recognition for this purpose. But if any other form of wording is

used, care must be taken to show legally that the parties did not intend to create a legally binding agreement (*see* 3:**2**). There is a difference between a tentative agreement (not binding) and a provisional agreement, which may be binding: *Branca* v. *Cobarro* (1947).

Chillingworth v. *Esche* (1924): The parties agreed on the sale of certain property 'subject to a proper contract to be prepared by the vendor's solicitors'. HELD: There was no contract between the parties.

Eccles v. *Bryant and Pollock* (1948): The parties agreed on the sale of certain property 'subject to contract'. The contract was drawn up and counterparts prepared for each party. The purchaser signed his counterpart and posted it to the vendor, but the vendor did not sign his counterpart. HELD: There was no contract between the parties.

Alpenstow Ltd v. *Regalian Properties plc* (1985): The plaintiffs, who were the registered owners of a property, wrote to the defendant property development consultants on 12 July, as a result of previous negotiations, agreeing as follows: that if, following the grant of planning permission, they wished to sell any part of their interest in the property (**a**) they would give notice to the defendants of their willingness to sell to the defendants at a stated price; (**b**) within 28 days of the notice the defendants would inform them of their acceptance of the notice, subject to contract, and within seven days thereafter the plaintiffs would submit a draft contract for the approval by the defendants; and (**c**) within 28 days of receipt of the draft contract the defendants would approve the contract and exchange contracts within seven days thereafter. In conclusion, the plaintiffs stated that they were awaiting confirmation of acceptance of the agreement set out in the letter. The defendants accepted the agreement.

Planning permission was later granted and the plaintiffs gave notice of their willingness to sell part of their interest in the property to the defendants. The defendants accepted the contract. On being requested for a draft contract as agreed, the plaintiffs contended that the agreement set out in the letter of 12 July was 'subject to contract' and, accordingly, was not binding. The defendants sought specific performance of the agreement. On the question of the effect of the words 'subject to contract' in the present circumstances it was HELD that the words 'subject to contract' had a clear prima-facie meaning, being in themselves merely conditional.

It was a condition precedent to the coming into existence of a contract that there should be an exchange of contracts in accordance with property conveyancing practice. Prior to that, either party could withdraw. However, in a strong and exceptional context the court would not give those words that meaning in a particular case. The facts of this case constituted such a strong and exceptional context. Accordingly, the court would not give the words 'subject to contract' their clear prima-facie meaning. The parties were bound by the agreement.

Branca v. *Cobarro* (1947): The parties signed an agreement by which B was to buy the lease and goodwill of C's mushroom farm. The agreement ended with the words, 'This is a provisional agreement until a fully legalized agreement drawn up by a solicitor embodying all the conditions herewith stated is signed'. B paid a deposit, but subsequently changed his mind over the transaction. B sued for the return of his deposit, contending that the agreement was not binding. HELD: The wording of the agreement showed that the parties intended it to be binding, and that it would remain in force until its provisions were embodied in a formally drawn up document.

12. Letters of intent

It is not unusual for a negotiating party to write to or telex the other party to the effect that it is his intention to enter into a contract at some time in the future. There is no hard and fast rule as to the legal effect of such letters. It is necessary to take each case separately and consider the wording and the facts existing at the time. In their usual form, letters of intent do not take effect as acceptances, for this would not be the intention of a party who merely wishes to state his present intention while keeping his option open to withdraw from negotiations should he subsequently change his mind. But where the words and facts show an intention to contract, then the letter of intent will be construed as an acceptance.

In *Wilson Smithett & Cape (Sugar)* v. *Bangladesh Sugar* (1986) the plaintiff presented to the defendant a tender for the supply of materials which was to remain open until 12 June. The defendant sent a letter of intent to the plaintiff for the supply of materials according to the tender and requiring the plaintiff to put up a performance bond within seven days. The plaintiff duly put up the bond. The defendant refused to go ahead with the transaction, contending that there was no binding contract. It was held that, on the facts of this case, the letter of intent constituted an acceptance of the plaintiff's tender offer. It created a binding contract.

Letters of intent often make provision for work to be done or services to be performed before the conclusion of the contract. It was explained in *British Steel Corporation* v. *Cleveland Bridge & Engineering Co.* (1984) that a contract could come into existence following a letter of intent, either by the letter forming the basis of an ordinary executory contract under which each party assumed reciprocal obligations to the other, or under a unilateral contract whereby the letter would constitute a standing offer which would result in a binding contract if acted on by the offeree.

British Steel Corporation v. *Cleveland Bridge & Engineering Co.* (1984): The defendants were contractors who had contracted to fabricate the steel work for the Sama Bank in Saudi Arabia. The design required steel nodes for the purpose of attaching steel beams to the frame. The defendants approached the plaintiffs for the production of the steel nodes. On 9 February the plaintiffs sent an estimated price based on incomplete information to the defendants. After further discussion, the defendants sent a letter of intent to the plaintiffs on 21 February as follows:

'We are pleased to advise you that it is the intention of Cleveland Bridge & Engineering Co. to enter into a subcontract with your company, for the supply and delivery of steel castings which form the roof nodes for this project. The price will be as quoted in you telex dated 9 February 1979. . . . The form of subcontract to be entered will be our standard form of subcontract for use in conjunction with the ICE General Conditions of Contract. We request that you proceed immediately with the works pending the preparation and issuing to you of the official form of subcontract.'

The plaintiffs went ahead with the construction of the nodes but were never able to agree to the onerous terms of the defendants' form of subcontract. By 28 December 1979 all nodes were delivered except one which was delayed until 11 April by the steel strike. The plaintiffs claimed the value of the nodes and the defendants counterclaimed for damages for late and out-of-sequence delivery. The plaintiffs argued that there was no contract and that they were entitled to reclaim the value of the nodes (*quantum meruit*). The defendants contended that a contract had been made when the plaintiffs constructed the nodes following the letter of intent. HELD: Important terms of contract had never been resolved and, accordingly, no contract had been made. The plaintiffs were entitled to the value of the nodes.

The communication of acceptance

13. Acceptance must be communicated

The general rule is that acceptance must be communicated to the offeror. Acceptance speaks from the moment it is communicated. Where the offeree merely intended to accept, but did not communicate his intention to the offeror, there is no contract, i.e. mere mental acceptance is not sufficient. Moreover, the offeror may not stipulate that he will take silence to be acceptance, and thus bind the offeree.

Felthouse v. *Bindley* (1863): F offered to buy his nephew's horse for £30 15*s*. In the letter containing the offer, F wrote, 'If I hear no more about him, I consider the horse mine at £30 15*s*.' The nephew did not reply to this letter. Six weeks later, when the nephew was about to sell his farming stock, he instructed B, an auctioneer, to keep the horse out of the sale as he was already sold. B inadvertently sold the horse, F sued B for conversion. (To succeed in conversion, F would have to show that he had a right to immediate possession of the horse, i.e. that there was a contract between himself and his nephew.) HELD: The nephew had not communicated his intention to sell the horse to F, therefore there was no contract, and no property in the horse had ever vested in F.

14. Where acceptance need not be communicated

There are two important exceptions to the rule that a contract is not made until acceptance is actually communicated to the offeror:

(a) Where performance constitutes acceptance, i.e. unilateral contracts.

(b) Where acceptance is duly made by post.

15. Unilateral contracts

In the case of a unilateral or 'if' contract, the offeror is deemed to have included in his offer a term providing that the described and required performance by the offeree will be a sufficient acceptance and communication is not necessary. The offeror is bound when the offeree performs whatever act is required of him according to the terms of the offer.

Carlill v. *Carbolic Smoke Ball Co.* (1892): The following advertisement appeared in newspapers: '£100 reward will be paid by the Carbolic Smoke Ball Company to any person who contracts the increasing epidemic influenza, colds, or any other disease caused by taking cold, after having used the ball three times daily for two weeks according to the printed directions supplied with each ball. One thousand pounds is deposited with the Alliance Bank, Regent Street, showing our good faith in this matter.' C, in reliance on this advertisement, bought a smoke ball and used it according to the directions but nevertheless suffered an attack of influenza. She claimed £100 from the company. HELD: **(a)** The deposit of £1,000 showed that the company intended to enter into legal relations; **(b)** the advertisement was an offer made to all the world, and a contract was made with that limited portion of the public who came forward and performed the condition on the faith of the advertisement; **(c)** the offer contained an intimation that performance of the condition was sufficient acceptance and that there was no need for notification of acceptance to be given to the offeror.

Note

The third part of the judgement in the *Smoke Ball Case* should be carefully distinguished from the rule in *Felthouse* v. *Bindley*, in which there was no performance required of the offeree.

In cases where a reward has been offered in return for a specific piece of information, or the finding of a specific thing, acceptance can be made once only, even though the offer was made to the public.

Lancaster v. *Walsh* (1838): An offer was made to pay £20 reward to any person who came forward with information leading to the conviction of the thief of certain property. The second person to give the information claimed £20 reward. HELD: Acceptance was made by the first person to give the information, and no further acceptance was possible.

16. Manner of acceptance

Acceptance may be communicated in any manner whatsoever. Generally, the offeree may decide for himself the manner of acceptance; but if the offeror prescribes, expressly or by implication, the mode of acceptance, the question arises whether communication of acceptance in any other manner will suffice. In *Manchester Diocesan Council for Education* v. *Commercial and General Investments* (1969), Buckley J explained the position as follows: 'It may be that an offeror, who by the terms of his offer insists on acceptance in a particular manner, is entitled to insist that he is not bound unless acceptance is effected or communicated in that precise way, although it seems probable that, even so, if the other party communicates his acceptance in some other way, the offeror may by conduct or otherwise waive his right to insist on the prescribed method of acceptance. Where, however, the offeror has prescribed a particular method of acceptance, but not in terms insisting that only acceptance in that mode shall be binding, I am of opinion that acceptance communicated to the offeror by any other mode which is no less advantageous to him will conclude the contract. Thus in *Tinn* v. *Hoffman & Co.* (1873), where acceptance was required by return of post, Honeyman J said: "That does not mean exclusively a reply by return of post, but you may reply by telegram or by verbal message, or by any means not later than a letter written and sent by return of post." If an offeror intends that he shall be bound only if his offer is accepted in some particular manner, it must be for him to make this clear.'

Compagnie de Commerce et Commissions SARL v. *Parkinson Stove Co. Ltd* (1953): P made an offer to C with the stipulation that acceptance should be made on a particular form and that no other manner of acceptance would be valid. C accepted by letter. HELD by the Court of Appeal: no valid acceptance had been made.

Quenerduaine v. *Cole* (1883): Q made an offer to C by post. C made a counter-offer by telegraph. Q immediately posted a letter accepting the counter-offer, but by the time it reached C he no longer wished to enter the contract. Q claimed that a contract had been made. HELD: The fact that the counter-offer was made by telegraph indicated an implied condition that prompt acceptance was required. The purported acceptance by letter reached C after the counter-offer had lapsed. No contract was made.

Holwell Securities v. *Hughes* (1974): An agreement was made on 19 October 1971, in which an option was granted to X to purchase certain land. The agreement provided that 'The said option shall be exercisable by notice in writing to [the offeror] an any time within six months from the date hereof'. On 14 April 1972, X posted a properly stamped and addressed letter to the offeror giving notice of the exercise of the option. This letter went astray in the post and was never delivered to the offeror. The offeror refused to sell the land and X brought this action for specific performance, contending that the option had been validly exercised by the mere posting of the letter. HELD by the Court of Appeal: Since the agreement prescribed the manner in which the option was to be exercised, it could only be exercised in that way, i.e. by actually serving notice on the offeror. The mere posting of the notice which went astray did not constitute a valid exercise of the option.

The *Wettern Electric* case provides a recent example of the offeror's power to control the manner of acceptance. In this case, a regional development agency offered a manufacturing company a licence to occupy a factory unit for 12 months on stated terms. The offer contained the following statement: 'If you accept this licence on the above terms, will you please complete acknowledgement and acceptance at the foot of the enclosed copy and return it to us at your earliest convenience.' The company did not accept the offer in the required manner: they went into occupation of the factory unit. It was held by Judge Newey QC that, since entry was not the prescribed method of communicating acceptance, it did not take effect as acceptance of the agency's offer. The legal position was that the occupation by the company constituted an offer to enter into a contractual licence on the terms already communicated by the agency. By allowing the occupation, the agency had accepted this offer. In other words, the parties made, by conduct, a contract for a licence: *Wettern Electric* v. *Welsh Development Agency* (1983).

There remains the following question to be considered: where acceptance has been made in a manner other than that prescribed, may the offeror waive his stipulation and treat the acceptance as valid and binding on the offeree? There is no clear authority on this point, but it was suggested *obiter* in the *Parkinson Stove Case* (1953) that such a waiver would be valid.

When a unilateral contract is made it seems that the offeror is bound from the time when the offeree began his performance of what was required of him by the offer.

Errington v. Errington and Woods (1952): X promised to give his house to his son and daughter-in-law provided they paid off the building society mortgage loan. The couple thereafter made regular payments to the building society on account of the mortgage. X died leaving all his property to his widow. The son then left his wife and went to live with his widowed mother, leaving his wife (X's daughter-in-law) in the house in question. She continued to make the regular payments to the building society. X's widow later sought to recover possession of the house.

HELD: X's promise had led to a unilateral contract — a promise of the house in return for their act of paying the instalments. X's promise could not be revoked after the couple had started to pay the instalments.

17. Acceptance by post

Where post is deemed to be the proper means of communicating acceptance, the acceptance takes effect from the moment the letter of acceptance is properly posted. This rule applies even where the acceptance is delayed or lost in the post.

Henthorn v. *Fraser* (1892): F, representing a building society, offered in writing to sell certain houses to H, the offer to remain open for 14 days. H received the offer in person. Next day the following events took place: midday: the society posted a letter to H revoking the offer. 3.50 p.m.: H posted a letter to the society accepting the offer. 5.00 p.m.: H received the society's revocation. HELD: A contract was made at 3.50 pm, when H posted his letter of acceptance. Per Lord Herschell: 'Where the circumstances are such that it must have been within the contemplation of the parties that, according to the ordinary usages of mankind, the post might be used as a means of communicating the acceptance of an offer, the acceptance is complete as soon as it is posted.'

Household Fire Insurance Co. v. *Grant* (1879): G applied for shares in the plaintiff company. The company sent a letter of allotment by post, but it never reached G. The company went into liquidation and the liquidator, on behalf of the company, sued for the balance outstanding on the shares. G contended that he was not bound to pay, since he had not received a reply to his offer to buy the shares. HELD: a contract was made at the moment the letter of allotment (i.e. the acceptance) was posted.

18. Payment of a deposit

In *Damon Cia* v. *Hapag-Lloyd* (1985), the question whether the payment of a deposit may be a condition precedent to the formation of a contract was considered. In this case the parties had concluded the negotiation for the sale of three ships on the standard terms of the Norwegian Shipbrokers' Association Form of Sale. Clause 2 of that form provides that 'As a security for the correct fulfilment of this contract, the buyers shall pay a deposit of 10% — ten per cent — of the purchase money on signing this contract'. Clause 13 further provided that, 'Should the purchase money not be paid as per clause 16, the sellers have the right to cancel this contract, in which case the amount deposited shall be forfeit to the sellers'. In the present case, the deposit was not paid. The sellers pressed the buyers to sign a memorandum of their agreement and to pay the deposit, but without success.

The sellers subsequently sold the ships to another purchaser and then claimed to recover the deposit under clause 2 of the Norwegian form. The buyers contended that no contract with them had been entered into since the memorandum of agreement had not been signed and the deposit had not been paid. It was held by the Court of Appeal that (a) the execution of the memorandum of agreement was not contemplated by the parties as being a prerequisite to the conclusion of the contract, the terms of the sale having already been agreed, and (b) the payment of the deposit was not necessarily a condition precedent to the formation of a contract, there being no reason to infer that a contract did not arise until the deposit had been paid.

Unless there is an express stipulation that payment of a deposit is a condition precedent to the coming into existence of the contract, the requirement to pay it will simply be an important obligation of the purchaser, but not a condition precedent. In the *Damon* case, it was mentioned that, in the case of contracts for the sale of land, a deposit is normally payable at the time of the exchange of contracts, at which point the vendor could refuse to exchange if the purchaser had not paid the deposit.

19. Place of contracting

In cases with an international element, it is sometimes necessary to establish *where* a contract was made. Where agreement is reached between parties present in a particular country, the contract is obviously made in that country. But where the parties are in different countries and they use the post as the means of communicating, the contract is made in the country where the acceptance is posted. Similarly, where acceptance is made by cable, the contract is made in the country from which the acceptance was sent: *Benaim & Co.* v. *Debono* (1924). If, however, the communication is instantaneous, for example by telex, the contract is made at the place where the acceptance is received: *Entores* v. *Miles Far East Corporation* (1955).

20. Cross offers

Consider the following: A makes an offer to B, and, by coincidence, B makes an offer to A in identical terms, and the two offers cross in the post. Is there a contract? There are no cases exactly on the point, but arguing from general principles, it appears that there has been no agreement between A and B in the manner required by law, i.e. there has been no acceptance of an offer.

Revocation

21. Continued negotiations

Where, after protracted negotiations, the parties differ as to whether or not a binding contract has been made, the court will consider the whole course of negotiations and decide whether agreement was reached at any point: *see Pagnam SpA* v. *Feed Products Ltd* (1987).

22. Termination of an offer

An offer may come to an end by revocation, lapse or rejection. In any case, the offer loses its legal effect and becomes incapable of acceptance.

23. When revocation is possible

The offeror may withdraw (i.e. revoke) his offer at any time before acceptance. But once a valid acceptance has been made, he is bound by the terms of his offer. An offer cannot be revoked after acceptance. In other words, no unilateral withdrawal is possible once the contract is formed.

> *Payne* v. *Cave* (1789): C made the highest bid for P's goods at an auction sale, but he withdrew his bid before the fall of the hammer. P contended that C was bound by the sale.
> HELD: C's bid was an offer and could be revoked before

acceptance, i.e. before the fall of the hammer. There was an effective revocation by C.

Re National Savings Bank Association (1867): An application for shares in a company was withdrawn before delivery of the letter of allotment. HELD: No contract to take the shares.

Routledge v. *Grant* (1828): An offer was made by the defendant to sell a house for a certain price. In his offer the defendant stipulated that acceptance should be within six weeks. On the question whether the defendant could withdraw his offer before the expiration of the six weeks, HELD: the defendant was free to withdraw his offer at any time within the six weeks provided that no acceptance had been made. (In this case the plaintiff had given no consideration to the defendant to keep the offer open.)

A unilateral contract is concluded when the offeree begins to perform the stipulations contained in the offer and from that moment the offeror is bound by his offer: *Errington* v. *Errington and Woods* (1952). Consider also *Carlill* v. *Carbolic Smoke Co*. (1892).

24. Options
Where the offeror gives an undertaking to keep the offer open for a stipulated period he is not bound by his undertaking unless the offeree gave consideration in return for it. Where the offeree gives consideration to keep the offer open for a period there is a separate binding contract known as an *option*, and revocation within the period will be in breach of contract. (*See Dickinson* v. *Dodds* (1876); *Routledge* v. *Grant* (1828).)

25. Communication essential
Revocation is effective only upon actual notice of it reaching the offeree. Where revocation is communicated by post, it takes effect from the moment it is received by the offeree, and not from the time of posting.

Byrne v. *Van Tienhoven* (1880): the following communications passed between the parties:

1 Oct: T posted an offer in Cardiff to B in New York.
8 Oct: T posted a revocation of the offer.

11 Oct: B sent a telegram accepting the offer of 1 Oct.
15 Oct: B sent a letter confirming the acceptance.
20 Oct: B received the revocation dated 8 Oct.

HELD: T's revocation was inoperative because it did not reach B until after acceptance had been made. A contract was made on 11 October, when B accepted the offer.

26. Indirect communication of revocation

Provided the offeror has shown, by words or conduct, a clear intention to revoke, and notice has reached the offeree, the revocation is effective. The means of communication do not matter.

Dickinson v. *Dodds* (1876): On 10 June P received from D an offer to sell houses, the offer 'to be left over until Friday, 9 o'clock a.m., 12 June'. On 11 June P was informed by X that D had offered or agreed to sell the houses to Y. P then delivered an acceptance of D's offer. D had, in fact, sold the houses to Y on 11 June. P contended that D was contractually bound to sell the houses to him. HELD: D's undertaking to keep the offer open for a certain time was not binding for the plaintiff had given no consideration for it. There was no need for an express withdrawal of the offer. It was sufficient that P knew that D had changed his mind and had offered the property to another. Effective revocation had taken place before the purported acceptance, and there was no contract between the parties.

Lapse

27. Lapse of an offer

An offer may lapse, and thus become incapable of acceptance:

(a) by passage of time, or
(b) by the death of one of the parties, or
(c) the non-fulfilment of a condition precedent — *see* 16:9.

28. Passage of time

An offer will lapse through passage of time in the following circumstances:

(a) Where acceptance is not made within the period prescribed by the offeror.

(b) Where no period is prescribed, and acceptance is not made within a reasonable time. (What is reasonable depends upon the circumstances of the case.)

> *Ramsgate Victoria Hotel Co.* v. *Montefiore* (1866): In June, M offered to buy shares from the company. In November, the company allotted shares to M, who refused to take them, contending that his offer had lapsed. HELD: The offer had lapsed through passage of time: acceptance had not been made within a reasonable period.

29. Death of a party

The death of the offeror or offeree sometimes causes the offer to lapse. The position is not free from doubt, and may be summarized as follows:

(a) The offer lapses when the offeree hears of the death of the offeror: *Re Whelan* (1897). But whether an acceptance made in ignorance of the offeror's death is effective is a matter of doubt: *Bradbury* v. *Morgan* (1862).

(b) It seems that the death of the offeree will cause the offer to lapse.

> *Duff's Executors' Case* (1886): D received an offer of some shares in return for certain shares held by D. D died without accepting, but his executors purported to accept. HELD: The offer had lapsed on D's death.

30. Non-fulfilment of a condition

Where the offeror makes his offer subject to the fulfilment of a condition, failure on the part of the offeree to fulfil the condition will prevent acceptance from taking place. Such a condition may be implied from the circumstances of the case. For example, in *Financings* v. *Stimson* (1962), it was held that a customer's offer to take a motor car under a hire-purchase agreement, the offer being made to a finance company, was subject to an implied term that the car remained in the same condition up to the time of the acceptance of the offer. In this case the car was stolen from the dealer's premises and damaged before the finance company accepted the customer's offer and, in consequence, the customer was not bound by any agreement.

Rejection

31. Rejection: express and implied
An offeree who has rejected an offer cannot subsequently accept it. Rejection may be express or implied.

32. Express rejection
Express rejection is effective when notice of it has reached the offeror. But where rejection is made by post it is not clear whether it operates from the moment of posting the letter or from the moment the letter reaches the offeror. For example, if X posts an offer to Y, and Y posts a letter rejecting the offer, but soon afterwards changes his mind and sends a telegram accepting the offer, what is the position if X receives the telegram before the letter?

It is suggested that a contract is made when X receives the telegram, and Y's letter has no legal effect.

33. Implied rejection
Rejection is implied by law:

(a) where the offeree makes a counter-offer: *Hyde* v. *Wrench* (1840);
(b) where the offeree makes a conditional acceptance: *Jordan* v. *Norton* (1838).

Note
There is no implied rejection of the offer where the offeree makes a request for further information: *Stevenson* v. *McLean* (1880).

Progress test 2

1. 'An offer must be definite.' Explain.

2. What is an invitation to treat? Give examples.

3. What is a referential bid and what rules govern?

4. Has an offer any validity before it is communicated to the offeree?

5. 'The communication of an offer may be particular or general.' Comment on this statement.

6. 'Acceptance must be unqualified and must correspond exactly with the terms of the offer.' Would it, therefore, be true to say that the terms of the offer become the binding contractual terms after acceptance has taken place?

7. What is the effect of a counter-offer?

8. Explain in detail and illustrate the effect of the words 'subject to contract'.

9. Are there any exceptions to the rule that a contract is not made until acceptance is actually communicated to the offeror?

10. What is a unilateral or 'if' contract?

11. May the offeror stipulate the manner in which acceptance is to be made?

12. What rules govern acceptance by post?

13. May an offeror always revoke before acceptance has taken place?

14. Explain how an offer may lapse (a) by passage of time, (b) by death, and (c) by the non-fulfilment of a condition.

15. In what circumstances will rejection of an offer be implied?

16. A borrowed £10 from B, saying that he would pay him back the following week, together with an extra £5 if business was good during the week. A has repaid the £10 and B wishes to know whether he can claim the £5. Advise him.

17. C sees a rare book in a bookshop window. It is labelled 'First Edition — £5'. C goes into the shop and puts a £5 note on the counter and asks for the book. The bookseller tells C that it was marked at £5 by mistake, and that its real price is £12. Is the bookseller bound to sell the book to C for £5? Give reasons for your answer.

18. D goes into a self service store, takes up a wire basket from the stack provided, and then fills the basket with goods from the shelves. He is about to leave the store, when he remembers that he has forgotten to bring money with him: so he starts to replace the goods on the shelves. The store manager stops him, saying that he has bought these goods and must pay for them. Advise the manager.

19. E says to F, 'How much would you sell your car for?' F replies, 'A hundred and fifty pounds'. Is there a contract between the parties?

20. G's lawn is infested with weeds, and his neighbour, H, treats the lawn with weed killer. G knows nothing of this until H presents him with a bill for £2.50, the price of the weed killer. Is G bound to pay H?

21. J applied for a post as a legal assistant in the secretary's department of XYZ Ltd. The company's appointments committee decided to appoint J. A committee member happened to meet J at his club and told him that he had been appointed. On the strength of this information, J immediately resigned from his present post, and ordered four new suits from his tailor. In the meantime, the committee decided to appoint K instead of J to the post. Two days later, J received a letter from

XYZ Ltd, signed by the chairman of the appointments committee, thanking J for his application, but regretting that he had not been successful, and that the post had gone to K. J, who now has no job, and cannot pay his tailor's bill, seeks your advice as to whether he has an action for breach of contract against XYZ Ltd.

22. Invitations to tender were made on a 'fixed bid' basis. One of the tenderers, L, put in a bid of '£50,000 or £3,000 in excess any other offer expressed as a fixed money amount, whichever is the higher.' M put in a bid of £51,000. What is the legal position?

23. L offered to sell his motor cycle to M for £80. M replied, 'I'll give you £75 for it.' L then shook his head. M then produced £80 from his pocket saying, 'Here you are then, eighty pounds.' L replies that he has changed his mind, and that he does not want to sell the motor cycle. Is he within his legal rights? State your reasons for your answer fully.

24. N and O entered into a written agreement containing a clause 'this is a provisional agreement until a proper agreement containing these terms is drawn up by a solicitor and signed'. Are the parties bound by this agreement? Would the result have been the same if the term was expressed 'this agreement is subject to a contract to be prepared by a solicitor'?

25. After prolonged and unfriendly negotiations between S and T for the sale of S's vintage car, T wrote to S offering to pay £850 for it. The letter went on to say, 'If I do not hear from you within a week, I shall assume that the car is mine at that price.' Three weeks later, S sells the car to U for £860. T asks you to advise him whether he can make any claim against S.

26. A building company tendered the price of £2,500,000 to carry out and complete the building of a new primary school for a local authority. The local authority wrote to the company saying, 'It is our intention to place the contract with you when the Standard Form of Building Contract has been prepared for execution.' Has a binding contract been made?

3
Intention to create legal relations

1. Intention to be bound is essential

The intention to create legal relations is an essential element in contract. Where no intention to be bound can be attributed to the parties, there is no contract. The test of intention is objective. The courts seek to give effect to the intentions of the parties, whether expressed or presumed. In *Rose and Frank Co.* v. *Crompton Bros.* (1925) Aitkin LJ said in the Court of Appeal that 'To create a contract there must be a common intention of the parties to enter into legal obligations, mutually communicated expressly or impliedly.' In the same case, Scrutton LJ said: 'Now it is quite possible for parties to come to an agreement by accepting a proposal with the result that the agreement does not give rise to legal relations. The reason for this is that the parties do not intend that their agreement shall give rise to legal relations. This intention may be implied from the subject matter of the agreement, but it may also be expressed by the parties. In social and family relations such an intention is readily implied, while in business matters, the opposite result would ordinarily follow.' It follows that, for present purposes, a broad distinction must be made between agreements of the commercial kind and agreements of the domestic kind.

2. Commercial and business agreements

The ordinary commonsense implication is that in a commercial or business agreement, the parties intended should be legally binding. If a party to a business agreement wishes to assert that legal relations were not intended when the agreement was entered, the onus is on him to show that no legal relations were intended and the onus is a heavy one. It is always open to parties to include a term in their agreement to the effect that it is 'not subject to the jurisdiction of the courts'. These are the devices which may be used to express the intention not to create legal relations: these expressions have the effect of rebutting the implication which ordinarily arises in contracts of the business kind: *Eccles* v. *Bryant and Pollock* (1948); *Chillingworth* v. *Esche* (1924); *Rose and Frank* v. *Crompton* (1925) CA (1925) HL; *Appleson* v. *Littlewood* (1939); *Kleinwort Benson Ltd* v. *Malaysia Mining Corporation* (1989) CA; *Orion Insurance Co.* v. *Sphere Drake* (1990). The subject-matter of the agreement may also be relevant to intention in respect of legal relations. In *Edwards* v. *Skyways* (1964), it was held that an employee air pilot was entitled to enforce his employer's promise to make an *ex gratia* payment equivalent to the employer's contribution to a pension fund on the termination of his employment. The employer failed in his contention that the use of the expression *ex gratia* was sufficient to show that the parties did not intend to create legal relations. In *Esso Petroleum Co.* v. *Commissioners of Customs and Excise* (1976), specially produced coins were distributed by Esso to their dealers who offered their customers a free coin with the purchase of four gallons of petrol. It was held by the House of Lords that, in these circumstances, the offer to make a gift in return for the purchase of petrol was not intended to be legally binding.

Kleinwort Benson Ltd v. *Malaysia Mining Corporation* (1989) CA: The plaintiff bank agreed with the defendant company to grant a loan facility of up to £10 million to the wholly-owned subsidiary of the defendant company. The wholly-owned subsidiary traded in tin on the London Metal Exchange. The loan facility was granted after the defendant had stated in two 'comfort letters' addressed to the plaintiff that, 'it is our policy to ensure that the business of (the subsidiary) is at all times in a position to meet its liabilities to you under the (loan facility) arrangements'. In 1985 the tin market collapsed when the subsidiary owed the plaintiff the entire amount of the facility. The plaintiff claimed against the defendant on the basis of the 'comfort letters'. The question to be decided was whether the 'comfort letters' constituted a contractual promise binding on the defendant. HELD by the Court of Appeal: The 'comfort letters' had stated the defendant's current policy: there was no express or implied promise that this policy would remain. The statement was one of present fact regarding the parent company's intentions. It was not a promise as to future conduct, and therefore, not a contractual promise. The statement was not intended to be other than a representation of fact giving rise to a moral responsibility.

Rose and Frank Co. v. *Crompton Bros.* (1925): An agreement was expressed to be 'not subject to legal jurisdiction in the law courts'. HELD by the House of Lords: No binding contract.

Appleson v. *Littlewood* (1939): A sent in football pools coupon containing a condition that it 'shall not be attended by or give rise to any legal relationship, rights, duties, consequences'. HELD by the Court of Appeal: The condition was valid and the agreement was not binding.

J.H. Milner & Son v. *Percy Bilton* (1966): In negotiations between solicitors and their clients, a letter was written stating, 'May we please take this opportunity of placing on record the understanding that all legal work of and incidental to the completion of the development and the grant of leases shall be carried out by us'. HELD: No contract.

Where a 'memorandum or note' in writing is expressed to be subject to contract, the requirements of the Law of Property Act 1925, s. 40, will not be satisfied because such a memorandum does not contain any recognition or admission of the existence of a contract: *Tiverton Estates* v. *Wearwell* (1975).

3.   Social and domestic agreements

In cases of social, family or other domestic agreements, the question of intention to create legal relations depends on the inferences to be drawn from the circumstances of each case and the language used by the parties. In *Merritt* v. *Merritt* (1970), Lord Denning MR said: 'In all these cases the court does not try to discover the intention by looking into the minds of the parties. It looks at the situation in which they were placed and asks itself: would reasonable people regard the agreement as intended to be binding?'

Balfour v. *Balfour* (1919): A husband agreed to send his wife £30 a month for her support while he was working abroad. HELD by the Court of Appeal: No contract.

Simpkins v. *Pays* (1955): A lodger and the members of the family with whom he lived agreed to go shares in a newspaper competition. They sent in a winning entry. HELD: There was an intention to be bound. The prize money should be shared according to the agreement.

Jones v. *Padavatton* (1969): In this action the plaintiff and defendant were mother and daughter respectively. There was an agreement between the parties to the effect that if the daughter gave up her very satisfactory pensionable job in the USA and came to London to read for the Bar with the intention of practising law in Trinidad (where the mother lived), the mother would pay an allowance of 200 dollars a month to maintain the daughter and her small son while in England. According to this agreement, the daughter began her legal studies in November 1962, continuing up to the time this action was brought. At the time of the agreement, the mother meant 200 West Indian dollars a month and the daughter understood it to be 200 US dollars. But once arrived, the daughter accepted the allowance in West Indian dollars without dispute.

In 1964, because the daughter was finding it difficult to live on her allowance, a house was found and the purchase price of £6,000 was provided by the mother, to whom the property was conveyed. The varied arrangement was that the daughter should live in part of the house and let the rest furnished, using the rent to cover expenses and the daughter's maintenance in place of the 200 dollars a month. In 1967 the parties quarrelled and the mother, complaining that she could not get any accounts, brought this action for possession of the house, on the grounds that the agreement between the parties was not made with the intention to create legal relations. HELD: The arrangement of 1964 by which the daughter had the use of the house was lacking in contractual intent. The mother was entitled to possession.

Merritt v. *Merritt* (1970): Husband and wife were married in 1941 and had three children. In 1966 the husband left home to live with another woman. The matrimonial home, a freehold house, was in the joint names of husband and wife and was subject to an outstanding mortgage of some £180. In order to make arrangements for the future, the wife met the husband in his car. He said that he would pay her £40 a month out of which she would have to pay off the outstanding mortgage. He gave her the building society mortgage book. Before leaving the car the wife insisted that he put into writing the following agreement: 'In consideration of the fact that you will pay all charges in connection with the house. . .until such time as the mortgage payment has been completed, when the mortgage payment has been completed I will agree to transfer the property into your sole ownership.' The husband signed and dated this agreement. When the mortgage was paid off, the husband refused to transfer the house as agreed. HELD by the Court of Appeal: The written agreement was intended to create legal relations because the presumption of fact against such an intention where arrangements were made by a husband and wife living in amity did not apply to arrangements made when they were not living in amity but were separated or about to separate, when it might safely be presumed that they intended to create legal relations. The surrounding circumstances of the present case showed that the parties did so intend; accordingly, the wife was entitled to sue on the agreement, and it being sufficiently certain and there being good consideration by the wife paying off the mortgage, she was entitled to a declaration that she was the sole owner of the house and to an order that the husband join in transferring it to her.

Progress test 3

1. 'The intention to create legal relations is an essential element in a binding contract.' Explain this statement.

2. Where the parties do not expressly state whether or not they intend to be legally bound by their agreement, how do the courts discover their intention in this respect?

3. Consider the legal effect of the two following stipulations:

(a) 'This agreement is binding in honour only and is not to give rise to legal rights and obligations.'

(b) 'This agreement is outside the jurisdiction of the courts, and the parties hereby agree not to bring any action in the courts on any question arising from this agreement.'

4. A invited B to his (A's) home for dinner, and B accepted the invitation. In an attempt to impress B, A arranged for a sumptuous and expensive meal to be prepared. B forgot about the invitation and did not arrive. The food was wasted. A now wishes to know whether he has any claim against B. Advise him.

5. C, D and E have agreed to form a syndicate for the purpose of making a weekly entry in a football pools competition. C and D, who know nothing about football, agree to give E a sum of money weekly, and to leave it to him to fill in the forms and send them off in his own name. Seven weeks after the start of this arrangement, E sends off an entry which wins £18,000, which he now refuses to share with C and D. Advise C and D.

4
Consideration

The nature of consideration

1. Nature and definition

A voluntary promise (i.e. one which is given for no consideration) is not binding even though there may have been some good moral reason for making the promise.

> *Eastwood* v. *Kenyon* (1840): The plaintiff was the executor of John Sutcliffe, who had died intestate as to his real property leaving as his heir-in-law his only child, Sarah, an infant at the time of his death. The plaintiff spent his own money on the improvement of the realty. To reimburse himself, the plaintiff borrowed £140 from one Blackburn, giving a promissory note. When Sarah reached full age she promised the plaintiff that she would pay to the plaintiff the amount of the note. After Sarah's marriage, her husband promised the plaintiff that she would pay to the plaintiff the amount of the note. The plaintiff sued Sarah's husband on this promise and was met by the defence that no consideration was given for the promise. HELD: the benefit conferred on the defendant (through his wife) by the plaintiff was not consideration to support the defendant's subsequent promise to pay the plaintiff.

It was said by Lord Denman in that case: 'Taking then the promise of the defendant, as stated on this record, to have been an express promise, we find that the consideration for it was past and executed long before; and yet it is not laid to have been at the request of the defendant nor even of his wife when sole. . . and the declaration really discloses nothing but a benefit voluntarily conferred by the plaintiff and received by the defendant with an express promise by the defendant to pay money. . . .

'In holding this declaration bad because it states no consideration but a past benefit not conferred at the request of the defendant, we conceive that we are justified by the old common law of England.'

The classic nineteenth-century definition to be found in the case of *Currie* v. *Misa* (1875) is that a valuable consideration 'may consist either in some right, interest, profit, or benefit accruing to the one party, or some forbearance, detriment, loss, or responsibility given, suffered, or undertaken by the other'. A more easily understandable definition is set out in *Pollock on Contracts*, 13th edn, p. 133, namely that '*An act or forbearance of one party, or the promise thereof, is the price for which the promise of the other is bought, and the promise thus given for value is enforceable.*' Pollock's definition was adopted by the House of Lords in *Dunlop* v. *Selfridge* (1915).

2. Executory and executed consideration

Valuable consideration may be something promised or something done. Regarding a simple contract as a transaction which is essentially a bargain, consideration may be a price promised, or a price paid. ('Price' is used here in the widest sense.)

(a) *Executory consideration* is the price *promised* by one party in return for the other party's promise.

(b) *Executed consideration* is the price *paid* by one party in return for the other party's promise.

Note

The party alleging the breach of contract must show that he gave consideration: generally, this is the plaintiff, but where a defendant brings a counter-claim for breach of contract — i.e. where he alleges that the plaintiff was in breach of contract — then he must show that he, the defendant, gave consideration.

3. Failure of consideration

Money paid or property transferred under a void contract can be recovered where there has been a total failure of consideration. The right to recover is not affected in cases where the payer has received some incidental benefit which was no part of the bargain.

The test whether consideration has failed totally is whether the party who relies on such failure has received any part at all of what he bargained for: *Films Rover International* v. *Cannon Film Sales* (1988) CA.

4. Rules governing consideration
The following rules govern consideration:

(a) Consideration must be real (or sufficient).
(b) Consideration need not be adequate.
(c) Consideration must move from the promisee.
(d) Consideration must not be past.
(e) Consideration must not be illegal.
(f) Consideration must not be vague.
(g) Consideration must be possible of performance.

Rules (a) to (d) above are fundamental to the nature of consideration. Rules (e) to (g) may be regarded as auxiliary.

5. Consideration must be real
Consideration must have some value. It matters not how small that value is, so long as it is worth something. Indeed, the word 'value' is sometimes used to mean consideration.

It follows that where a party performs an act which is merely a discharge of a pre-existing obligation, there is no consideration, but where a party does more than he was already bound to do, there may be consideration. The pre-existing obligation may arise out of a contract between the same parties, under the public law or out of a contract with a third party. The test question in each of these cases is:

(a) Did the party claiming to have given consideration do any more than he was bound to do under a previous contract with the other party? *Stilk* v. *Myrick* (1809); *Hartley* v. *Ponsonby* (1857); but *see Williams* v. *Roffey Bros. and Nichols* (1990).
(b) Did the party claiming to have given consideration do any more than he was already obliged to do under the public law? *Glasbrook Brothers* v. *Glamorgan County Council* (1925); *Ward* v. *Byham* (1956).
(c) Did the party claiming to have given consideration do any more than he was bound to do under a pre-existing contract with

a third party? *Shadwell* v. *Shadwell* (1860); *Scotson* v. *Pegg* (1861); *New Zealand Shipping Co.* v. *Satterthwaite* (1975).

Stilk v. *Myrick* (1809): The captain of a ship promised his crew that, if they shared between them the work of two seamen who had deserted, the wages of the deserters would be shared out between them. HELD: The promise was not binding because the seamen gave no consideration: they were already contractually bound to do any extra work to complete the voyage.

Hartley v. *Ponsonby* (1857): A ship's crew had been seriously depleted by a number of desertions. The captain promised the remaining crew members £40 extra pay if they would complete the voyage. HELD: The promise was binding. It was dangerous to put to sea in a ship so undermanned. The seamen were not obliged to do this under their contracts of service and were, therefore, free to enter into a fresh contract for the remaining part of the voyage.

Williams v. *Roffey Bros. & Nichols* (1990): The plaintiff subcontractors undertook to carry out certain carpentry work for a main contractor who was refurbishing a block of twenty-seven flats. Fearing that delay on the part of the plaintiff would cause the main contractor to become liable to pay liquidated damaged under the main contract, he .promised orally to pay the plaintiff an additional sum for each flat completed on time. The contractor declined to pay this additional money and the plaintiff sued for it. The contractor contended that the plaintiff had given no consideration to support the promise to pay extra money and that by completing on time, the plaintiff had done no more than he was already contractually bound to do under his contract with the contractor. HELD by the Court of Appeal: as a result of his promise to pay extra money, the contractor obtained certain benefits, i.e. the plaintiff continued to work, liquidated damages were avoided and the contractor was saved from the expense and trouble of engaging others to complete the plaintiff's work. There was no economic duress or fraud on the part of the plaintiff. There was, accordingly, consideration for the contractor's promise to pay additional money and the promise was accordingly binding. The principle in *Stilk* v. *Myrick* (1809) was approved.

Glasbrook Brothers v. *Glamorgan County Council* (1925): At the time of a strike at a colliery, the managers asked for police protection of the colliery property. The superintendent of police thought that a mobile patrol would be sufficient, but he agreed to supply a standing guard on payment by the colliery. It was claimed that the promise to pay was not binding as the police were under a duty to protect property, and there was, therefore, no consideration. HELD by the House of Lords: The promise was binding because the police had done more than they were bound to under their public duty.

Ward v. *Byham* (1956): The father of an illegitimate daughter promised the mother £1 a week provided 'that she will be well looked after and happy'. HELD by the Court of Appeal: The promise was binding because the woman's undertaking amounted to more than her bare legal obligations to the child.

Shadwell v. *Shadwell* (1860): After becoming engaged to marry, the plaintiff received a letter from his uncle stating that he was glad to hear of the intended marriage and that he would make an annual payment of £150 yearly to assist the plaintiff in starting his career as a barrister. The plaintiff did marry. At the time of the uncle's death the promised payments were not all made and the plaintiff brought this action against the personal representatives for their recovery. The defendants contended that the plaintiff had given no consideration to support the uncle's promise because he was already contractually bound to marry his fiancée at the time his uncle made the promise. HELD: The plaintiff's marriage was 'an object of interest' to the uncle and was, therefore, sufficient consideration to support the promise of the annual payments.

Scotson v. *Pegg* (1861): By a previous contract with X, the plaintiffs had undertaken to deliver a cargo of coal to X or to the order of X. X then directed the plaintiffs that they

would unload the cargo at a stated rate. The plaintiffs sued
for breach of this promise. The defendants contended that
the promise was not binding for lack of consideration. It
was argued that the plaintiffs were already bound under the
previous contract with X to deliver the cargo and that,
therefore, no consideration moved from the plaintiffs to the
defendants. HELD: The delivery of the coal was a benefit to
the defendants and was, therefore, consideration. The
defendant's promise was binding.

In *New Zealand Shipping Co.* v. *A.M. Satterthwaite & Co.* (1975),
on appeal to the Privy Council, the rule in *Scotson* v. *Pegg* was
applied. In this case it was decided that 'An agreement to do an act
which the promisor is under an existing obligation to a third party
to do, may quite well amount to valid consideration and does so in
the present case: the promisee obtains the benefit of a direct
obligation which he can enforce. This proposition is illustrated and
supported by *Scotson* v. *Pegg* which their Lordships consider to be
good law.'

6.   Consideration need not be adequate

According to the doctrine of freedom of contract, the courts
will not interfere with a bargain freely reached by the parties. It is
not part of the court's duty to assess the relative value of each
party's contribution to the bargain. Once it is established that a
bargain was freely reached, it will be presumed that each party
stipulated according to his wishes and intentions at the time. There
is no reason, for example, why a party should not be bound by a
promise to sell a new Rolls-Royce motor car for one penny. If the
agreement is freely reached, the inadequacy of the price is
immaterial to the existence of a binding contract.

Thomas v. *Thomas* (1842): The plaintiff was the widow of one
Thomas who, just before his death, said that he wished that
his wife should go on living in his house after his death. His
will made no mention of this wish but his brothers, as his
executors, knew of it. After the death of one of the

executors, the remaining executor dispossessed the plaintiff
of the house and she brought this action for breach of
contract. It was argued that the motive of the executors —
their respect for the wish of the deceased — was
consideration: but this argument was rejected by the court.
HELD: The stipulation for the payment towards the ground
rent was consideration quite independent of the moral
feeling which disposed the executors to enter into such a
contract. (An important factor in this case is the admission
of the executor's counsel that he could not base his
argument upon the manifest inadequacy of the
consideration.)

Bainbridge v. *Firmstone* (1838): The plaintiff, at the request of
the defendant, consented to allow the defendant to weigh
two boilers. In return, the defendant promised to return the
boilers in perfect and complete condition. The defendant
took the boilers to pieces and refused to put them back
together again. The plaintiff sued for damages and the
defendant contended that the plaintiff had given no
consideration to support the promise to return the boilers
in complete condition. HELD: The plaintiff's consent given
at the defendant's request amounted to consideration and
the defendant's promise was binding. Per Lord Denman CJ,
'The defendant had some reason for wishing to weigh the
boilers; and he could do so only by obtaining permission
from the plaintiff, which he did obtain by promising to
return them in good condition. We need not enquire what
benefit he expected to derive.'

Chappell & Co. v. *Nestlé Co.* (1960): The Nestlé company
offered to the public gramophone records of a certain dance
tune for 1s 6d each together with three chocolate bar
wrappers. The wrappers were thrown away on receipt by
the company. On the question whether the wrappers were
part of the consideration given for each record it was HELD
by the House of Lords that the wrappers were part of the
consideration even though they were of no further value
once received by the company.

7.   Consideration must move from the promisee

No stranger to the consideration may by himself sue on a contract. Any action for breach of contract must be brought by a party who gave consideration. This rule is related to, but must be distinguished from, the doctrine of privity of contract. In *Dunlop Pneumatic Tyre Co.* v. *Selfridge & Co.* (1915), Lord Haldane said that the two principles were fundamental.

The question whether a party to a contract who gave no consideration may sue on the contract has not yet come squarely before the courts in England. However, in *Coulls* v. *Bagot's Executor and Trustee Co.* (1967), the Australian High Court took the view that a joint promisee could sue on a contract even though it was only the other joint promisee who gave consideration to support the promise made to them jointly.

> *Price* v. *Easton* (1833): X and the defendant agreed that if X did specified work for him, he, the defendant, would pay £19 to P. X did the work but the defendant did not pay the money to P. P sued for the money. HELD: The plaintiff could not succeed because no consideration had passed from him to the defendant.

Consider the following situations:

(a) X, Y and Z enter into an agreement under which X promises to do certain work for Y if Y will pay £10 to Z. If X does the work, he can sue Y on his promise: but Z cannot sue by himself, for he gave no consideration to Y.

(b) X and Y enter into an agreement under which X promises to do certain work for Y if Y will pay £10 to Z. If X does the work, he can sue Y on his promise: but Z cannot sue by himself, for he gave no consideration to Y, nor is he a party to the contract. (*See* Chapter 14.)

8.   Consideration must not be past

Where one party has performed an act before the other party's promise was made, that act cannot be consideration to support the promise. See *Eastwood* v. *Kenyon* (1840).

Thus A offers to drive B from London to Cambridge in his motor car. On arrival at Cambridge, B promises A to pay one pound fifty pence towards the cost of the petrol. B's promise is not binding because the 'consideration' for which it was given was past.

Roscorla v. *Thomas* (1842): At T's request, R bought T's horse for £30. After the sale, T promised R that the horse was sound and free from vice. The horse proved to be vicious. HELD: There was no consideration to support T's promise and he was not bound. The sale itself could not be valuable consideration, for it was completed at the time the promise was given.

Re McArdle (1951): M and his wife lived in a house which was part of the estate of M's father, in which M and his brothers and sister were beneficially interested expectant on the death of their mother, who was tenant for life. In 1943 and 1944, Mrs M paid £488 for improvements and decorations to the house. In 1945, the beneficiaries all signed a document addressed to Mrs M which provided: 'In consideration of your carrying out certain alterations and improvements to the house, we the beneficiaries under the will (of their father) hereby agree that the executors shall repay you from the said estate when so distributed the sum of £488 in settlement of the amount spent on such improvements.' In 1945, the tenant for life died and Mrs M claimed payment of £488. HELD by the Court of Appeal that, as the work had been done and paid for before the beneficiaries made their promise to repay Mrs M, the consideration was past and the promise contained in the document was not binding.

9. Bills of Exchange 1882, s. 27(1)

Section 27(1) of the Bills of Exchange Act 1882 provides an exception to the rule that past consideration is no consideration.

Section 27(1). 'Valuable consideration for a bill may be constituted by:

(a) Any consideration sufficient to support a simple contract;
(b) An antecedent debt or liability. Such debt or liability is deemed valuable consideration whether the bill is payable on demand or at a future time.'

It has been held that the 'antecedent debt or liability' must not be that of a stranger to the bill: *Oliver* v. *Davis* (1949).

10. Apparent exceptions to the rule of past consideration

Section 27 of the Bills of Exchange Act 1882 provides the only real exception to the rule of past consideration. There are, however, two circumstances which are often quoted as apparent exceptions:

(a) Where the plaintiff performs a service at the request of the defendant and the defendant subsequently makes a promise to pay, an action is allowed on the defendant's promise. In *Re Casey's Patents* (1892) Bowen LJ said, 'The fact of a past service raises an implication that at the time it was rendered it was to be paid for, and, if it was a service which was to be paid for, when you get in a subsequent document a promise to pay, that promise may be treated as an admission which evidences or as a positive bargain which fixes the amount of that reasonable remuneration on the faith of which the service was originally rendered.' This dictum of Bowen LJ was applied by the Privy Council in *Pao On* v. *Lau Yiu Long* (1980). In that case Lord Scarman stated the principle as follows: 'An act done before the giving of a promise to make a payment or to confer some other benefit can sometimes be consideration for the promise. First the act must have been done at the promisor's request; secondly, the parties must have understood that the act was to be remunerated either by a payment or the conferment of some other benefit; and thirdly, payment, or the conferment of a benefit, must have been legally enforceable had it been promised in advance'.

(b) Where a right of action to recover a debt or other liquidated claim is barred by the Limitation Act 1980, and the person liable acknowledges the claim or makes any payment in respect thereof, the right shall be deemed to have accrued on and not before the date of the acknowledge or the last payment: Limitation Act 1980, s. 29(5). This means that a promise by a debtor to pay a statute-barred debt is actionable. Notice that s.29 provides for a fresh accrual of a *right of action*: the section concerns procedural rights and not the accrual of substantive contractual rights. The acknowledgment does not create a fresh course of action. Thus, the section provides only an apparent exception to the rule that past consideration is no consideration.

11. Consideration must not be illegal
Where the consideration is either contrary to a rule of law or immoral, the courts will not usually allow an action on the contract: the rule is *ex turpi cause non oritur actio* (no action arises from a base cause). *See* Chapter 11.

12. Consideration must not be vague
The general rule is that the promise by a contracting party must be clear and definite. A vague promise is not binding unless the vagueness can be cured by the implication of terms: *Scammell & Nephew* v. *Ouston* (1941); *Hillas & Co.* v. *Arcos* (1932); *White* v. *Bluett* (1853). *See* 2:**1** and 5:**10**.

13. Consideration must be possible of performance
A promise to do something which is physically or scientifically impossible cannot be binding. Such a promise cannot constitute consideration. Promises to do what is obviously impossible may be perhaps regarded as lacking the essential intention to create legal relations.

Thus, A promises B that he will swim the Atlantic Ocean from Brighton to New York. No consideration moves from A to B.

Waiver must be supported by consideration

14. Waiver of a contractual right
Where a contracting party waives his rights under the contract, wholly or in part, the waiver is not binding unless consideration is given for it. For example, if X owes Y £100, and Y tells X that he will take £90 in full satisfaction of the debt, X will not be discharged from his obligation to pay the £100. If X pays £90 to Y, he will remain liable to the extent of £10.

15. Consideration makes a waiver binding
Where a debtor gives consideration in return for the waiver,

there is accord and satisfaction, and the waiver becomes a part of a new binding contract between the parties (*see* 16:**7**).

16. Where payment of a lesser sum discharges an obligation to pay a greater sum

Where a debtor pays a lesser sum to his creditor than that which is due, the debtor is not discharged from his obligation to pay the balance. At common law the debtor remains liable even where the creditor has agreed to release him from further liability, for the creditor's promise is not supported by any consideration moving from the debtor: *Foakes* v. *Beer* (1884). But if, at the creditor's request, some new element is introduced, such as payment at a different place, or at a different time, compliance with this request will amount to consideration for the waiver. In *Sibree* v. *Tripp* (1846), Baron Alderson said: 'It is undoubtedly true that payment of a portion of a liquidated demand, in the same manner as the whole liquidated demand ought to be paid, is payment only in part; because it is not one bargain, but two; namely payment of part and an agreement, without consideration, to give up the residue . . . But if you substitute a piece of paper or a stick of sealing wax, it is different, and the bargain may be carried out in its full integrity. A man may give, in satisfaction of a debt of £100, a horse of the value of £5, but not £5. Again, if the time or place of payment be different, the one sum may be in satisfaction of the other.'

Thus if D is under a contractual obligation to pay C the sum of £1,000 in London on 28 June, and he (C) requests D to pay £800 in London on 2 June, saying that he will take the lesser sum in full discharge of the greater, C will have no further claim against D if he complies.

Note

There must be some element introduced at the request of the creditor. But *see D & C Builders* v. *Rees* (1965).

Pinnel's Case (1602): Pinnel sued Cole for a debt of £8 10*s* due on 11 November. Cole pleaded that, at Pinnel's request, he had paid £5 2*s* 6*d* on 1 October, and that this had been accepted by Pinnel in full satisfaction. The court found for the plaintiff Pinnel, on a technical point of pleading, but it was made clear in the judgment that, but for this flaw, the court would have found for the defendant, Cole, because the payment of the lesser sum had been made on an earlier date and at the plaintiff's request.

Foakes v. *Beer* (1884): On 11 August 1875 judgment was entered against Dr Foakes and in favour of Mrs Beer, for £2,077 17s 2d for debt and £13 1s 10d for costs. By the Judgments Act 1838, all judgment debts carry interest until paid. On 21 December 1876, the parties agreed in writing that if Dr Foakes paid £500 immediately and the balance of the £2,090 19s by instalments of £150 at stated intervals, Mrs Beer would not take any proceedings whatever on the judgment. Dr Foakes paid all sums as they fell due under the agreement. Mrs Beer then claimed interest, contending that she was not bound by the agreement since there was no consideration from Dr Foakes. HELD by the House of Lords: Payment of only part of a judgment debt is not sufficient consideration to support an agreement by the judgment creditor not to take any proceedings whatever.

Where a third party enters into an agreement with a creditor by which the creditor accepts payment of a lesser sum than the debt in full satisfaction of the debtor's obligation, the creditor cannot sue the debtor for the difference: *Hirachand Punamchand* v. *Temple* (1911).

Promissory estoppel

17. The doctrine as a defence

Where a party has waived his contractual rights against another, and that other party has changed his position in reliance on the waiver, it would be unjust to allow an action against him on the original contract to succeed. In equity, the party who waived his rights may be estopped from denying that he intended the waiver to be binding.

The modern law of promissory estoppel stems from the decision of the House of Lords in *Hughes* v. *Metropolitan Rail Co.* (1877). In this case it was held that a landlord was not entitled to eject his tenant six months after giving notice to repair the premises as provided in the lease on the grounds that, during the six-month period, the landlord had entered into negotiations with the tenant for the sale of the reversion to him. It was held that the negotiations should be regarded as a promise by the landlord that, so long as negotiations continued, the notice would not be enforced. The principle applied in this case was stated in wide terms by Lord Cairns: 'It is the first principle upon which all Courts of Equity proceed, that if parties who have entered into definite and distinct terms involving certain legal results — certain penalties or legal forfeiture — afterwards by their own act or with their own consent enter upon a course of negotiations which has the effect of leading one of the parties to suppose that the strict rights arising under the contract will not be enforced or will be kept in suspense or held in abeyance, the person who otherwise might have enforced those rights will not be allowed to enforce them where it would be inequitable having regard to the dealings which have thus taken place between the parties.'

18. What the defendant must prove

In order to raise the defence of promissory estoppel, the following conditions must be satisfied:

(a) There must have been an original agreement between the parties out of which the defendant owed an obligation to the plaintiff.

(b) The plaintiff must have waived, partly or wholly, his rights against the defendant.

(c) The defendant must have given no consideration for the waiver so as to make it binding at law.

(d) The defendant must have altered his position in reliance on the waiver, so that it would be inequitable to allow the plaintiff to insist on the terms of the original agreement.

19. A shield and not a sword

It is important to note that *the doctrine does* not *create a cause of action*. The doctrine does not relieve a plaintiff from the need to show that he gave consideration for the defendant's promise. In the language of counsel in *Combe* v. *Combe* (1951), the doctrine is a shield and not a sword. Promissory estoppel was explained in the

High Trees case (1947), and in *Combe* v. *Combe* (1951). It was applied by the House of Lords in *Tool Metal Manufacturing Co.* v. *Tungsten Electric Co.* (1955). In the *Tool Metal* case, Viscount Simonds emphasized that the gist of the equitable right lies in the fact that one party has by his conduct led the other to alter his position. He indicated that mere acts of indulgence in commercial transactions are not likely to create rights and that the statement of principle in *Combe* v. *Combe* may well be far too widely stated.

> *Central London Property Trust* v. *High Trees House* (1947): The property company let a block of flats to High Trees House Ltd, the tenants, at a ground rent of £2,500 p.a. in 1937. Owing to war conditions prevailing in London, few of the flats could be let off by the tenants, and they consequently found it difficult to pay £2,500 ground rent. Accordingly, the landlords agreed in writing to reduce the rent to £1,250 p.a. *There was no consideration given for this reduction.* By 1945 the tenants found no difficulty in letting off the flats. The whole block became full. The landlords brought this action to recover the whole balance of rent for the last two quarters of 1945 at the original contract rate. HELD: **(a)** The landlords' promise to reduce the rent was intended to be legally binding and to be acted on, and having been acted on by the tenants, the landlords would not be permitted to act in a manner inconsistent with it, but **(b)** the promise to reduce the rent was a temporary measure and was to be effective only so long as war conditions prevented the tenants from letting the full block. Since the block was fully let early in 1945, the landlords were entitled to the full rent with effect from the quarter ending September 1945.

> *Combe* v. *Combe* (1951): In 1943 a wife obtained a decree nisi against her husband, and immediately afterwards her solicitors wrote to her husband's solicitors asking whether the husband was prepared to make an allowance of £100 a year to the wife. The husband's solicitors replied that the husband agreed. The husband never paid the allowance. In 1950, the wife brought this action, claiming arrears of payment under the husband's promise. At first instance, the judge found for the wife. He held that, although the agreement was not supported by consideration, the

husband's promise was enforceable because it was an absolute acceptance of liability, which was intended to be binding and acted on, and was in fact acted on by the wife. The husband appealed, contending that the judge had misapplied the *High Trees* principle, which could be used 'as a shield and not a sword'. HELD by the Court of Appeal: The wife had given no consideration for the husband's promise, therefore she could not succeed in an action on it. Lord Denning said, 'It [the *High Trees* principle] does not create new causes of action where none existed before. It only prevents a party from insisting on his strict legal rights when it would be unjust to allow him to do so, having regard to the dealings which have taken place between the parties. Thus a creditor is not allowed to enforce a debt which he has deliberately agreed to waive if the debtor has carried on some business or in some other way changed his position in reliance on the waiver.'

However, in the Australian case *Walton Stores (Interstate) Ltd* v. *Maher* (1988), it was held that the doctrine of promissory estoppel could be used to enforce a pre-contractual promise where the other party relied to his detriment on the promise of the first party.

20. Is the estoppel irrevocable?

In the Privy Council case, *Emmanuel Ayodeji Ajayi* v. *R.T. Briscoe (Nigeria)* (1964), the question whether a promissory estoppel is revocable was considered. In this case the position was stated in the form of qualifications to the doctrine as follows:

'(a) that the other party has altered his position,
(b) that the promisor can resile from his promise on giving reasonable notice, which need not be a formal notice, giving the promisee a reasonable opportunity of resuming his position,
(c) the promise only becomes final and irrevocable if the promisee cannot resume his position.'

Lord Denning MR considered the same question in *W.J. Alan & Co.* v. *El Nasr Export and Import Co.* (1972), stating his view as follows: '. . . the one who waives his strict rights cannot afterwards insist on them. His strict rights are at any rate suspended so long as the waiver lasts. He may on occasion be able to revert to his strict legal rights for the future by giving reasonable notice in that behalf, or otherwise making it plain by his conduct that he will thereafter insist on them: *see Tool Metal Manufacturing Co.* v. *Tungsten Electric Co.* (1955). But there are cases where no withdrawal is possible. It may be too late to withdraw; or it cannot be done without injustice to the other party. In that event he is bound by his waiver. He will not be allowed to revert to his strict legal rights. He can only enforce them subject to the waiver he has made.'

See also *Brikom Investments* v. *Carr* (1979) at 16:8.

Progress test 4

1. How was consideration defined in *Currie* v. *Misa*?

2. Distinguish between executory consideration and executed consideration.

3. State the rules governing consideration. Comment on the exceptions, real and apparent, to the rule that past consideration is no consideration.

4. 'Where a party performs an act which is merely a discharge of a pre-existing obligation, there is no consideration: but where a party does more than he was already bound to do, there may be consideration.' Explain this statement, using decided cases to illustrate your explanation.

5. Are the courts concerned with the adequacy of consideration?

6. From whom must consideration move?

7. Explain the difference between past consideration and executed consideration.

8. Where a party waives a contractual right, is he bound by the waiver?

9. Does payment of a lesser sum ever discharge an obligation to pay a greater sum? Give full reasons for your answer.

10. What do you understand by the statement, 'The *High Trees* principle does not create new causes of action where none existed before'?

11. Explain fully the circumstances in which a party may benefit from the doctrine of promissory estoppel.

12. A is under a contractual obligation to pay £1,000 to B. According to the agreement, the sum is payable in Paris on 4 November. Six weeks before the money is due, B asks A if he will pay the debt into his (B's) New York bank account on 4 October. B tells A that if he complies with this request, £900 will be taken as full discharge of the debt of £1,000. A agrees to do this and, in fact, pays £900 into B's New York account. On 15 November B writes to A demanding the balance of £100, which he claims is still outstanding. Advise A.

13. C is a teacher in a state primary school, and D, aged 10, is one of her pupils. E, D's father, promises C that he will pay her £100 if she will give private tuition to D on the four Saturday mornings preceding a scholarship examination for which D has been entered. C agrees, and gives D private tuition accordingly. E now refuses to pay the agreed £100 to C, contending that C was obliged to teach D in any case, and that there was, therefore, no consideration. Advise C. Would it affect your answer if **(a)** D took the examination and failed; **(b)** D was unable to take the examination due to sickness?

14. F's motor car has broken down on a lonely country road. F asks G, who is passing that way in his Land-Rover, if he will tow the car to the nearest garage. G agrees and tows the car 20 miles to the nearest garage. On arrival at the garage, F promises to send G £5 as payment for his services. Is F bound by his promise to pay, or is the consideration for it past?

15. H, a tailor, agrees to make a suit for J at a price of £135. Shortly afterwards, J loses his job and he tells H that he cannot now afford to pay £135 for the suit. H then promises orally that he will reduce the price to £100.

(a) If H delivers the suit to J, and J pays £100 for it, can H subsequently claim the original contract price of £135? Would it make any difference to your answer if J obtained a highly paid job before the suit was finished?

(b) If H sells the suit to another customer for £120, can J bring an action against H for breach of contract? Give your answer on the footing that J is not able or willing to pay more than £100.

5
The terms of a contract

1. Terms

The terms of a contract are its contents, and these determine the extent to which the parties are in agreement. Accordingly, the terms of a contract define the rights and obligations arising from the contract. In the event of a breach of primary obligation, the secondary obligation to pay monetary compensation is substituted. Contractual terms may be expressed or implied:

(a) *Express terms* are express statements made by the parties and by which they intended to be bound.

(b) *Implied terms* are those which have been implied by the law either:

    (*i*) according to the provisions of a statute, or
    (*ii*) to give effect to the presumed intentions of the parties.

Express terms

2. Statements made during negotiations

Material statements made by the parties during negotiations leading up to a contract can be divided into two groups:

(a) Statements made, but which the parties did not intend to be binding terms. These statements are mere representations if they helped to induce the making of the contract.

(b) Statements by which the parties intended to be bound. These are terms of the contract and may be warranties or conditions.

Thus, the parties are bound by statements by which they intended to be bound: where there is no such intention, the parties are not bound. In this connection, the court discovers intention by the application of an objective test. The test question is: *'What would a reasonable man understand to be the intention of the parties, having regard to all the circumstances?'* In applying this test, the court will take notice of all the circumstances of the negotiations between the parties.

3.   Express terms of contract

Where a statement is made during negotiations for the purpose of inducing the other party to enter the contract, there is prima-facie ground for inferring that the statement was intended to be a binding term of contract: but the inference can be rebutted if the party making the statement can show that it would not be reasonable to hold him bound by it: *Dick Bentley Productions* v. *Harold Smith (Motors)* (1965).

In seeking to discover whether to parties intended to be bound by a statement made by one of them, the court will take into account any factor which appears to be relevant. There are no hard and fast rules to be applied. An important factor is the time of making of the statement. If it was made at the time of the contract it is more likely to be a term of contract than if it was made at an early stage of the negotiations. In *Bannerman* v. *White* (1861) the statement was made at the time of the contract; in *Routledge* v. *McKay* (1954) the statement was made at the beginning of negotiations, a week before the contract was concluded.

Where the party who made the statement had exclusive access to information or a special knowledge as compared with the plaintiff, this is likely to be taken into account in the plaintiff's favour: *Couchman* v. *Hill* (1947), *Oscar Chess* v. *Williams* (1957) and *Harling* v. *Eddy* (1951). If the contract is put into writing and the previous oral statement is not included, it tends to show that the statement was a mere representation: *Routledge* v. *McKay* (1954). But this is not always the result when other factors are taken into account. In *Birch* v. *Paramount Estates* (1956) and in *J. Evans & Son (Portsmouth)* v. *Andrea Merzario* (1976) previous oral statements were held to be binding even though not included in the written contract. In *Routledge* v. *McKay* (1954) and *Harling* v. *Eddy* (1951) previous oral statements were held to prevail over the printed conditions of contract.

Where a condition is particularly onerous or unusual, and would not be generally known to the other party, the party seeking to enforce that condition has to show that it has been fairly and reasonably brought to the attention of the other party: *Interfoto Picture Library Ltd* v. *Stiletto Visual Programmes Ltd* (1988). In this case, the Court of Appeal applied *Parker* v. *South Eastern Railway Co.* (1877) and *Thornton* v. *Shoe Lane Parking Ltd* (1971) (which were cases on exclusion clauses) thus making it clear that *Parker* and *Thornton* were applicable to onerous or unusual conditions regardless of whether they were exclusion clauses.

Oscar Chess v. *Williams* (1957): The plaintiffs were car dealers and the defendant was a customer. The parties agreed on a trade-in of the defendant's old car as part of the arrangement when he purchased another from the plaintiffs. The registration book of the car traded in gave its date as 1948. The defendant confirmed this date in good faith. Some months later it was discovered that the date should have been 1939. The car was thus worth much less that the amount allowed for it in the trade-in arrangement. HELD by a majority of the Court of Appeal: The age of the car was not a term of the contract and that there was no breach of contract by the defendant.

Couchman v. *Hill* (1947): C bought a heifer at an auction sale. The heifer was described in the sale catalogue as 'unserved'. The printed conditions of sale contained the following stipulation: 'The lots are sold with all faults, imperfections, and errors of description, the auctioneers not being responsible for the correct description, genuineness, or authenticity of, or any fault or defect whatever.' Before he bid for the heifer, C asked the auctioneer and H, the owner, 'Can you confirm heifer unserved?' Both answered in the affirmative. The heifer died two months later as the result of a miscarriage. C sued H for breach of contract. HELD by the Court of Appeal: The substance of the conversation between the parties before the sale amounted to a contractual term overriding the stultifying exemptions clause in the printed conditions.

Routledge v. *McKay* (1954): B bought a motor cycle from S by private sale. A week before the sale S told B in good faith that it was a 1941 or 1942 model. The written memo-

randum of the sale did not mention the year of the model.
The motor cycle was a 1930 model and B sued S for breach
of contract. HELD by the Court of Appeal: The oral
statement as to the year of the model was a mere
representation and not a term of contract (NB: The
statement was made (a) a full week before the sale, and (b)
it was not included in the written memorandum.)

Heilbut, Symons & Co. v. *Buckleton* (1913): The defendants
underwrote a large number of shares in Filisola Rubber and
Produce Estates, Ltd. The defendants instructed one
Johnston, their Liverpool manager, to obtain applications
for shares. The plaintiff telephones Johnston, saying, 'I
understand that you are bringing out a rubber company.'
To which Johnston replied 'We are.' The plaintiff then
asked Johnston whether he had any prospectuses, and he
replied that he had not. The plaintiff then asked 'if it was all
right', to which Johnston replied, 'We are bringing it out'.
The plaintiff then said, 'That is good enough for me.' As a
result of this telephone conversation a large number of
shares were allotted to the plaintiff. At this time, there was a
rubber boom and the Filisola shares were at a premium.
Shortly afterwards, the shares fell in value. The plaintiff
brought this action for fraudulent misrepresentation by the
defendants through their agent Johnston, and,
alternatively, damages for breach of warranty that the
Filisola company was a rubber company whose main object
was to produce rubber. At Liverpool Assizes before Lush J
and a special jury, the jury found that there was no fraud:
but that the company could not properly be described as a
rubber company and that the defendants or Johnston or
both had warranted that the company was a rubber
company. The jury based its findings as to warranty on the
telephone conversation, there being no other evidence. The
defendants appealed without success to the Court of Appeal.
The defendants then appealed to the House of Lords. HELD
by the House of Lords: Johnston's telephone statements did
not amount to a warranty. There was, accordingly, no
breach of contract.

Dick Bentley Productions v. *Harold Smith (Motors)* (1965): The second plaintiff, Mr Bentley, told Mr Smith of the defendant company that he was on the look-out for a well-vetted Bentley car. Mr Smith subsequently obtained a Bentley car and Mr Bentley went to see it. Mr Smith told Mr Bentley that the car had done 20 thousand miles only since the fitting of a new engine and gearbox. (The mileometer showed 20 thousand miles.) Later that day Mr Bentley took his wife to see the car and Mr Smith repeated his statement. Mr Bentley took the car out for a run and then bought it for £1,850, paying by cheque. The car was a disappointment to Mr Bentley and it soon became clear that the car had done more than 20 thousand miles since the change of engine and gearbox. The action for £400 damages was brought against the defendant company in the county court, the plaintiffs alleging fraud. The defendants counterclaimed for £190 for works carried out on the car. His Honour Judge Herbert held that there was no fraud, but that there was a breach of warranty, awarding £400 damages to the plaintiffs and £77 to the defendants on their counterclaim. The defendants appealed, contending that their representation did not amount to a warranty. HELD: The representation was a warranty.

Interfoto Picture Library Ltd v. *Stiletto Visual Programmes Ltd* (1988) CA: The defendants were an advertising agency and the plaintiffs ran a library of photographic transparencies. They had not dealt with each other before. The defendants needed period photographs of the 1950s for a presentation. On 5 March 1984, they telephoned the plaintiffs, enquiring whether they had any photographs of that period which might be suitable. On the same day, the plaintiffs dispatched to the defendants 47 transparencies packed in a jiffy bag together with a delivery note. At the top right-hand corner of the delivery note the date for return was clearly stated as 19 March. Across the bottom of this document, under the heading 'Conditions' fairly prominently printed in capitals, there were nine conditions, printed in four columns. Condition no.2 in the first column read as follows: 'All transparencies must be returned to us within 14 days from the date of delivery. A holding fee of £5.00 plus VAT per day will be charged for each transparency which is retained by you longer than the said period of 14 days save where a copyright licence is granted or we agree a longer period in writing with you.' The defendants accepted delivery of the transparencies but did not use them for their presentation. They put the transparencies aside and forgot about them. They were not returned until 2 April. The plaintiffs sent an invoice for the holding charge calculated at £5 per transparency per day from 19 March to 2 April, total £3,783.50. The defendants refused to pay and the plaintiffs sued for the amount invoiced. Judgment was given for the plaintiffs and the defendants appealed to the Court of Appeal. HELD: Condition 2 was an unreasonable and extortionate clause which the plaintiffs had not brought to the attention of the defendants and therefore it did not become part of the contract. The defendants were ordered to pay a sum which the trial judge would have awarded on a *quantum meruit* on his alternative findings, i.e. the reasonable charge of £3.50 per transparency per week for the retention of the transparencies beyond a reasonable period fixed as 14 days from the date of their receipt by the defendants.

4. Certainty of terms

The parties should make their contracts in terms which are certain or the contract may fail: *Scammell and Nephew* v. *Ouston* (1941). Meaningless terms will be ignored and the contract will operate without them: *Nicolene* v. *Simmonds* (1953). A contract couched in uncertain or vague terms may be saved if the contract contains a term which will resolve the uncertainty: *Foley* v. *Classique Coaches* (1934). The court will declare an implied term to give effect to the presumed intentions of the parties (*see* below): but where the parties have not agreed on a matter fundamental to the contract, there can be no binding contract: *Courtney and Fairbairn* v. *Tolaini Brothers* (1975). A contract to negotiate, even though supported by consideration, is not known to the law, since it is too uncertain to have any binding force and, further, no court could estimate the damages for breach of such an agreement: *Courtney and Fairbairn* v. *Tolaini Brothers* (1975).

Nicolene v. *Simmonds* (1953): The plaintiff ordered a quantity of iron bars, specifying his requirements in detail. The defendant accepted the order saying, in his letter, 'I assume that we are in agreement that the usual conditions of acceptance apply' and 'I thank you very much indeed for entrusting this contract to me'. The plaintiff merely acknowledged this letter, saying that he awaited the invoice, making no reference to the 'usual conditions of acceptance'. The defendant failed to deliver the iron bars and the plaintiff sued for breach of contract. The defendant contended that, since there had been no agreement on the 'usual conditions of acceptance', there was no contract concluded. The plaintiff contended that the defendant's letter accepting the order was a contractually binding acceptance of the plaintiff's offer to buy the goods. HELD by the Court of Appeal: Since there were no such 'usual conditions' and hence nothing to which the expression could apply, it was meaningless and capable of being rejected without impairing the contract as a whole; the defendant's letter accepting the plaintiff's order constituted an unqualified acceptance of the plaintiff's offer, and, therefore, there was a concluded contract between the parties.

Courtney and Fairbairn v. *Tolaini Bros.* (1975): The plaintiff, a building contractor, after preliminary discussions with the defendant, a developer, concerning three projects — a motel, a filling station and a hotel — wrote to say: 'I would be very happy to know that. . . you will be prepared to instruct your Quantity Surveyor to negotiate fair and reasonable contract sums in respect of each of the three projects as they arise.' The defendant wrote: 'In reply to your letter. . . I agree to the terms specified therein, and I look forward to meeting the interested party regarding finance.' The defendant, taking advantage of finance made available through the introductions and influence of the plaintiff, engaged another building contractor to do the work. The plaintiff brought this action for breach of contract, contending that the letters, taken together, formed a binding contract. HELD by the Court of Appeal:

There was no contract because there was no agreement on the price or on any method by which the price was to be calculated (the price in a building contract being of fundamental importance); the agreement was only an agreement to negotiate fair and reasonable contract sums.

Bushwall Properties v. *Vortex Properties* (1976): The parties entered into an agreement for the sale of 51 acres of land by phased completion at a price of £500,000. By the terms of the agreement the purchase price was to be 'phased as to £250,000 upon first completion, as to £125,000 a further 12 months thereafter and as to the balance of £125,000 a further 12 months thereafter'. The agreement further provided that 'on the occasion of each completion a proportionate part of the land shall be released forthwith' to the plaintiffs. The defendants then, in breach of this agreement, conveyed the land to a third party who subsequently sold the land to the plaintiffs for £500,000 payable immediately on completion. The plaintiffs brought this action for breach of the agreement for the sale by phased completion. The defendants contended that the reference to 'a proportionate part of the land' was too uncertain because the agreement did not contain a provision governing the power of either party to select the 'proportionate part'. HELD by the Court of Appeal: In the absence of any express term as to how the land to be included in each phase was to be selected, the agreement was void for uncertainty.

Malcolm v. *University of Oxford* (1990): The Oxford University Press made an agreement with M by telephone to the effect that the OUP gave a 'commitment' to publish M's book in return for a 'fair royalty'. HELD by the Court of Appeal: There was an enforceable contract between M and the OUP. Where there was a practice which left certain matters of detail to the discretion of the publisher, failure to agree on any such matter in an informal bargain that otherwise possessed the attributes of a binding contract did not mean that a contract did not exist because in practice either the parties would agree upon those matters later or the publisher would decide.

5.   Construction of a contract

The court will construe a contract as follows:

(a)   Words are presumed to have their ordinary literal meaning, but legal terms are presumed to have their technical meaning.

(b)   Where a contract is ambiguous so that it may have either a legal or an illegal meaning, the legal meaning will be preferred.

(c)   Where the meaning of words used is not clear, or where two terms cannot be reconciled, the intention of the parties will prevail: indeed, an oral term may thus prevail over a contradictory written term as in *Couchman* v. *Hill* (1947). Where a contract is made up of a standard printed form together with specially prepared documents which conflict with the standard form, the court will generally take the view that the intention of the parties should be gathered from the specially prepared documents, and that the conflicting provision in the standard form should be disregarded.

(d)   The contract will be construed most strongly against the party who drew it up. Thus, where there is an ambiguous passage in a contract so that the words will bear two different meanings the court will choose that meaning which is against the interest of the party who drew up the document, to the benefit of the other party. This is known as the *contra proferentum* rule, and is most important in connection with exemption clauses.

(e)   In construing the written terms of a contract, evidence of the preceding negotiations is not receivable in proceedings, nor is evidence of the parties' intentions during negotiations. However, evidence of the factual background known to the parties at or before the date of the contract is receivable: *Prenn* v. *Simmonds* (1971) HL.

6.   Contract and professional negligence

A professional person will usually seek to avoid contracting to produce an absolute result. A structural engineer does not expressly undertake that his bridge will not collapse, although he will usually contract, expressly or by implication, to exercise all reasonable skill and care in the carrying out of his design work. Similarly, a surgeon does not in practice give an absolute undertaking that an operation will be concluded successfully. In short, professional people understandably try to avoid giving express contractual undertakings which would have the effect of increasing their liabilities under the law of negligence.

Thake v. *Maurice* (1986): The first and second plaintiffs were, respectively, husband and wife. They were the parents of four children with a fifth on the way and were finding it difficult to manage on the husband's pay as a railway guard. The husband arranged for a vasectomy to be performed by the defendant in 1975. Notwithstanding the vasectomy, the wife became pregnant again in 1977. As she thought that her husband was by then sterile, she failed to recognize the symptoms of pregnancy until it was too late for an abortion. She gave birth to a girl.

The plaintiffs brought this action claiming that the defendant had contracted to sterilize the first plaintiff and that this contract had been broken when he became fertile again: or, alternatively, that the plaintiffs were induced to enter the contract by a warranty or misrepresentation that the operation would render the first defendant permanently sterile: or, alternatively, that the defendant had failed to warn them of the small risk that the first plaintiff would become fertile again. HELD by the Court of Appeal:

(a) A doctor or surgeon could not be regarded as guaranteeing the success of any operation or treatment unless he expressly undertook as much in clear and unequivocal terms. Accordingly, the defendant contracted to perform a vasectomy operation with reasonable care and skill — he did not contract to sterilize the first defendant.
(b) However, the defendant owed to the plaintiffs a duty of care to warn against the possibility of a recovery of fertility because a warning was necessary to alert the second plaintiff to the risk of pregnancy and so enable her to seek an abortion at an early stage. Failure to give such a warning amounted to a breach of the defendant's duty of care. The risk of the second plaintiff's failure to appreciate at an early stage that she had once again become pregnant must have been in the reasonable contemplation of the defendant.

The plaintiffs were entitled to damages under the following heads: the cost of the layette, the cost of the child's upkeep until the age of 17, loss of the second plaintiff's earnings during this period; also the plaintiffs were entitled to damages for distress, pain and suffering and for the discomfort and pain of a normal pregnancy and delivery. The relief and joy after the birth of a normal healthy baby did not cancel out the plaintiff's entitlement for distress, pain and suffering.

The above case should be compared with *Eyre* v. *Measday* (1986) CA in which a surgeon had performed a sterilization operation on the female plaintiff. The defendant surgeon had emphasized the irreversible nature of the operation but failed to say that there was a small risk (less than one per cent) of pregnancy occurring after the operation. The plaintiff claimed damages for breach of contract, contending that the statement that the operation was irreversible and the failure to warn of the slight risk amounted to breach of a contractual term or breach of an express or implied collateral warranty, that he would render her irreversibly sterile. The main problem of the Court of Appeal in this case was to decide whether or not the defendant had given an implied guarantee that the operation would succeed. Slade LJ said: 'But in my opinion, in the absence of any express warranty, the court should be slow to imply against a medical man an unqualified warranty as to the result of an intended operation, for the very simple reason that, objectively speaking, it is most unlikely that a responsible medical man would intend to give a warranty of this nature.' Accordingly, the plaintiff's claim failed.

Implied terms

7. Unexpressed terms
There is a general presumption that the parties have expressed, orally or in writing, every material term which they intend should govern their contract. But there are circumstances where terms which have not been expressed by the parties are inferred by the law. An implied term is binding to the same extent as an express term. A term may be implied in a contract:

(a) to give effect to the presumed but unexpressed intentions of the parties, or
(b) by statute.

In *Scancarriers* v. *Aotearoa International* (1985), the Privy Council made it clear that the process of implication is available only where a binding contract has been made. The process of implication is not relevant until the formation of a contract has been completed.

8. Implied terms and presumed intentions

In order to discover the unexpressed intention of the parties, the courts may take notice of trade customs, the conduct of the parties, or the need to give 'business efficacy' to a contract.

It must be emphasized that, where the parties have made an unambiguous express provision in their contract, the court will not imply a term to the contrary: *see Trollope & Colls* v. *North West Regional Hospital Board* (1973), a House of Lords decision.

9. Trade or professional customs

In *Hutton* v. *Warren* (1836), Baron Parke said, 'It has long been settled that in commercial transactions extrinsic evidence of custom and usage is admissible to annex incidents to written contracts in matters with respect to which they are silent. The same rule has also been applied to contracts in other transactions in life in which known usages have been established and prevailed; and this has been done upon the principle of presumption that, in such transactions, the parties did not mean to express in writing the whole of the contract by which they intended to be bound, but to contract with reference to those known usages.' Although Baron Parke spoke only of terms implied in written contracts, the same principle applies to oral contracts.

⌐Where a term is implied on the grounds of a custom, the implication is based on the assumption that it was the intention of the parties to be bound by the custom⌐A custom can, of course, be excluded from an agreement by an express term to that effect.

An example of a term implied by custom occurs in contracts of marine insurance, where there is an implied undertaking by the broker that agreed premiums will be paid, i.e. he is deemed to promise the insurer that he will be liable for payment of premiums in the event of default on the part of the assured.

10. Conduct of the parties

A term may be implied by reason of the conduct of the parties.

For example, when a customer selects goods from the shelves of a self-service store and presents them at the cashier's desk, and the cashier rings up the price, which the customer immediately pays, there is a contract. There is an express term as to price, i.e. the sum of the prices on the labels of the selected items, the remaining terms being implied by the conduct of the parties: *Pharmaceutical Society of GB* v. *Boots Cash Chemists* (1953).

> *Hillas & Co.* v. *Arcos* (1932): There was an agreement between the parties for the supply of 22,000 standards of timber during 1931, the agreement containing an option clause allowing the buyers to take 100,000 standards during 1932. The agreement was vague as to the kind of timber, the terms of shipment, and other important details usually expressed in commercial contracts: however, the parties managed to get through the part of the agreement relating to the 22,000 standards in 1931. In 1932 the sellers claimed that they were not bound to deliver the 100,000 standards: they contended that the clause was vague and was merely a basis for further negotiations. HELD by the House of Lords: The option clause was not specific as to details, but it was couched in the same language as the agreement to supply timber in 1931. The unexpressed details of the option clause could, therefore, be inferred from the course of dealing between the parties during 1931.

11. 'Business efficacy'

A term may be implied to give to a contract what has become known as 'business efficacy'. Bowen LJ said in *The Moorcock* (1889), 'The implication which the law draws from what must obviously have been the intention of the parties, the law draws with the object of giving efficacy to the transaction and preventing such a failure of consideration as cannot have been within the contemplation of either side. . . In business transactions. . . what the law desires to effect by the implication is to give such business efficacy to the transaction as must have been intended at all events by both parties who are business men. . . .' As a result of the decision in this case, the courts were often asked to imply a term on vague or uncertain grounds.

In 1941, however, the rule in *The Moorcock* was given some

precision by the House of Lords in *Luxor (Eastbourne)* v. *Cooper* (1941). In this case, Lord Wright said, 'It is agreed on all sides that the presumption is against the adding to contracts of terms which the parties have not expressed. The general presumption is that the parties have expressed every material term which they intended should govern their agreement, whether oral or in writing. It is well recognized, however, that there may be cases where obviously some term must be implied if the intention of the parties is not to be defeated, some term of which it can be predated that "it goes without saying", some term not expressed, but necessary to give the transaction such business efficacy as the parties must have intended. . . The implication must arise inevitably to give effect to the intention of the parties.'

> *The Moorcock* (1889): There was a contract between the defendants, who owned a Thames-side wharf and jetty, and the plaintiffs that the plaintiffs' vessel *Moorcock* should be unloaded and reloaded at the defendants' wharf. The *Moorcock* was, accordingly, moored alongside the wharf but, as the tide fell, she took to the ground and sustained damage on account of the unevenness of the river bed at that place. The plaintiffs brought this action for breach of contract. HELD: There was an implied term in the contract that the defendants would take reasonable care to see that the berth was safe: both parties must have known at the time of the agreement that if the ground were not safe the ship would be endangered when the tide ebbed: there was a breach of the implied term.

It is important to notice that no term will be implied to give the contract efficacy unless the implication must arise inevitably. In order to imply a term it is necessary to say not merely that it would be a businesslike arrangement to make, but that any other arrangement would be so unbusinesslike that sensible people could not be supposed to have entered into it: *see Brown & Davis* v. *Galbraith* (1972) CA. The *Moorcock* was followed in *Eyre* v. *Measday* (1986), *Wettern Electric* v. *Welsh Development Agency* (1983) and *Fraser* v. *Thames Television* (1983).

In *Shirlaw* v. *Southern Foundries* (1939) CA, it was said, 'Prima facie that which in any contract is left to be implied and need not be expressed is something so obvious that it goes without saying;

so that, if while the parties were making their bargain an officious bystander were to suggest some express provision for it in their agreement, they would testily suppress him with a common, "Oh, of course".'

In *Baylis* v. *Barnett* (1988) CA, an employer claimed that there was an implied term binding his employee to the payment of interest which he alleged to be outstanding on a loan made to that employee by the employer. In this case it was said that, 'There was no doubt whatever that if the "officious bystander" had asked the parties whether they intended that the employee should indemnify the employer for any interest which he had to pay to the bank they would have said "yes". *Baylis* was one of those rare cases where the court was right in implying such a term on the basis that it was certain that such had been the intention of the parties.'

In *Fraser* v. *Thames Television* (1983), there was a contract between a three-woman rock group and their manager on the one hand, and Thames Television on the other, by which Thames acquired the right to use the idea of such a group as a television series. Thames gave the women first refusal of a part in the proposed series. It was held that there was implied into the agreement a negative covenant that if all three women were willing to appear in the series then Thames would not make use of the idea without employing them. The court may imply a term into a contract where, and only to the extent that, it is necessary in order to achieve business efficacy; but the court will avoid the temptation to rewrite the contract in a more efficient and attractive way: *Express Newspapers* v. *Silverstone Circuits* (1989) CA.

A term will not be implied on grounds of mere reasonableness. In *Liverpool City Council* v. *Irwin* (1976), a House of Lords decision, Lord Wilberforce said that the implication of reasonable terms would be 'to extend a long, and undesirable, way beyond sound authority'. This case was concerned with the obligations of a local authority towards its tenants in a high-rise block of flats. The court was simply concerned to establish what the contract was, the parties themselves not having fully stated the terms. It was in this sense that the court was searching for what must be implied. Lord Wilberforce said further: 'In my opinion such obligation should be read into the contract as the nature of the contract itself implicitly requires, no more, no less; a test in other words of necessity. The relationship accepted by the corporation is that of landlord and tenant; the tenant accepts obligations accordingly, in relation, *inter alia*, to the stairs, the lifts and the rubbish chutes. All these are not just facilities, or conveniences provided at discretion; they are essentials of the tenancy without which life in the dwellings, as a tenant, is not possible. . . . The subject-matter of the lease (high-rise blocks) and the relationship created by the tenancy demands, of its nature, some contractual obligation on the landlord.'

Lord Wilberforce concluded that, since there was no obligation to maintain and repair stairs, lifts and chutes undertaken by the tenants, then the nature of the contract and the circumstances required that the obligation be placed on the landlord. On the question of standard of maintenance, Lord Wilberforce resorted again to the concept of necessity, holding that the standard must not exceed what is necessary having regard to the circumstances, i.e. an obligation to keep in reasonable repair and usability, taking into account the responsibilities of the tenants themselves. Applying this test, the House of Lords unanimously decided that the council was not in breach of its obligations with regard to the maintenance of stairs, lifts and chutes.

The dictum of Lord Wilberforce in *Liverpool City Council* v. *Irwin* was applied in *Sim* v. *Rotherham Metropolitan Borough Council* (1986) in which the question arose whether teachers were contractually bound to 'cover' for absent colleagues — a matter not expressly contained in the teachers' contracts of employment. It was held that, since cover arrangements (like the timetable) were administrative directions from the head teacher and necessary for the proper conduct of the school and, since teachers have always accepted a professional obligation to comply with timetable and cover arrangements, it followed that the teachers were under a contractual duty to comply with a request to cover.

12. Terms implied by statute

Certain statutes provide for the implication of terms in contracts. Statutory implied terms will operate irrespective of the intention of the parties, unless there is a valid exclusion clause. Examples of statutory implied terms are to be found in ss. 12–15 of the Sale of Goods Act 1893. The provisions of the 1893 Act have now been consolidated with their amendments in the Sale of Goods Act 1979. These Acts provide for the implication of certain very important undertakings by the seller in contracts of sale of goods. It is necessary now to consider the implied terms separately (**13–17** below) and then to consider the restrictions on the seller's power to contract out of the implied undertakings (**18**).

13. Implied terms as to title (s. 12)

The 1979 Act provides for the implication of three terms as to title to the goods, namely,

(a) a condition that the seller has the right to sell the goods, and
(b) a warranty that the goods will be free from any undisclosed encumbrance, and
(c) a warranty that the buyer will enjoy quiet possession.

> *Rowland* v. *Divall* (1923): After a buyer had used a motor car for four months, the police took it away because it had been stolen before it had come into the seller's possession. The buyer sought to recover the full price on the ground that the consideration had wholly failed. HELD by the Court of Appeal: There was a breach of the implied condition arising under s. 12 of the Sale of Goods Act. The seller had no title and the buyer, therefore, received nothing from him. There was a complete failure of consideration and the full purchase price was recoverable. The fact that the buyer had enjoyed the use of the car for four months was not a benefit conferred by the seller under the contract.

14. Correspondence with description (s. 13)

Where there is a contract for the sale of goods by description, there is an implied condition that the goods will correspond with the description. A sale of goods will not be prevented from being a sale by description by reason only that, being exposed for sale (as, for example, in a self-service store) they are selected by the buyer.

Where a sale is by sample as well as by description, it is not sufficient that the bulk of the goods corresponds with the sample if the goods do not also correspond with the description.

The following cases indicate the strictness with which the court has applied s. 13.

> *Wilensko Slaski, etc.* v. *Fenwick & Co.* (1938): There was a contract for the sale of a quantity of pit props of specified

lengths. The buyer undertook that he would 'not reject the goods. . . or any part of them'. One per cent of the goods delivered did not comply with the specification and the buyer claimed to be able to reject them. HELD: Notwithstanding his undertaking, the buyer was entitled to reject the goods because the seller was in breach of the implied condition in s. 13.

Re Moore & Co. and Landauer & Co. (1921): The terms of a contract for the sale of tinned pears provided that the goods were to be packed in cases of 30 tins each. When the buyers inspected the tendered consignment they found that about half the cases contained 24 tins each, the remainder containing 30 tins each. The buyers rejected all these cases. HELD by the Court of Appeal: It was part of the contract description of the goods that there should be 30 tins to the case and that, accordingly, the sellers were in breach of the implied condition in s. 13. Further, by s. 30(3), the buyer was entitled to reject the whole consignment.

Macpherson Train & Co. v. *Howard Ross & Co.* (1955): There was a contract for the sale of 5,064 cases of cans of peaches. The contract included a clause which provided as follows: 'Shipment and destination: afloat per SS *Morton Bay* due London approximately 8 June.' The *Morton Bay* did not arrive in London until 21 June. The buyers refused to accept the goods, contending that there was a breach of condition, as 'afloat per SS *Morton Bay* due London approximately 8 June' was part of the description of the goods. The sellers contended that 8 June was not intended to be the delivery date. HELD: The clause was part of the implied condition in s. 13. The buyers were entitled to refuse to accept the goods.

These cases should be seen in the light of *Harlingdon & Leinster Enterprises Limited* v. *Christopher Hill Fine Art Limited* (1990), where it was held that, for there to be a sale by description, it must be established that the parties shared a common intention that the description should be a term of the contract and that this would be established if the buyer relied on the description. Slade LJ stated: 'The presence or absence of reliance on the description may be very relevant insofar as it throws light on the intentions of the parties at the time of the contract. If there was no such reliance by the purchaser, this may be powerful evidence that the parties did not contemplate that the authenticity of the description should constitute a term of the contract, in other words, that they contemplated that the purchaser would be buying goods as they were.'

15. Merchantable quality (s. 14)

Where the seller sells goods in the course of a business, there is an implied condition that the goods supplied under the contract are of merchantable quality. But there is no such condition as regards defects specifically drawn to the buyer's attention before the contract was made, or, if the buyer examines the goods before the contract is made, as regards defects which that examination ought to reveal. Nor where the sale is not in the course of a business.

> *Wilson* v. *Rickett, Cockerell & Co.* (1954): W bought from the defendant coal merchants 'a ton of Coalite'. When part of the consignment was being burnt in the grate, there was an explosion which caused damage to W's goods in the room. The explosive matter was not Coalite, but some foreign matter which had got mixed with the Coalite. W claimed damages under s. 14. HELD by the Court of Appeal: There was a breach of the implied condition of merchantable quality under s. 14.

> *Wren* v. *Holt* (1903): The buyer bought a glass of beer in a public house and later became ill because the beer was contaminated with arsenic. HELD: There was a breach of the implied condition as to merchantable quality under s. 14.

16. Fitness for purpose (s. 14)

Where the seller sells goods in the course of a business and the buyer, expressly or by implication, makes known to the seller any particular purpose for which the goods are being bought, there is an implied condition that the goods supplied under the contract are reasonably fit for that purpose. The implied condition arises whether or not the purpose is one for which such goods are

commonly supplied. There is, however, no implied condition as to
fitness for purpose where the circumstances show that the buyer
does not rely, or that it is unreasonable for him to rely, on the
seller's skill or judgment. Nor where the sale is private, i.e. not in
the course of a business.

Where goods have a self-evident purpose, e.g. a hot-water
bottle or a pair of underpants, the purpose for which the goods are
being bought is made known to the seller by implication.

Priest v. *Last* (1903): There was a retail sale of a hot-water
bottle. The bottle burst and injured the buyer's wife. The
buyer brought this action to recover damages for the
medical expenses incurred. HELD: The seller was in breach
of the implied condition as to fitness for purpose, the
purpose being self-evident in the case of goods of this kind.

Ashington Piggeries v. *Christopher Hill* (1971): The defendants
were two mink companies concerned with the breeding of
mink and with the supply of equipment and foodstuffs to
other mink breeders. The plaintiffs, who manufactured
compounds for animal feeding, entered into an agreement
with the defendants for the manufacture of a mink food to
be called King Size. The formula was supplied by the
defendants, and the plaintiffs had made it clear that they
knew nothing about the nutritional requirements of mink.
The plaintiffs did, however, suggest as a variation in the
formula, the substitution of herring meal for fishmeal. For
about a year, King Size was used by about 100 mink farms
without complaint. But in March 1961 the plaintiffs bought
a large consignment of herring meal which had been
contaminated by a chemical known as DMNA, toxic to mink
but harmless to other animals. The inclusion of
contaminated herring meal in the manufacture of King Size
resulted in serious losses on some mink farms.

The defendant buyers refused to pay for a consignment
of King Size containing contaminated meal and the plaintiff
sellers brought this action for breach of payment. The
defendants counterclaimed for breach of contract. HELD by
the House of Lords:

(a) There was a breach of the implied condition in s. 14 that

the goods were reasonably fit for purpose, the buyers
having relied on the skill and judgment of the sellers;
(b) the sellers were also in breach of the implied condition
that the goods were of merchantable quality.

17. Sale by sample (s. 15)

In the case of a contract of sale by sample there are the
following further implied conditions:

(a) that the bulk will correspond with the sample in quality, and
(b) that the buyer will have a reasonable opportunity of
comparing the bulk with the sample, and
(c) that the goods will be free from any defect, rendering them
unmerchantable, which would not be apparent on reasonable
examination of the sample.

18. Contracting out the implied terms

The right of the seller to exclude or restrict his liability under
ss. 12, 13, 14 and 15 of the Sale of Goods Act 1979 is controlled by
s. 55 and the provisions of the Unfair Contract Terms Act 1977.
For the details of these *see* Appendix 2.

19. The Supply of Goods and Services Act 1982

This Act provides for the implication of terms **(a)** in certain
contracts for the transfer of property in goods, **(b)** contracts for
the hire of goods and **(c)** contracts for the supply of services. The
Act also governs the exclusion of such implied terms.

20. Contracts for the transfer of property in goods

For the purposes of the 1982 Act, a 'contract for the transfer
of goods' means a contract under which one person transfers or
agrees to transfer to another the property in goods other than any
of the following:

(a) a contract of sale of goods;
(b) a hire-purchase agreement;
(c) a contract under which the property in goods is or is to be
transferred in exchange for trading stamps;
(d) a transfer made by deed for which there is no consideration
other than presumed consideration;
(e) a contract intended to operate by way of security: s. 1.

In any contract for the transfer of goods, terms will be implied corresponding to those which are implied in the case of contracts for the sale of goods. They are implied terms about title (s. 2), implied terms where transfer is by description (s. 3), implied terms about quality or fitness (s. 4) and implied terms where transfer is by sample (s. 5).

21. Contracts for the hire of goods

For the purposes of the 1982 Act, a 'contract for the hire of goods' means a contract under which one person bails or agrees to bail goods to another by way of hire other than any of the following:

(a) a hire-purchase agreement;
(b) a contract under which goods are bailed in exchange for trading stamps: s. 6.

In any contract for the hire of goods, terms will be implied corresponding to those which are implied in the case of contracts for the sale of goods. They are, implied terms about the right to transfer possession (s. 7), implied terms where hire is by description (s. 8), implied terms about quality or fitness (s. 9) and implied terms where hire is by sample (s. 10).

22. Contracts for the supply of services

The 1982 Act provides for implied terms regarding **(a)** care and skill, **(b)** time of performance and **(c)** consideration, in any contract for the supply of a service.

(a) *Care and skill.* Where the supplier is acting in the course of a business, there is an implied term that the supplier will carry out the service with reasonable care and skill: s. 13.
(b) *Time of performance.* Where the supplier is acting in the course of a business and the time for the service to be carried out is not fixed by the contract, left to be fixed in a manner agreed by the contract or determined by the course of dealing between the parties, there is an implied term that the supplier will carry out the service within a reasonable time: s. 14.
(c) *Consideration.* Where the consideration for the service is not determined by the contract, left to be determined in a manner to be agreed by the contract or determined by the course of dealing

between the parties, there is an implied term that the party contracting with the supplier will pay a reasonable charge: s. 15.

23. Contracting out of terms implied under the 1982 Act

In the case of contracts for transfer of goods or the hire of goods, a supplier may contract out subject to s. 11 which reflects s. 55 of the Sale of Goods Act 1979 and takes the Unfair Contract Terms Act into account. In the case of contracts for the supply of services, a supplier may contract out of the implied terms under the 1982 Act subject to s. 16 which also brings into operation the Unfair Contract Terms Act 1977. *See* Appendix 2.

Relative significance of terms

24. Conditions and warranties

The traditional view is that each term of a contract, express or implied, is either a condition or a warranty, depending upon its importance with regard to the purpose of the contract, and any other term is a warranty. The question whether a term is a condition or a warranty becomes significant in case of breach of contract.

According to the traditional approach, the difference between a condition and a warranty is as follows. If a promisor breaks a *condition* in *any* respect, however slight, the other party has a right to elect to treat himself as discharged from future obligations under the contract and to sue for damages immediately. If he does not exercise the right to elect to treat the contract as at an end he will remain bound by the contract, but can sue for damages with respect to the other party's breach. If, on the other hand, a promisor breaks a warranty in any respect the only remedy available to the other party is to sue for damages, i.e. there is no right to treat the contract as at end.

Where the parties describe a term as a condition it is open to the court to hold that the term is, nevertheless, a mere warranty: *Schuler* v. *Wickman Machine Tool Sales* (1973).

The traditional division was adopted in the drafting of the Sale of Goods Act 1893, where a condition is defined in s. 11 as a term 'the breach of which may give rise to a right to treat the contract as repudiated': a warranty is defined as a term 'the breach of which may give rise to a claim for damages but not a right to reject the goods and treat the contract as repudiated'. The Act provides by s. 62 that a warranty is 'collateral to the main purpose of the contract'. These provisions are included without alteration in the 1979 Act.

Since there is, usually, a stronger remedy available for breach of condition than for breach of warranty, it is not usual for the parties to be in dispute as to whether a term is a condition or a warranty. The difference is conveniently illustrated by the following cases.

Poussard v. *Spiers and Pond* (1876): An actress was under a contractual obligation to play in an operetta as from the beginning of its London run. The producers were forced to use a substitute for her as she was ill until a week after the show opened. HELD: The obligation to perform as from the first night was a condition and the breach of it entitled the other party to repudiate the contract.

Bettini v. *Gye* (1876): A singer was under contractual obligation to sing in a series of concerts and to take part in six days of rehearsals before the first performance. He arrived three days late, thus leaving only three days for rehearsals. HELD: The undertaking to take part in the rehearsals for six days was a warranty and not a condition. The breach entitled the other party to damages but not to repudiate the contract.

25. The modern approach

The traditional distinction between conditions and warranties is no longer regarded as exhaustive for it took no account of stipulations which were neither conditions nor warranties strictly so-called. Such stipulations were of a different character and their effect depended on the consequences of breach. In the *Hong Kong Fir* case (1962), the charterers of a ship sought to treat the charter-party as repudiated by the owners on the grounds that there was a breach of the owners' undertaking that the ship was 'in every way fitted for ordinary cargo service'. The ship had broken down on a number of occasions due to the incompetence of the engine room crew. It was held by the Court of Appeal that in these circumstances there was no breach of condition and, therefore, no right to treat the contract as repudiated. In this case, Upjohn LJ said, 'the question to be answered is, does the breach of the stipulation go so much to the root of the contract that it makes further commercial performance impossible, or, in other words, is the whole contract frustrated? If yea, the innocent party may treat the contract as at an end. If nay, his claim sounds in damages only.' In the same case, Diplock LJ expressed the view that many contractual undertakings cannot be categorized as being 'conditions' or 'warranties', and that of such undertakings, 'all that can be predicated is that some breaches will, and others will not, give rise to an event which will deprive the party not in default of substantially the whole benefit which it was intended that he should obtain from the contract; and the legal consequences of such an undertaking, unless provided for expressly in the contract, depend on the nature of the event to which the breach gives rise and do not follow automatically from a prior classification of the undertaking as a "condition" or a "warranty".'

In the *Hong Kong Fir* case (*see* 16:11) the Court of Appeal took the view that the legal consequences of a breach of contract depend on the consequences of the breach — or, to use the words of Diplock LJ 'the nature of the event to which the breach gives rise'. This is quite different from the traditional approach based on the distinction between minor terms (warranties) and important terms (conditions) — the distinction resting on the intention of the parties at the time they made their contract. In *Behn* v. *Burness* (1863), Williams J said that a term 'is more or less important in proportion as the object of the contract more or less depends upon it.'

The distinction was once more before the Court of Appeal in the *Mihalis Angelos* (1970): *see* 17:3. In this case the approach was different from that taken in *Hong Kong Fir*. The term in question was an 'expected readiness' clause in the light of the expectations or intentions of the parties rather than with the events consequent upon the breach of the clause. In holding that the 'expected readiness' clause was a condition, Lord Denning said that the clause was 'an assurance by the owner that he honestly expects that the vessel will be ready to load on that date and that his expectation is based on reasonable grounds'. Edmunds Davies LJ held that the 'expected readiness' clause was a condition, 'particularly having regard to the importance to the charterer of the ability to be able to rely on the owner giving no assurance as to expected readiness save on grounds both honest and reasonable'. Megaw LJ took the same view on the grounds, *inter alia*, 'that it would only be in the rarest case, if ever, that a ship-owner could legitimately feel that he had suffered an injustice by reason of the law having given to a charterer the right to put an end to the contract because of the breach by the ship-owner of a clause such as this. If a ship-owner has chosen to assert, contractually, but dishonestly or without reasonable grounds, that he expects his vessel to be ready to load on such and such a date, wherein does the grievance lie?'

In *The Hansa Nord* (1976), Lord Denning MR explained that: 'The task of the court can be stated simply in the way in which Upjohn LJ stated it (in the *Hong Kong Fir* case). First, see whether the stipulation, on its true construction, is a condition strictly so called, that is a stipulation such that, for any breach of it, the other party is entitled to treat himself as discharged. Second, if it is not such a condition, then look to the extent of the actual breach which has taken place. If it is such as to go to the root of the contract, the other party is entitled to treat himself as discharged; but otherwise not. To this may be added an anticipatory breach. If one party, before the day on which he is due to perform his part, shows by his words or conduct that he will not perform it in a vital respect when the day comes, the other party is entitled to treat himself as discharged.'

In *The Hansa Nord* the seller of a cargo of citrus pulp pellets was in breach of contract as a result of part of the cargo not being in good condition. The entire cargo was rejected by the buyer who later bought it when it was offered for sale under a court order in Rotterdam. The buyer then used the pellets for the original purpose, i.e. animal food. When the buyer's action for damages came before the Court of Appeal, it was held that not all terms were either conditions or warranties, even in a sale of goods contract: it was therefore possible to decide on general principles and the effect of the breach which was not serious. It was decided that the buyers had no right to reject the cargo. The House of Lords took the same approach in *Reardon Smith Line* v. *Yngvar Hansen-Tangen* (1976). In this case there was a contract to charter a tanker as yet unbuilt and described in the specification as Osaka 354. The Osaka Company subcontracted the building of the ship to the Oshima yard. The management and workforce were provided in part by Osaka and the ship was of identical technical specification to the one described as Osaka 354. It was held by the House of Lords that the charterers were not entitled to refuse delivery.

26. Time for performance or completion

Time is of greater or lesser importance to the parties in most kinds of contract. It is quite usual for the contracting parties to stipulate for a date for a contract for the sale of goods. Failure to comply with such a stipulation is, obviously, a breach of contract. Whether there is a breach of condition or whether the breach sounds in damages only will depend on the intention of the parties. This intention will be gathered from the express terms of the contract and, where appropriate, the nature and circumstances of the contract.

A time clause in a mercantile contract is not necessarily a condition: *Sarah D* (1989) CA. Where a requirement as to time is essential to the contract, the traditional phrase is that 'time is of the essence'. Where time is not of the essence, it can usually be made so as against a party already in delay by giving that party notice to that effect. Such notice must contain a stipulated completion date reasonably ascertained.

Many contracts do not contain stipulations as to time of performance of any part of the contract or its overall completion. It is then implicit that performance or completion, as the case may be, will be achieved within a reasonable time. For example, in the much-used JCT Standard Form of Building Contract, the architect has a duty to nominate and re-nominate certain subcontractors. He does so by issuing an instruction to the contractor. There are no stipulations governing the time of issue of such instructions. It was held by the House of Lords in *Percy Bilton* v. *GLC* (1982) that, with regard to the duty to re-nominate, it must be carried out within a reasonable time of the contractor's request for the instruction.

The court may not imply an extension of time on the grounds that the agreed dates for completion appear to it to be unreasonable: *Trollope & Colls* v. *North West Regional Hospital Board* (1973).

Where one party is bound by a date for completion and the

other party, by his default, causes a delay in the progress of the contract work, then the completion date ceases to be binding and a reasonable time for completion is substituted. In such a case, if there is a liquidated damages clause governing delay by the contractor, then that will cease to have effect: *Peak Construction (Liverpool)* v. *McKinney Foundations* (1970).

In contracts for the sale or lease of land, the problem of time of performance is linked with the question whether specific performance is available. In equity, the time fixed for completion was not of the essence. Thus, a plaintiff was not denied specific performance merely because he had failed to comply with the time for completion. But where a vendor, by his conduct, loses the right to specific performance, he has no equity left to restrain the other party's common law claim based on non-compliance with a stipulation as to time: *Stickney* v. *Keeble* (1915), a House of Lords case.

Section 41 of the Law of Property Act provides that: 'Stipulations in a contract, as to time or otherwise, which according to rules of equity are not deemed to be or have become of the essence of the contract, are also construed and have effect at law in accordance with the same rules.' In *Raineri* v. *Miles* (1980), the House of Lords gave this section to mean that, in a contract for the sale of land where time is not of the essence in equity, late completion gives rise to a right to damages at law, but not to a right to elect to have the contract discharged.

In all types of contract, time is of the essence only where the parties have shown, expressly or implicitly, that such was their intention. Where there is no stipulation that time is of the essence, the court will look at the nature of the contract to discover whether or not such is the presumed intention of the parties. *See*, for example, the approach of the House of Lords in *United Scientific Holdings* v. *Burnley Borough Council* (1978).

Collateral contracts

27. Express collateral contracts

There is no reason why the consideration given by a party to a contract should not be to enter, or promise to enter, another contract. Where two or more contracts bear this kind of relationship, they may be described as collateral to one another. A collateral contract may be between the same parties as the other contract, as in *City and Westminster Properties* v. *Mudd* (1958); or the collateral contract may be between one only of the parties to the other contract and a third party, as in *Shanklin Pier* v. *Detel Products* (1951). The collateral contract is, in effect, a device by which a promise may be enforced even though it forms no part of a primary contract with the promisee. In *Heilbut, Symons & Co.* v. *Buckleton*, a House of Lords case decided in 1913, it was stated that the courts should be slow to hold that there was a collateral contract. This was referred to by Lord Denning MR in *Evans* v. *Merzario* (1976), when he said:' . . . we have a different approach nowadays to collateral contracts. When a person gives a promise, or an assurance to another, intending that he should act on it by entering into a contract, we hold that it is binding.' In that case Lord Denning MR held that the oral assurances that the goods would be stowed below deck amounted to a collateral contract: but the other two judges did not agree, holding that there was one single contract made up of the oral statement and the printed conditions.

In *Dick Bentley Productions* v. *Harold Smith (Motors)* (1965), the plaintiff told the defendant that he was 'looking for a well vetted Bentley car'. The defendant then showed him a Bentley car saying that it had 'done only 20,000 miles' since change of engine and gearbox. It was held by the Court of Appeal that the statement as to mileage by the defendant (Mr Smith) was a term of the contract. It was untrue and accordingly there was a breach of contract. In that case, Salmon LJ said that, in effect, Mr Smith said: 'If you will enter into a contract to buy this motor car from me for £1,850, I undertake that you will be getting a motor car which has done no more than 20,000 miles since it was fitted with a new engine and a new gearbox.'

> *City and Westminster Properties* v. *Mudd* (1958): The landlords offered to M a renewal of his lease, the draft renewal containing a covenant for M 'to use the demised premises as and for showrooms, workrooms and offices only'. The landlord informed M that if he signed the lease they would not object to his continuing to reside on the premises. M entered the lease. Later, the landlords claimed that the lease

was forfeit because M had continued to live on the premises in breach of his covenant. HELD: The claim to forfeit the lease failed because M signed it in reliance on the promise not to enforce the covenant. This promise was part of a contract, separate from, but collateral to, the lease.

Shanklin Pier v. *Detel Products* (1951): The plaintiffs, the owners of a pier, entered into a contract with a contractor to have the pier repaired and repainted. Under the terms of this contract, the plaintiffs had the right to specify the paint to be used by the contractor. On the faith of statements made by the defendants to the plaintiffs with regard to the defendants' paint and its fitness for painting the pier, the defendants specified the paint to the contractor who bought the necessary quantity from the defendants. The paint proved to be quite unsuitable for painting the pier. The plaintiffs contended that the statements made to them by the defendants with regard to the suitability of the paint were enforceable warranties given in consideration of their specifying the paint to their contractor. HELD: The defendants' statements constituted a binding warranty, the breach of which entitled the plaintiffs to damages.

28. Implied collateral contracts.

In proper circumstances, the court will imply a collateral contract so as to give effect to the presumed intentions of the parties. The rules governing the discovery of intention will be applied. Thus, where A enters a contract with B on the faith of an express or implied promise by C, there is a collateral contract between A and C. This principle is of general application, but it is of special significance with respect to the relationship between a guarantor and the principal debtor, and to the relationship between dealer and hirer in contracts of hire-purchase.

Note
_____

In hire-purchase transactions the relationships of the parties are often as follows: dealer and customer arrange the transaction and the dealer then sells the article to a finance company which lets the goods on hire-purchase to the customer. Thus the *express* contract of hire-purchase is between the customer and the finance company, but the courts now recognize there may be an *implied collateral contract* between the dealer and the customer: *See Andrews* v. *Hopkinson*, below.

Clarke v. *Dunraven, The Satanita* (1897): C and D, who were competitors in a yacht regatta, each gave an undertaking to X to abide by certain rules. HELD by the House of Lords: A contract had been created between C and D. It was presumed that, by entering the competition, each had given to the other an undertaking to abide by the rules.

Andrews v. *Hopkinson* (1956): H, car dealer, induced A to enter a hire-purchase agreement with a finance company by praising a second-hand car which he wished to supply to A. H said, 'It's a good little bus. I would stake my life on it.' A week later the car was wrecked and A was injured in an accident caused by the faulty steering mechanism of the car. HELD: There was a contract between A and H, collateral to the hire-purchase contract. H was in breach of this collateral contract.

Progress test 5

1. Explain briefly what you understand by the expression 'term of contract'.

2. Distinguish between representations and terms of contract.

3. How may an agreement be affected by the uncertainty of its terms?

4. By what rules will the court construe a contract?

5. State briefly the basis on which the court will imply a term in a contract.

6. Explain in detail how the courts imply on the basis of (*a*) customs, (*b*) conduct and (*c*) the need to give a contract business efficacy.

7. What are the terms implied by the Sale of Goods Act 1979?

8. What is a contract for work and materials? What terms are implied in such contracts?

9. Distinguish between conditions and warranties.

10. When is time of the essence of a contract?

11. Summarize the provisions of the Supply of Goods and Services Act 1982.

12. What is a collateral contract? What did Lord Denning MR say about them in *Evans* v. *Merzario*?

6
Exclusion clauses

1. The scope of the topic

An exclusion clause is a contract term which purports to limit or exclude obligations which would otherwise attach to one of the parties to the contract. The obligations affected by exclusion clauses may arise out of contract or tort. A contracting party who introduces an exclusion clause is usually seeking to limit his liability for breach of contract or negligence. The most valuable definition was given by Lord Diplock in *Photo Productions* v. *Securicor Transport* (1980). He said that an exclusion clause 'is one which excludes or modifies an obligation, whether primary, general secondary or anticipatory secondary' (*see* 16:**10**).

The law of exclusion clauses falls naturally into three main parts. First, the question of how an exclusion clause becomes an integral part of a contract must be examined. Second, there must be a careful examination of the effectiveness of exclusion clauses under the rules of common law. Third, those provisions of the Unfair Contract Terms Act 1977 which have a bearing on the effectiveness or validity of exclusion clauses must be considered. The remaining paragraphs of this chapter will follow this pattern.

The exclusion clause as a term of contract

2. Integral term of chapter contract

The court will not construe an exclusion clause unless it is satisfied beyond doubt that the clause is an integral term of the contract. Problems have arisen in this connection as a result of the many ways in which contracting parties have sought to introduce these clauses. Although it is most usual to find exclusion clauses in the small print of standard form conditions, they are also to be found in wall notices, on shop counters, on the backs of tickets, invoices and receipts and, in one recent case, on the cover of a cheque book.

Where the question arises whether an exclusion clause is a term of contract, the usual rules of offer and acceptance are applied. The clause must be an integral part of an offer or a counter-offer. If such an offer or counter-offer is accepted, the contract is formed on that basis and the exclusion clause is an express term of it. Otherwise, the clause will not be part of the contract unless it can be implied, e.g. by previous dealings as in *Spurling* v. *Bradshaw* (1956). *See* also *Mitchell* v. *Finney Lock Seeds* (1983), per Lord Denning MR. The most important characteristic of agreement through offer and acceptance is that the express provisions must be communicated. They must be sufficiently brought to the attention of the other party. This must be done before the contract is concluded. It follows that any clause (exclusion or otherwise) will not be a binding term if it was communicated after the contract was made: *Olley* v. *Marlborough Court Hotel* (1949). Nor will an exclusion clause be a binding term of contract if it is written (or printed) on a document which is not intended to bear contractual terms, e.g. a receipt or the cover of a cheque book: *Chapelton* v. *Barry Urban District Council* (1940) and *Burnett* v. *Westminster Bank* (1966) respectively. Where a ticket, e.g. a railway or a bus ticket, purports to be issued subject to certain conditions set out elsewhere, those conditions will become part of the contract only if they have been sufficiently drawn out to the attention of the purchaser. Attention is drawn to the offer and acceptance analysis in the following two cases discussed further below: *Parker* v. *South Eastern Railway Co.*(1877); *Thornton* v. *Shoe Lane Parking* (1971). Where an exclusion clause is contained in a mass of small print in standard form conditions put forward by one party, the question whether the exclusion is binding depends on whether it was brought sufficiently to the attention of the other party. In *L'Estrange* v. *Graucob* (1934) the plaintiff had signed without reading the written conditions proffered by the defendant. It was held that she was bound by them including an exclusion clause.

Where a clause was brought to the notice of the other party during previous dealings it may be implied in a subsequent transaction to give effect to the presumed intentions of the parties: *Spurling* v. *Bradshaw* (1956) and *Circle Freight International* v. *Medeast Gulf Exports* (1988). The party relying on previous dealings must discharge the burden of showing that the clause in question was brought to the attention of the other party. This cannot be achieved unless the course of dealing was consistent over a period of time: *McCutcheon* v. *MacBrayne* (1964); *Mitchell* v. *Finney Lock Seeds* (1983).

A party cannot claim to have sufficiently drawn the other party's attention to a clause where he has orally misrepresented the meaning of that clause: *Curtis* v. *Chemical Cleaning and Dyeing Co.*(1951). Similarly, where an overriding oral assurance will disentitle the contract-breaker from reliance on any of those printed clauses: *Evans* v. *Merzario* (1976).

Parker v. *South Eastern Railway Co.*(1877): P deposited a bag in the defendants' cloakroom. He paid two pence and was given a ticket on the face of which was printed 'See Back'. On the back of the ticket was a printed notice saying that the company would not be responsible for any item whose value was more than £10. P's bag, which was worth more than £10, was lost and he brought this action for damages from the company. P had not read the notice on the back of the ticket. HELD: P had notice of the condition on the back of the ticket, the condition was part of a counter-offer by the defendant company which was accepted by P. The printed notice was, therefore, part of the contract and the company could rely on it in their defence.

Thornton v. *Shoe Lane Parking* (1971): The plaintiff drove his car to a multi-storey automatic car park which he had never used before. On the outside of the park there was a notice under the heading 'Shoe Lane Parking'. The notice contained the parking charges and other information. At the end of the notice were the following words: 'ALL CARS PARKED AT OWNERS RISK'. When the plaintiff reached the entrance there was no one in attendance. A traffic light turned from red to green and a ticket was pushed out from a machine. The plaintiff took the ticket and drove into the car park. He left his car there and returned for it several hours later. As he attempted to put his belongings into his

car, the plaintiff was severely injured. The trial judge held
that the accident was half the fault of Shoe Lane Parking,
and half the fault of the plaintiff himself. The defendants
claimed that they were exempted from liability by certain
conditions which had become part of the contract. The
defendants claimed that the ticket was a contractual document and that it incorporated a condition exempting them
from liability. On the ticket appeared the words: 'This ticket
is issued subject to the conditions of issue as displayed on
the premises'. The plaintiff, who had looked at the ticket to
see the time printed on it, had not read the other printing
on the ticket. He did not read the words which provided
that the ticket was issued subject to conditions. Nor did he
read the conditions which where set out on a pillar opposite
the ticket machine. One of these conditions provided that
the defendants would not be responsible or liable for injury
to the customer occurring when the customer's motor
vehicle was in the parking building. It was this condition
which the defendants relied upon. HELD by the Court of
Appeal: The exempting condition did not bind the plaintiff
because he did not know of it and the defendants did not do
what was reasonably sufficient to give him notice of it.

In *Thornton* v. *Shoe Lane Parking*, Lord Denning MR explained
the principle as follows: 'Assuming that an automatic machine is a
booking clerk in disguise, so that the old fashioned ticket cases still
apply to it, we then have to go back to the three questions put by
Mellish LJ in *Parker* v. *South Eastern Railway Co.*, subject to this
qualification: Mellish LJ used the word "conditions" in the plural,
whereas it would be more apt to use the word "condition" in the
singular, as indeed Mellish LJ himself did at the end of his
judgment. After all, the only condition that matters for this
purpose is the exempting condition. It is no use telling the
customer that the ticket is issued subject to some "conditions" or
other, without more; for he may reasonably regard "conditions"
in general as merely regulatory, and not as taking away his rights,
unless the exempting condition is drawn specifically to his
attention. Telescoping the three questions, they come to this: the
customer is bound by the exempting condition if he knows that
the ticket is issued subject to it; or, if the company did what was

reasonably sufficient to give him notice of it. Counsel for the defendants admitted here that the defendants did not do what was reasonably sufficient to give the plaintiff notice of the exempting condition. That admission was properly made. I do not pause to enquire whether the exempting condition is void for reasonableness. All I say is that it is so wide and so destructive of rights that the court should not rule any man bound by it unless it is drawn to his attention in the most explicit way. It is an instance for what I had in mind in *Spurling* v. *Bradshaw*. In order to give sufficient notice, it would need to be printed in red ink with a red hand pointing to it, or something equally startling.

'However, although reasonable notice of it was not given, counsel for the defendants said that this case came with the second question propounded by Mellish LJ, namely that the plaintiff "knew or believed that the writing contained conditions". There was no finding to that effect. The burden was on the defendants to prove that they did not do so. Certainly there was no evidence that the plaintiff knew of this exempting condition. He is not, therefore, bound by it.'

Chapelton v. *Barry Urban District Council* (1940): The council hired out deckchairs and by the stack of chairs was a notice containing the terms of hire. C hired two chairs, paid his money and received two tickets which he put in his pocket. When C sat in one of the chairs, it broke and caused him injury. The chair was not fit for use. C sued the council for negligence and was met with the defence that the words printed on the back of his ticket included: 'The Council will not be liable for any accident or damage arising from the hire of the chair.' HELD by the Court of Appeal: the terms of the contract of hire were contained in the notice by the stack of chairs. The ticket issued was a mere receipt, therefore the writing on the back of it could not be included in the contract. The council could not rely on the exemption clause.

Olley v. *Marlborough Court Hotel* (1949): O locked the door of her hotel room and deposited the key at the reception desk, and then left the hotel for a few hours. On returning, she found that her key was missing from the reception desk and some of her belongings had been stolen from her room. O

sued the hotel company for negligence and was met with
the defence that she was contractually bound by the terms
of a notice in her room providing that: 'The proprietors will
not hold themselves responsible for articles lost or stolen
unless handed to the manageress for safe custody'. HELD by
the Court of Appeal: **(a)** the company was negligent; **(b)** the
notice was not a term in O's contract with the company, for
she did not see it before the contract was made, nor was she
aware of its existence then. A party may be fixed with notice
of an exemption clause communicated in previous dealings
Spurling v. *Bradshaw* (1956) and *Circle Freight International* v.
Medeast Gulf Exports (1988).

L'Estrange v. *Graucob* (1934): E signed a printed contract of
sale of a slot machine without reading it. The machine
proved unsatisfactory and E claimed damages for breach of
the implied condition as to fitness for purpose under the
Sale of Goods Act 1893, s. 14(1). She was met with the
defence that one of the printed terms excluded the implied
conditions. HELD: the printed condition excluded the
implied condition under the Act. Since E had signed the
contract, it was irrelevant that she had not read it.

Curtis v. *Chemical Cleaning and Dyeing Co.* (1951): C took a
wedding dress to the cleaning company for cleaning and
was asked to sign a document which contained a clause that
the garment is 'accepted on the condition that the company
is not liable for any damage'. C asked why she had to sign it
and was told that the company would not accept liability for
damage done to the beads and sequins on the dress. C
signed the document. The dress was stained badly while
being cleaned and C brought this action for damages. The
company raised the exemption clause in their defence.
HELD by the Court of Appeal: the clause gave no protection
to the company because of misrepresentation as to its
extent.

McCutcheon v. *MacBrayne* (1964): The appellant asked his
brother-in-law, one McSporran, to have his car sent by the
respondents from the isle of Islay to the Scottish mainland.

McSporran went to the respondents' office where he was quoted the freight for the return journey of the car. He paid the money, for which he was given a receipt, and he delivered the car. The car was shipped on a vessel which subsequently sank owing to the negligent navigation of the respondents' servants. The car was lost and the appellant sued in negligence for the value of it. The respondents' practice was to require consignors to sign risk notes which included their elaborate printed conditions, one of which excluded liability for negligence. On the occasion in question, McSporran was not asked to sign a risk note. McSporran had previously consigned goods to the mainland and had sometimes signed a risk note and sometimes not. He had never read the risk notes on those occasions when he had signed them. He did not know that, by the conditions of the risk note, the consignor agreed to send the goods at owner's risk. The appellant had consigned goods on four previous occasions and each time he had signed a risk note, but he had never read the conditions and did not know what they meant. The respondents contended that the appellant was bound by the conditions in the risk note by reason of the knowledge gained by the appellant and his agent in previous transactions. The conditions were also displayed in the respondents' office and in the respondents' ship, but neither the appellant nor McSporran had read them. On the question whether the exemption clause in the conditions was part of the contract, HELD by the House of Lords that the contract was an oral contract and the printed conditions were not part of it because the respondents had not discharged the burden of showing the appellant had knowledge of the printed conditions — accordingly, the liability of the appellants in negligence was not excluded.

Per Lord Devlin: 'In my opinion, the bare fact that there have been previous dealings between the parties does not assist the respondents at all. The fact that a man has made a contract in the same form 99 times (let alone the three or four times which are here alleged) will not of itself affect the hundredth contract, in which the form is used. Previous dealings are irrelevant only if they prove knowledge of the terms, actual and not constructive, and assent to them.'

J. Evans & Son (Portsmouth) v. *Andrea Merzario* (1976): The plaintiffs were importers of machines from Italy. Since 1959 they had contracted under standard form conditions with the defendants to make arrangements for the carriage of the machines to England. The defendant forwarding agents proposed in 1967 to change to container transportation. They gave an oral assurance to the plaintiffs that their machines would be transported in containers shipped under deck. On the faith of this assurance the plaintiffs accepted the defendants' new quotations. Owing to an oversight on the part of the defendants, a container with one of the machines inside was shipped on deck. During the voyage this machine was lost overboard. By the standard form conditions, **(a)** the defendants were free in respect of the means and procedures to be followed in the transportation, **(b)** they were exempted from liability for loss or damage to goods unless in their personal custody and **(c)** that their liability should not, in any event, exceed the value of goods. The plaintiffs claimed damages for the loss of the machine, alleging that the carriage of the container on deck was a breach of contract. HELD by the Court of Appeal: The oral statement made by the defendants was a binding warranty which was to be treated as overriding the printed conditions and the plaintiffs were entitled to damages for its breach.

Effectiveness of exclusion clauses

3. Construction of exclusion clauses

To discover the meaning and effectiveness of an exclusion clause it is necessary to construe the contract as a whole — including the exclusion clause. This basic rule applies even where there is a fundamental breach or, indeed, any breach of contract by the party seeking to invoke the clause. The principle underlying the House of Lords decision in the *Suisse Atlantique* case (1966) may be stated thus: *the question whether, and to what extent, an exclusion clause is to be applied to* any *breach of contract is a matter of the construction of the contract.* This proposition was affirmed and applied in the *Photo Productions* case (1980). In that case the House

of Lords made it quite clear that there was no rule of law by which
an exclusion clause could be eliminated from a consideration of a
party's position when there was a breach of contract (whether
'fundamental' or not) or by which an exclusion clause could be
deprived of effect regardless of the terms of the contract. The
general rule is that contracting parties are free to agree to
whatever exclusion or modification of their obligations they
choose. This rule is subject to statute, particularly under the Unfair
Contract Terms Act 1977.

The *Photo Productions* decision overruled *Harbutt's Plasticine* v.
Wayne Tank Co. (1970) and *Wathes* v. *Austins* (1976) and certain
other cases in which the Court of Appeal propounded and applied
the so-called doctrine of 'fundamental breach'. By this doctrine, a
party who was in fundamental breach could not avail himself of
the terms of an exclusion clause at all, no matter how strongly it
was worded. By this doctrine, the clause was deprived totally of
effect. It is important to understand that this doctrine no longer
applies.

Exclusion clauses may modify primary, general secondary or
anticipatory secondary obligations because parties are free to
agree to whatever exclusion or modification of all three types of
obligation as they please. This freedom to exclude is subject to the
equitable rule against penalties (*see* 17:**17,18**). By this rule, no
contract clause can validly impose on the breaker of a primary
obligation, a general secondary obligation to pay the other party
a sum of money that is manifestly intended to be in excess of the
amount which would fully compensate the other party for the loss
sustained by him in consequence of the breach of the primary
obligation, per Lord Diplock in *Photo Productions*. The freedom to
exclude is further subject also to the provisions of the Unfair
Contract Terms Act 1977 (*see* **6** below). The court must construe
an exclusion clause strictly and *contra proferentem*, i.e. in case of
doubt or ambiguity, against the interests of the party introducing
the clause. *See*, for example, *White* v. *John Warrick & Co.* (1953);
Hollier v. *Rambler Motors* (1972). The court cannot reject an
exclusion clause, however unreasonable it may seem to the court,
if the words are clear and fairly susceptible of one meaning only:
Photo Productions v. *Securicor Transport* (1980).

The duty of the court in approaching the construction of
clauses purporting to exclude liability for negligence was

summarized by Lord Morton of Henryton in the Privy Council case of *Canada Steamship Lines* v. *R.* (1952) as follows:

(a) If the clause contains language which expressly exempts the person in whose favour it is made (hereafter called the *proferens*) from the consequence of negligence of his own servants, effects must be given to that provision.

(b) If there is no express reference to negligence, the court must consider whether the words used are wide enough, in their ordinary meaning, to cover negligence on the part of the servants or the *proferens*. If a doubt arises at this point, it must be resolved against the *proferens*.

(c) If the words are used wide enough for the above purpose, the court must then consider whether the head of damage may be based on some ground other than that of negligence. The 'other ground' must not be so fanciful or remote that the *proferens* cannot be supposed to have desired protection against it but, subject to this qualification, the existence of a possible head of damage other than that of negligence is fatal to the *proferens* even if the words used are, prima facie, wide enough to cover negligence on the part of his servants.

In *Ailsa Craig Fishing Co.* v. *Malvern Fishing Co.* (1983), Lord Fraser referred to this summary by Lord Morton, saying that the principles were not applicable in their full rigour when considering the effect of clauses merely limiting liability (*see* **4** below). *See* also *White* v. *John Warrick & Co.* (1953) and *Hollier* v. *Rambler Motors* (1972).

Suisse Atlantique Société d'Armement Maritime v. *Rotterdamsche Kolen Centrale* (1966): The plaintiffs agreed by a charter-party dated 1956 to charter their ship to the defendants for carrying coal from the USA to Europe. The charter was expressed to remain in force for two years' consecutive voyages between USA and Europe. By the charter, if the vessel was delayed beyond the agreed loading time, the defendants were to pay £1,000 a day demurrage. Similarly, demurrage was payable if the vessel was delayed beyond the agreed unloading time. In September 1957 the plaintiffs regarded themselves as being entitled to treat the charter-party as repudiated by reason of the defendants' delays in loading and unloading the vessel. The defendants did not accept this contention, and it was agreed (without prejudice to this dispute) that the charter-party should be continued.

From October 1957 the vessel made eight round voyages under the charter. It was contended by the plaintiffs that each round voyage ought reasonably to have been completed in 30 to 37 days, including loading and unloading. On this basis, the eight voyages which took 511 days should have taken 240 or 296 days. From this the plaintiffs argued that they had lost the freights which they would have earned on nine or, alternatively, six voyages. The plaintiffs claimed damages of $773,000 or alternatively, £467,000.

The basis of the plaintiffs' contention was that the charter-party gave them a contractual right to the number of voyages which would be made in the event of both parties carrying out their contractual obligations, and that in the event of both parties carrying out their contractual obligations, and that their claim was not limited to their entitlement to demurrage. The plaintiffs (who had failed before Mocatta J and before the Court of Appeal) appealed to the House of Lords. An argument, not advanced in the courts below, was put forward, namely that if the delays were such as to entitle the appellants to treat the charter-party as repudiated, the demurrage clauses did not apply, and that the appellants would then be entitled to recover their full loss on the basis they claimed. HELD by the House of Lords: the appellants, having elected in 1957 to form the charter-party, were bound by its provisions, including the demurrage clauses which operated as agreed damages. The appellants were not entitled to damages for loss of freight, nor would they be so entitled if the respondent's breaches were deliberate.

Photo Productions v. *Securicor Transport* (1980) HL: The defendants (Securicor) contracted to provide night security patrols at the plaintiffs' factory. While on patrol , a Securicor employee lit a small fire which got out of control and destroyed the plaintiffs' factory and stock. The plaintiffs sued for damages and the defendants pleaded an exclusion

clause in the contract which provided that 'under no
circumstances' were the defendants to be 'responsible for
any injurious act or default of any employee unless such act
or default could be foreseen and avoided by the exercise of
due diligence on the part of Securicor as his employer; nor,
in any event, were Securicor to be held responsible for any
loss suffered by the plaintiffs through fire or any other
cause except in so far as such loss was solely attributable to
the negligence of Securicor's employees acting within the
course of their employment'. There was no allegation that
Securicor were negligent in employing the employee
involved.

At first instance it was held that Securicor could rely on
the exclusion clause. The Court of Appeal reversed this
decision, holding that there had been a fundamental breach
which precluded reliance on the clause. On appeal the
House of Lords, HELD: **(a)** The parties were free to agree to
whatever exclusion or modification of their obligations as
they chose: there was no rule of law by which an exclusion
clause could be eliminated from consideration when there
was a breach of contract (fundamental or not) or by which
an exemption clause could be deprived of effect regardless
of the terms of the contract. Therefore, the question
whether an exemption clause applied when there was a
fundamental breach, breach of a fundamental breach or any
other breach, turned on the construction of the whole of the
contract, including any of the exemption clauses. **(b)** The
exclusion clause was clear and unambiguous and it
protected Securicor from the breach of their obligations.

White v. *John Warrick & Co.* (1953): A contract for the hire of
a tradesman's bicycle provided that 'nothing in this
agreement shall render the owners liable for any personal
injury'. The saddle was defective, causing the plaintiff to
injure himself while riding. HELD: These words excluded
liability for breach of contract but they did not exclude
liability in tort (negligence).

Hollier v. *Rambler Motors* (1972): There was a contract by
which the defendants took in the plaintiff's car for repair. As
a result of the defendants' negligence, the car was damaged

by fire. The defendants argued that the contract included their usual conditions, one of which was 'the company is not responsible for damage caused by fire to customers' cars on the premises'. HELD: by the Court of Appeal that if the clause formed part of the contract (which it did not) it was not sufficiently unambiguous to exclude liability for negligence.

Note

The two cases above show that negligence must be specifically and unambiguously excluded if that is the intention of the parties.

4. Exclusion or mere limitation of liability?

The expression 'exclusion clause' is used to indicate either the total exclusion of liability or the restriction of liability, for example a restriction of liability in damages to a stated amount. In both cases the *contra proferentem* rule applies to the construction of the clause. The rule is not, however, applied with the same degree of severity in each case. In *Ailsa Craig Fishing Co.* v. *Malvern Fishing Co.* (1981), Lord Wilberforce said: 'Clauses of limitation are not regarded by the courts with the same hostility as clauses of exclusion: this is because they must be related to other contractual terms, in particular to the risk to which the defending party may be exposed, the remuneration which he receives, and possibly also the opportunity of the other party to insure.' In the same case, Lord Fraser referred to the Privy Council case of *Canada Steamship Lines* v. *R.* (1952) which summarized the strict principles to be applied when considering the effect of clauses of exclusion or indemnity. He pointed out that these principles had recently been applied by the House of Lords in *Smith* v. *U.M.B. Chrysler (Scotland)* (1978) and he went on to say that: 'In my opinion these principles are not applicable in their full rigour when considering the effect of clauses merely limiting liability. Such clauses will of course be read *contra proferentem* and must be clearly expressed, but there is no reason why they should be judged by the specially exacting standards which are applied to exclusion and indemnity clauses. The reason for imposing such standards on these clauses is the inherent improbability that the other party to a contract including such a clause intended to release the *proferens* from a liability that would otherwise fall upon him. But there is no such high degree of improbability that he would agree to a limitation of the liability of the *proferens*, especially when...the potential losses that might be caused by the negligence of its servants are so great in proportion to the sums that can reasonably be charged for the services contracted for.'

Ailsa Craig Fishing Co. v. *Malvern Fishing Co.* (1981): The issue in this case was whether Securicor had succeeded in limiting their liability under a contract between themselves and the Aberdeen Fishing Vessels Owners' Association Limited (the Association) who were acting on behalf of a number of owners of fishing vessels, including the appellants'. It was not relevant that the appellants were not a party to the contract in question. The appellants owned a vessel (*Strathallan*) which sank while berthed in Aberdeen harbour on 31 December 1971, when Securicor were bound under a contract with the Association to provide security cover in the harbour. Her gallows fouled a neighbouring vessel, causing them both to sink together. On a rising tide there was a special risk that the vessels might slide under the deck of the quay and become caught or snubbed by the bow. This is just what happened to the *Strathallan*. She took the *George Craig* with her. The sinkings would not have occurred if the Securicor employee had not been negligent in carrying out his duties. The contract in question was headed 'Temporary Contract or Contract Ltd to carry out the services detailed below subject to the Special Conditions printed overleaf'. The form requested 'continuous security cover for your vessels from 1900 hours on 31/12/71 until 0700 hours on 5/1/72' stating that the area covered the Fish Market Area. This contained the open quay where the sinkings occurred. The relevant paragraph of the Special Conditions was 2(*f*) which provided as follows:

'If, pursuant to the provisions set out herein, any liability on the part of the company shall arise (whether under the express or implied terms of this contract or at common law, or in any other way) to the customer for any loss or damage of whatever nature arising out of or connected with the provision or, or purported provision of, or failure in provision of, the services covered by this contract, such liability shall be limited to the company by way of damages of a sum:

(i) In the case of all services other than the Special Delivery Service:

(a) Not exceeding £1,000 in respect of any one claim arising from any duty assumed by the company which involves the operation, testing, examination, or inspection of the operational condition of the machine, plant or equipment in or about the customer's premises, or which involves the provision of any service not solely related to the prevention or detection of fire or theft:

(b) Not exceeding a maximum of £10,000 for the consequences of any incident involving fire, theft or any other cause of liability in the company under the terms hereof; and further provided that the total liability of the company shall not in any circumstances exceed the sum of £10,000 in respect of all and any incidents during any consecutive period of twelve months.'

The appellants argued that condition 2(*f*) applied only to liability which arose 'pursuant to' the provisions of the contract. This argument failed because clause (*f*) itself proclaims unambiguously that it applies to liability which shall arise under the 'express or implied' terms of the contract. It was also argued that sub-paragraph (*f*) was confused and uncertain in itself because the provisions of sub-paragraph (*i*) (*a*) and (*b*) did not make it clear whether the limit of liability in any particular case was £1,000 or £10,000. It was held that sub-clause (*a*) relates to any claim rising in any of the ways mentioned and it limits the liability of Securicor to £1,000 for each claim. Sub-paragraph (*b*) relates to any one incident. The two provisions were held to overlap but not to be inconsistent. It was held by the House of Lords that clause 2(*f*) was, in its context, sufficiently clear and unambiguous to receive effect in limiting the liability of Securicor for its own negligence or that of its employees.

Note

The contract in question in this case was made before the Supply of Goods (Implied Terms) Act 1973 came into force. This Act was the precursor to the present Unfair Contract Terms Act 1977.

Mitchell v. *Finney Lock Seeds* (1982): Farmers (George Mitchell Ltd) ordered 30 lb of cabbage seed from the seed merchants (Finney Lock). When it was delivered it looked just like cabbage seed and was planted over 63 acres. The resulting crop was not cabbages and was commercially useless. The price of the seed was £192 and the loss suffered by the farmers was over £61,000. They claimed damages from the seed merchants. At first instance they were awarded the sum with interest — a total of nearly £100,000. The seed merchants brought this appeal to the Court of Appeal, contending that their liability was limited by a printed clause in the contract to the price of the seed, i.e. £192. Their argument was based largely on the two House of Lords cases, *Photo. Productions* and *Ailsa Craig*. The limitation clauses provided:

'All Seeds, Bulbs, Corms, Tubers, Roots, Shrubs, Trees and Plants (hereinafter referred to as "Seeds or Plants") offered for sale or sold to us by which the Seeds Act 1920 or the Plant Varieties and Seeds Act 1964 as the case may be and the Regulations thereunder apply have been tested in accordance with the provisions of the same. In the event of any seeds or plants sold or agreed to be sold or with any representation made by us or by any duly authorized agent or representative on our behalf prior to, at the time of, or any way such contract, or any seeds or plants proving defective in varietal purity we will, at our option, replace the defective seeds or plants, free of charge to the buyer or will refund all payments made to us by the buyer in respect of the defective seeds or plants and this shall be the limit of our obligation. We hereby exclude any liability for any loss or damage arising from the use of any seeds or plants supplied by us and for any consequential loss or damage arising out of such use or any failure in the performance of or any defect in any seeds or plants supplied by us or for any other loss or damage whatsoever save for, at our option, liability for any such replacement or refund as aforesaid.... The price of any seeds or plants sold or offered for sale by us is based upon the foregoing limitations upon our liability. The price of such seeds or plants would be much greater if a more extensive liability were required to be under taken by us.'

It was HELD by the Court of Appeal: **(a)** that the provision was not sufficiently clear and unambiguous to limit or exclude the seed merchant's liability in negligence, and **(b)** it would not be fair and reasonable to allow reliance on the provision. The contract was made before 1 February 1978 and was subject to a provision, s. 55(4) of the Sale of Goods Act 1893, that, 'In the case of a contract of sale of goods any terms that... contract exempting from all or any of the previous section 13, 14 or 15 above... is... not enforceable to the extent that it is shown that it would not be fair or reasonable to allow reliance on the term'. Under the provisions of s. 55 of the Sale of Goods Act 1979 and the Unfair Contract Terms Act 1977, a new regime came into force in case of contracts entered into after 1 February 1978. With regard to the type of contract in the instant case, the new requirement is that the term must 'satisfy the requirements of reasonableness'. *See* **5** below.

The House of Lords held unanimously **(a)** that the clause in question unambiguously limits the appellant's liability and, that being the case, there is no principle of construction which can properly be applied to confine the effect of the limitation to breaches of contract arising without negligence and **(b)** the clause did not satisfy the statutory requirement of reasonableness. The appeal was dismissed.

5.　The position summarized

The propositions which emerge from the trilogy of House of Lords cases (*Suisse Atlantique*, *Photo Productions* and *Ailsa Craig*) were clearly summarized by Oliver LJ as follows in *Mitchell* v. *Finney Lock Seeds* :

'(1) There is no rule of law that the effect of a fundamental breach of contract, whether or not accepted by the innocent party as a repudiation, is to preclude reliance upon an exclusion clause in the contract inserted for the protection of the party in breach.

'(2) The effect of an exclusion clause has to be ascertained simply by constructing the contract as a whole. What has to be determined is whether, as a matter of construction, the clause applies to excuse or limit liability for the particular breach which has occurred, whether "fundamental" or otherwise.

'(3) There is a presumption that any breach of the primary obligations of the contract will result in a continuing secondary obligation on the party in breach to pay compensation for the breach. A clause in the contract excluding modifying or limiting that secondary obligation is, therefore, to be constructed restrictively and *contra proferentem.*

'(4) The contract has to be construed as whole for the exclusion clause is part of an entire contract and may, as a matter of construction, be an essential factor in determining the extent of the primary obligation. Thus, for instance, Securicor 1 (*Photo Productions*) was a case not of a clause excluding liability for a fundamental breach but of a clause which, on its true construction, demonstrated that there had been no breach at all of the primary obligation, which was simply to exercise reasonable care.

'(5) Since such clauses may not only modify or limit the secondary obligation to pay damages for breach but may also show the extent of the primary obligation, a clause totally excluding liability for a fundamental breach tends to be constructed more restrictively than a clause merely limiting damages payable for breach, for a total exclusion of liability, if widely constructed, might lead to the conclusion that there was no primary obligation at all and thus no contract. This is to say no more than that, when it is called upon to construe a commercial document clearly intended by both parties to have contractual force, the court will lean against a construction which leads to an absurdity.

'(6) Where the language is unclear or susceptible fairly of more than one construction, the court will construe it in the manner which appears more likely to give effect to what must have been the common intention of the parties when they contracted. But where, even construing the contract *contra proferentem* and allowing for the presumption of the continuance of a secondary obligation to pay for damages for breach of the primary contractual duty, the language of the contract is clear and is fairly susceptible of only one meaning, the court is not entitled to place upon an exclusion clause a strained construction for the purpose of rejecting it.'

Unfair Contract Terms Act 1977

6.   Effect of the Act

The purpose of the Act is to impose further limits on the extent to which liability for breach of contract or for negligence can be avoided by means of contract terms. This purpose is achieved by provisions which ensure:

(a) that certain types of exclusion clause are to have no effect, and
(b) that certain other types of exclusion clause are effective only in so far as they satisfy the requirements of reasonableness.

These two groups of exclusion clauses are listed in **8** and **9** respectively. The lists should be read against the relevant sections of the Act, Part 1 of which is set out in Appendix 2. The Act does not apply to contracts entered into before 1 February 1978.

7.   Definitions

The main provisions of the Unfair Contract Terms Act 1977 are set out in Appendix 2.

There are two important concepts defined in the Act, namely 'business liability' and 'dealing as a consumer'. These definitions are set out in the Act in ss. 1(3) and 12(1).

(a) *Business liability*. In the case of both contract and tort, ss.2 to 7 apply (except where the contrary is stated in s. 6(4)) only to business liability, that is liability for breach of obligations or duties arising.

   (*i*) from things done to or to be done by a person in the course of a business (whether his business or another's); or
   (*ii*) from the occupation of premises used for business purposes of the occupier; and references to liability are to be read accordingly.

(b) *Deals as a consumer*. A party to a contract 'deals as a consumer' in relation to another party if:

   (*i*) he neither makes the contract in the course of a business; nor holds himself out as doing so; and (*ii*) the other party does not make the contract in the course of a business; and

(*iii*) in the case of a contract governed by the law of sale of goods or hire-purchase, the goods passing under or in pursuance of the contract are of a type ordinarily supplied for private use or consumption. See *R & B Customs Brokers Co. Ltd* v. *United Dominions Trust Ltd* (1988).

8. Exclusions rendered ineffective by the Act

The following categories of exclusion clauses are made totally ineffective and void:

(a) Clauses excluding or restricting liability for death or personal injury resulting from negligence: s. 2(1).

(b) Clauses excluding or restricting liability for breach of obligations arising from the Sale of Goods Act 1979, s.12 (seller's implied undertakings as to title) and the equivalent in relation to hire-purchase: s. 6(1).

(c) As against a person dealing as consumer, clauses excluding or restricting the seller's liability for breach of obligations arising from ss. 13, 14 or 15 of the Sale of Goods Act 1979 or the corresponding things in relation to hire-purchase: s. 6(2). For the Sale of Goods Act 1979 *see* 5: **13-16**. The concept of 'consumer dealing' is defined in s. 12 of the 1977 Act.

(d) As against a person dealing as a consumer, clauses in any contract by which possession or ownership of goods passes, other than by sale or hire-purchase, excluding or restricting obligations in respect of the goods' correspondence with description or sample, or their quality or fitness for any special purpose: s. 7(2).

(e) Clauses to which s. 5 applies. This section provides that, in the case of goods of a type ordinarily supplied for private use or consumption, where loss or damage

(*i*) arises from the goods proving defective while in consumer use; and

(*ii*) results from the negligence of a person concerned in the manufacture or distribution of the goods,

liability for the loss or damage cannot be excluded or restricted by reference to any contract term or notice contained in or operating by reference to a guarantee of the goods.

9. Exclusions which are effective only in so far as they satisfy the requirements of reasonableness.

The statutory requirement of reasonableness is the key characteristic of the scheme under the Act. It is that the exclusion clause in question must be fair and reasonable having regard to the circumstances which were, or ought reasonably to have been, known to or in the contemplation of the parties when the contract was made: s. 11. Guidelines for the application of the reasonableness test are contained in Schedule 2 of the Act (*see* Appendix 2). The following categories of exclusion clauses are valid and effective only in so far as they satisfy the requirements of reasonableness:

(a) Clauses excluding or limiting liability for negligence other than liability for death or personal injury: s. 2(2).

(b) Clauses to which s. 3 applies. This section applies as between contracting parties where one of them deals as a consumer or on the other's written standard terms of business. 'As against that party, the other cannot by reference to any contract term

> (*i*) when himself in breach of contract, exclude or restrict any liability of his in respect of the breach; or
>
> (*ii*) claim to be entitled either to render a contractual performance substantially different from that which was reasonably expected of him, *or*, in respect of the whole or any part of his contractual obligation, to render no performance at all, except in so far as... the contractual term satisfies the requirements of reasonableness': s. 3(2).

(c) Clauses to which s. 6(3) applies. This subsection applies as against a person dealing otherwise than a consumer as defined in s. 12. Liability for breach of the obligations arising from ss. 13, 14 and 15 of the Sale of Goods Act 1979 or the corresponding things in relation to hire-purchase.

This means that, in the case of contracts between business or manufacturing companies, exclusion and limitation of liability clauses in their contracts will be ineffective unless they satisfy the requirements of reasonableness. This is an important and far-reaching provision since it is normal practice in all sectors of business and commercial activity to set out protective exclusion clauses in standard form contracts.

(d) Clauses to which s. 7(3) applies. This subsection applies as against a person dealing otherwise than a consumer and covers contracts other than sale or hire-purchase under which possession or ownership of goods passes. It provides that clauses can exclude or restrict obligations in respect of the goods correspondence with description or sample, or their quality or fitness for any particular purpose, only in so far as the clause satisfies the requirement of reasonableness.

(e) Clauses to which s. 7(4) applies. This subsection provides further in regard to contracts other than sale of goods or hire-purchase under which possession or ownership of goods passes. Liability in respect of:

    (*i*) the right to transfer ownership of the goods, or give possession; or

    (*ii*) the assurance of quiet possession to a person taking goods in pursuance of the contract,

cannot be excluded or restricted by reference to any term of contract except in so far as the term satisfies the requirements of reasonableness.

10. The 'reasonableness' test

In deciding whether an exclusion clause satisfies the requirements of reasonableness, the court will have regard to the circumstances which were, or ought reasonably to have been, known to the parties when the contract was made. *See* s. 11 and Schedule 2. A useful light on the judicial approach to 'reasonableness' in this context is thrown by the Court of Appeal in *Mitchell* v. *Finney Lock Seeds* (1983). In this case the contract was governed by the substituted s. 55 contained in Schedule 1, paragraph 11 to the Sale of Goods Act 1979. This makes the following material provision: 'In the case of a contract for the sale of goods, any term of that ... contract exempting from all or any of the provisions of section 13, 14 or 15 ... is not enforceable to the extent that it is shown that it would not be fair or reasonable to allow reliance on the term.' By s. 55(9), this provision is extended to terms which, though not making express reference to ss. 13, 14 and 15, have a similar operation. Thus the clause in question in the *Mitchell* case was caught. The Court of Appeal was unanimous in deciding that it would not be reasonable to allow the suppliers to rely on the clause. The facts pointing to this conclusion were:

(a) the clause was not negotiated, but was imposed unilaterally as part of a set of trading conditions;

(b) as between the parties, all the fault lay on the defendants — in fact the damage could not have been incurred without their negligence, the buyers having no way of knowing or discovering that the seed was not cabbage seed;

(c) the buyers could not have insured against this kind of disaster, whereas there was some cover available to the suppliers; and

(d) to limit the suppliers' liability to the price of the seed as against the magnitude of the losses which farmers can incur in a disaster of this kind would be grossly disproportionate as an allocation of risk.

With regard to the approach of the Court of Appeal to the question of reasonableness, the clear injunction of the House of Lords in the *Mitchell* case must be complied with. In that case it was said that, 'the appellate court should treat the original decision with the utmost respect and refrain from interference with it unless satisfied that it proceeded on some erroneous principle or was plainly and obviously wrong'. This was the approach of the Court of Appeal in *Phillips Products Ltd* v. *Hyland* (1987).

In *Thompson* v. *T. Lohan Plant Hire Ltd* (1987), the first defendants were a plant hire company. This company hired an excavator together with driver to a third party for use at the third party's quarry. The first defendants had written to the third party stating that the hiring would be under the Contractors' Plant Association conditions. Condition 8 headed 'Handling of plant' read as follows: 'When driver or operator is supplied by the Owner with the plant, the Owner shall supply a person competent in the working of the plant and such person shall be under the direction and control of the Hirer. Such drivers and operators shall be for all purposes in connection with their employment in the working of the plant regarded as the servants or agents of the Hirer (but without prejudice to any of the provisions of Clause 13) who alone shall be responsible for all claims arising in connection with the operation of the plant by the said drivers and operators. The Hirer shall not allow any other person to operate such plant without the Owner's previous consent to be confirmed in writing.' Condition 13, headed 'Hirer's responsibility for loss and damage' read as follows: '(a) For the avoidance of doubt it is hereby declared and agreed that nothing in this Clause affects the operation of Clauses 5, 8 and 9 of this Agreement. (*b*) During the continuance of the hire period the Hirer shall subject to the provisions referred to in sub-paragraph (*a*) make good to the Owner all loss or damage to the plant from whatever cause the same may arise, fair wear and tear excepted and except as provided in Clause 9 herein, and shall also fully and completely indemnify the Owner in respect of all claims by any person whatsoever for injury to person or property caused by or in connection with or arising out of the use of the plant and in respect of all costs and charges in connection there-with whether arising under statute or common law. In the event of loss or of damage to the plant, hire charges shall be continued at idle time rates until settlement has been effected . . .'. There was an accident in the third party's quarry involving the excavator while driven by the driver supplied by the first defendants. The plaintiff's husband was killed in this accident. The plaintiff sued the first defendants for damages for negligence. The trial judge found that the driver had been negligent and awarded damages to the plaintiff against the first defendants. The first defendants sought to be indemnified by the third party by Conditions 8 and 13 of the CPA conditions. The third party contended that **(a)** the CPA conditions were not expressly incorporated in the contract, that **(b)** neither Condition 8 nor 13 expressly excluded the first defendants' liability in negligence and, alternatively, **(c)** that if Condition 8 had validly and effectively excluded or restricted liability for negligence, it was, nevertheless, contrary to s. 2(1) of the Unfair Contract Terms Act 1977. That section provides that, 'A person cannot by reference to any contract terms . . . exclude or restrict his liability for death or personal injury resulting from negligence'. The judge held that Conditions 8 and 13 had the effect of transferring liability for the driver's negligence from the first defendants to the third party. The first defendants were entitled to be indemnified by the third party. The third party appealed to the Court of Appeal, where it was held that where the parties showed a clear intention that, as between themselves, liability for negligence was to be transferred from one to the other, it was effective at common law as between the parties. The Unfair Contract Terms Act s.2(1) was intended to prevent the restriction of exclusion of liability in relation to the victim of negligence. The section was not concerned with arrangements made by a wrongdoer with others for sharing or transferring the burden of compensating the victim. It followed that s. 2(1) did not apply to strike down Condition 8, since the only relevant 'liability' for the purposes of s. 2(1) was that owed to the plaintiff, who had obtained a judgment which she could enforce against the first defendants and which was not affected by the operation of Condition 8. The condition was, therefore, effective to transfer liability for the driver's negligence to the third party who was, accordingly, required to indemnify the first defendants under Condition 13. The appeal was, accordingly, dismissed.

Thompson v. *Lohan* should be compared to *Phillips Products* v. *Hyland* (1987) which was also concerned with a version of Condition 8 of the CPA conditions. In *Phillips Products* a plant hire company (second defendants) hired an excavator together with driver to the plaintiffs for use in the construction of an extension to the plaintiff's factory. The contract of hire incorporated the CPA conditions mentioned in *Thompson* v. *Lohan* above. An accident occurred as a result of the driver's negligence causing damage to the plaintiffs' factory. The plaintiffs claimed damages against both defendants. The second defendants denied liability contending that Condition 8 gave a complete defence. The plaintiffs contended that either Condition 8 did not cover the driver's negligence or, if it did, that it purported to 'exclude or restrict' liability and thus by s. 2(2) of the Unfair Contract Terms Act 1977 was required to be a fair and reasonable term and was one which the plaintiffs contended was not fair and reasonable. The trial judge found that Condition 8 was not fair and reasonable and gave judgment against both defendants. The second defendants appealed contending that Condition 8 did not purport to exclude or restrict liability, but rather operated to transfer liability to the hirers, so that s. 2(2) did not apply. It was decided by the Court of Appeal that Condition 8 had the effect of excluding liability and, accordingly, fell within section s. 2(2) of the 1977 Act. The trial judge's finding that Condition 8 was not fair and reasonable must stand for it was neither plainly wrong nor based on erroneous principle. The appeal was therefore dismissed.

Progress test 6

1.   What is an exclusion clause?

2.   How does the court approach the question whether an exclusion clause is part of the contract?

3.   What is the underlying principle in the *Suisse Atlantique* case?

4.   Assess the significance of the *Photo Productions* case.

5.   Explain why the *Harbutt's Plasticine* case was overruled.

6.   Summarize the propositions contained in the trilogy of House of Lords cases on exclusion clauses *Suisse Atlantique, Photo Productions* and *Ailsa Craig*.

7.   List the types of exclusion clauses rendered ineffective by the Unfair Contract Terms Act 1977.

8.   List those kinds of clauses which are, by statute, effective only in so far as they satisfy the requirements to reasonableness.

9.   Specify those provisions of Part I of the Unfair Contract Terms Act 1977 which take effect as measures for the protection of consumers.

10.   Specify those provisions of Part I of the Unfair Contract Terms Act 1977 which take effect in contracts other than 'consumer dealings'.

11.   B bought a motor car from C by private sale. C had described the car as being a 1971 model. Three months after the sale, B discovered that it was a 1966 model. Advise B.

12.   D took his girlfriend, E, for a ride in the 'Tunnel of Love' at a fairground. He paid the fare for two and put the tickets into his pocket without looking at them. During the ride, their

vehicle overturned due to a defect in its construction. D and E were both seriously injured. Advise them, **(a)** on the footing that there was a large notice at the entrance saying that 'All passengers ride at their own risk', and **(b)** that on the back of the tickets were the words, 'The proprietor is not to be held liable for injuries to riders in the Tunnel of Love, no matter how caused'.

13. When F stayed in London he always had a room at the Fritz Hotel. On the last occasion, his room key was taken from the reception desk by a thief, who then stole F's diamond tie-pin from his room. In the room, there was a notice to the effect that the management of the hotel did not accept liability for theft, and advised guests to deposit valuables with the manager for safe keeping. F's solicitor has told the hotel manager that F intends to sue him for negligence. Advise the manager.

14. G, a structural engineer, contracts to design a bridge for the Department of the Environment. To what extent, if at all, will G be liable to the Department in the case of a design failure leading to a partial collapse of the bridge?

15. G, a shipowner, had bought coal from H for the past three years. Although there was never an express stipulation as to delivery, H had always delivered the consignments into G's ships. He has ordered 10 tons for his ship *Sylvester*, now lying in dock. H has accepted the order, but refuses to deliver it to the *Sylvester*, saying that he never promised to do this. H has told G that the 10 tons of coal are ready for collection at H's yard. Is G bound to arrange for the collection of the consignment?

16. J, a farmer, hired a threshing machine from K. When the machine arrived at J's farm, it was found that the engine was worn out and would not work at all. J had to wait a fortnight before K could replace the engine. J was unable to hire another machine at that time and, in consequence, much of his wheat crop was spoiled. Advise J.

17. L bought an electric blanket from M, a dealer in electrical goods. When L used the blanket for the first time, it set the bed alight, and L's wife was seriously burnt. L wishes to know whether he has any remedy against M.

18. N ordered a 'Snip' lawnmower from O, who promised to deliver it to N's house on the following Friday. The mower was not delivered as promised, and on the day following, N, who was worried because his lawn looked unkempt, bought a 'Snip' mower from P, who delivered it immediately. Three days later, O delivered a 'Snip" mower to N, who refused to accept it. Advise O.

19. Q contracted to buy a new car from R. In the printed standard form contract there was a clause, 'All conditions, express or implied, are hereby excluded'. After taking delivery of the car, Q discovered that it was not new. It has been used for demonstration purposes. R refuses to take the car back. Advise Q.

20. R is considering taking a 10-year lease of certain property from a landlord, S. One of the lessee's covenants in the lease states that 'All outside woodwork shall be painted every two years'. S tells R that if he signs the lease, he will be satisfied if the woodwork is painted at the end of the 10-year period. R is thus induced to sign the lease. Is he bound by his covenant to have the woodwork painted every two years?

21. Harry parked his car in a car park owned and operated by Parkings Ltd. On entry, he received a ticket which provided, *inter alia*, that 'vehicles are left in the company's car park expressly at the owner's risk'. On returning later, Harry found that his car had gone and that the attendant had no explanation. Harry now wishes to sue Parkings Limited for the value of the car. Advise him whether the exemption provision is sufficient to defeat his claim.

22. Farmer Giles bought a quantity of turnip seed from Seedmaster Ltd. He sowed the seed over three fields totalling seven acres. The crop produced by these seeds was a plant not even fit for animal feed. Yet the seed looked just like turnip seed before it was sown. There was a clause in the contract

providing that 'Seedmasters would not be liable in damages for
a sum greater than the contract price in the event of any breach
of contract whatsoever or any negligence on their part'.

Advise Farmer Giles of his legal position as against Seedmaster
Ltd.

7
Mistake

Mistake — its effect upon agreement

1. Agreement affected in two ways

Where there was some kind of misapprehension or misunderstanding as to a material fact at the time of reaching agreement, the factual circumstances will fall into one of the two following classes:

(a) Where agreement has been reached on the basis of a mistake common to both parties.

(b) Where there was a mere appearance of agreement because of mutual or unilateral mistake.

2. Common mistake

Common mistake occurs where both parties to an agreement are suffering from the same misapprehension. Where this kind of mistake occurs, offer and acceptance correspond, i.e. there has been agreement between the parties. It is necessary to consider whether the underlying common mistake affects the validity of the contract. An example of common mistake would be where X agrees to sell certain goods to Y, and at the time of the agreement, the goods have perished unknown to both parties.

3. Mutual and unilateral mistake

(a) *Mutual mistake* occurs where the parties have negotiated at cross-purposes, e.g. where A agrees to sell a horse to B, and A intended to sell his white horse, while B thought he was agreeing to buy A's grey horse.

(b) *Unilateral mistake* occurs where one party only is mistaken and the other party knows, or is deemed to know of the mistake. An example would be where C makes an offer to D only and it is accepted by X, who knows that the offer was made to D only; C thinks, mistakenly, that acceptance was made by D.

Where mutual or unilateral mistake has occurred, the acceptance may not correspond with the offer, and there is, consequently, doubt as to the validity of the agreement.

4.   Mistake at law and mistake in equity

Lord Denning said in *Solle* v. *Butcher* (1950), '. . . mistake is of two kinds: first, mistake which renders the contract void, that is, a nullity from the beginning, which is the kind of mistake which was dealt with by the courts of common law, and secondly, mistake which renders the contract not void, but voidable, that is, liable to be set aside on such terms as the court thinks fit, which is the kind of mistake which was dealt with by the courts of equity.' Since 1875 the court has had the power to give equitable relief or legal relief for mistake, according to the circumstances of the case, and according to the kind of relief asked for by the parties.

Mistake at law and mistake in equity need not be confused. They should be considered separately. It should be noticed that where the court has declared a contract void for operative mistake, no question of equitable mistake can arise: the contract is void *ab initio*. The rules relating to mistake in equity can apply only in cases where the court has not found operative mistake at law.

Mistake at common law

5.   Operative mistake

Where there is a mistake of fact which prevents the formation of any contract at all, the court will declare the contract void. This kind of mistake is known as operative mistake: any other kind of mistake does not affect the contract in the eyes of the common law, e.g.

Harrison & Jones v. *Bunton & Lancaster* (1953): There was a contract for the sale of a quantity of Calcutta Kapok 'Sree' brand. Buyer and seller thought this to be tree kapok, whereas, in fact, it contained an admixture of bush cotton.

The true nature of 'Sree' brand kapok was generally known in the trade. HELD: Goods answering the contract description had been supplied and there was no operative mistake.

Operative mistake is an exceptional occurrence. It is exceptional to the general rule of contract that parties are bound by the terms of their agreement and must rely on their contractual stipulations for protection from the effect of facts unknown to them.

6. Examples of operative mistake

Operative mistake may be common, mutual or unilateral. It must be of such a nature that it cannot be deemed that there was any contract at all.

The circumstances in which operative mistake can occur are as follows:

(a) Common mistake as to the existence of the subject-matter of the contract.

(b) Common mistake as to a fact fundamental to the entire agreement.

(c) Mutual mistake as to the identity of the subject-matter of the contract.

(d) Unilateral mistake by the offeror in expressing his intention, the mistake being known to the offeree.

(e) Unilateral mistake as to the nature of a document signed or sealed.

Note

In all these cases, the mistake is operative only where the mistake prevented the formation of any real agreement between the parties. If any party is under some misapprehension at the time of making the contract, and the mistake is not operative, then the contract is valid at common law in spite of the mistake. The mistaken party is then bound by the contract unless there is fraud or illegality, or some relief for the mistake in equity.

Unilateral mistake as to identity should be regarded as a separate category of mistake at common law for, in this instance, the contract may become voidable only.

7. Common mistake as to the existence of the subject-matter

If, at the time of the contract and unknown to the parties, the subject-matter of the contract is not in existence (*res extincta*), there can be no contract. In *Couturier* v. *Hastie* (1852), there was a contract for the sale of a cargo of corn in transit in the Mediterranean. Unknown to buyer and seller, the ship's captain had been forced to sell his cargo as it had fermented in the hold. The case was decided on the basis that the contract required that something in existence should be bought and sold, and since there was no such thing in existence at the time of the contract there could be no contract. Since the Sale of Goods Act 1893 came into force this situation has been covered by the provision that 'Where there is a contract for the sale of specific goods, and the goods without the knowledge of the seller have perished at the time when the contract was made, the contract is void.' Where, however, the circumstances are such that the seller is deemed to have warranted the existence of the goods, the seller is probably liable to the buyer for breach of contract if the goods are non-existent: *McRae* v. *Commonwealth Disposals Commission* (1951), a case before the High Court of Australia.

8. Common mistake as to a fact or quality fundamental to the agreement

Where the parties have made a contract based on a common misapprehension relating to the fundamental subject-matter of the contract, there is operative mistake. In *Bell* v. *Lever Brothers* (1932), Lord Atkin suggested that the test should be: 'Does the state of the new facts destroy the identity of the subject-matter as it was in the original state of the facts?' But this kind of mistake is not operative unless it is the common mistake of the parties as to the existence of a fact or quality which makes the subject-matter of the contract essentially different from what they believed it to be. The doctrine of common mistake will operate only where the mistake existed at the date of the contract. Where a subsequent event causes a party to regard himself as mistaken to have entered the contract the doctrine does not apply: *Amalgamated Investment and Property Co.* v. *John Walker & Sons* (1976).

Bell v. *Lever Bros.* (1931): B was under a contract of service with Lever Bros. as chairman of a subsidiary company in

Africa. Lever Bros. entered into a contract with B by which it was agreed that B should resign from his post before the expiry of the contract of employment and that, in return, he would be paid a specified sum as compensation. After Lever Bros. had paid the agreed sum to B they discovered that B had previously engaged in private trading contrary to the terms of the contract of service. Had they known of this before the completion of the compensation agreement, they could have treated the contract of service as repudiated and there would have been no need to negotiate the compensation agreement. But B had always been under the impression that his private trading activities were not such as to entitle Lever Bros. to have the service contract set aside, and that the contract could be prematurely terminated only by agreement. Lever Bros. claimed the return of the compensation on the grounds that the compensation agreement was not binding because of the mistake of the parties. HELD by the House of Lords: The common mistake that the service contract was not determinable except by agreement merely related to the quality of the subject-matter and was not sufficiently fundamental to constitute an assumption without which the parties would not have entered the compensation agreement. An agreement to terminate a broken contract is not fundamentally different from an agreement to terminate an unbroken contract. The mistake was not operative and the compensation agreement was binding.

Galloway v. *Galloway* (1914): The parties, believing themselves to be married, entered into a separation agreement under seal by which the man undertook to make money payments to the woman. It was later discovered that they were not, in fact, married. The woman claimed the promised payments. HELD: The deed was void on the grounds of the parties' mistake.

Sybron Corporation v. *Rochem Ltd* (1983): A company employee, who was a member of the company pension scheme, retired in September 1973. Under the scheme, the employee was entitled to the immediate repayment of his cash contributions but the balance of accrued benefits was to be applied entirely at the company's discretion. In the exercise of that discretion, the company paid the employee a lump sum of £13,200 and purchased life assurance policies which it held in trust and from which annuities were paid to the employee and his wife as beneficiaries. Subsequently it was discovered that the employee had been party to fraudulent misconduct in conjunction with certain other employees who were subordinate to him. The company sued all those involved in the fraud and also claimed the return of the lump sum of £13,200 and a declaration that the life assurance policies were held by the company free of any trust in favour of the employee and his wife. The court found in favour of the company, ordering the repayment of all sums paid by them and granting a declaration as sought by the company. The employee and his wife appealed on the grounds that the employee was under no legal obligation to his employer to disclose breaches of his obligations under the contract of employment. HELD by the Court of Appeal: Although the employee was not under a duty to disclose his own misconduct, he was under a duty to disclose misconduct of his subordinates even though that disclosure would have revealed his own part in the fraud. The employee was thus in serious breach of contract and had the company known of it at the time of his retirement, they would have refused to exercise their discretion to pay him the lump sum and pension. The payments had been made under a mistake of fact. The wife was in no better position than the employee for, although she was not a party to the fraud, she was a volunteer and thereby disentitled as a beneficiary under the pension trust. Appeal dismissed.

Strickland v. *Turner* (1852): There was a contract of sale of an annuity and, unknown to the parties, the annuitant was already dead. HELD: The purchaser was entitled to the return of his money. The contract was void for total failure of consideration.

Note

There was a failure of consideration because of the mistake of fact relating to that consideration.

9. **Mutual mistake as to the identity of the subject-matt**
   Where the parties have negotiated complet
cross-purposes, it cannot be said that they were ever in agreement.
In this connection, Austin's concept of 'the sense of the promise'
has come to be accepted as the description of what the court looks
for in each of promises exchanged by the parties. It is a particular
aspect of the objective test of intention. If the court discovers that
the sense of the promise given by one party was quite different
from the sense in which it was accepted by the other, there will be
operative mistake.

> *Raffles* v. *Wichelhaus* (1864): There was a contract for the
> sale of 125 bales of cotton 'to arrive ex *Peerless* from
> Bombay'. It happened that there were two ships named
> *Peerless* leaving Bombay at about the same time: the buyer
> meant one and the seller meant the other. HELD: The
> contract was void for mistake.

> *Scriven* v. *Hindley* (1913): In an auction sale, the auctioneer
> was selling tow. X bid for a lot, thinking that he was buying
> hemp. HELD: No contract.

10. **Unilateral mistake as to the expression of intention**
    Where the offeror makes a material mistake in expressing his
intention, and the other party knows, or is deemed to know, of the
error, the mistake may be operative.

> *Hartog* v. *Colin & Shields* (1939): H claimed damages for
> breach of contract, alleging that C had agreed to sell him
> 30,000 Argentinian hare skins and had failed to deliver
> them. C contended that the offer contained a material
> mistake and that H was well aware of this mistake when he
> accepted the offer. The mistake alleged by C was that the
> skins were offered at certain prices *per pound* instead of *per
> piece*. In the negotiations preceding the agreement,
> reference had always been made to prices *per piece*,
> moreover, this was the custom of the trade. C contended (a)
> that the contract was void for mistake, and (b) if there was a
> contract, rescission should be allowed. HELD: The contract
> was void for mistake. H could not reasonably have supposed

that the offer expressed C's real intention: H must have known it was made under a mistake.

Note that, in this case, the defendants asked for a declaration that the contract was void for mistake at common law and, in the alternative, for the equitable remedy of rescission. Since the court declared the contract void, there was no need to consider the question of rescission.

11. Unilateral mistake as to the nature of the document signed

The general rule is that a person is bound by the terms of any instrument which he signs or seals even though he did not read it, or did not understand its contents: *see L'Estrange* v. *Graucob* (1934), and *Blay* v. *Pollard & Morris* (1930). An exception to this general rule arises where a person signs or seals a document under a mistaken belief as to the nature of the document and the mistake was due to either

(a) the blindness, illiteracy, or senility of the person signing, or
(b) a trick or fraudulent misrepresentation as to the nature of the document, provided that person took all reasonable precautions before signing.

Where a person signs a document or executes a deed in these circumstances, he may raise the ancient defence of *non est factum* (it is not his deed). Until the decision of the House of Lords in *Saunders* v. *Anglia Building Society* (1971) it was thought that the defence was available even where there had been negligence on the part of the claimant, unless the instrument signed was negotiable. In the *Saunders* case, Lord Reid said: 'The plea of *non est factum* obviously applies when the person sought to be held liable did not in fact sign the document. But at least since the sixteenth century it has also been held to apply in certain cases so as to enable a person who in fact signed a document to say that it is not his deed. Obviously any such extension must be kept within narrow limits if it is not to shake the confidence of those who habitually and rightly rely on signatures when there is no obvious reason to doubt their validity. Originally this extension appears to have been made in favour of those who were unable to read owing to blindness or illiteracy and who therefore had to trust someone to tell them what they were signing. I think that it must also apply in favour of those who are permanently or temporarily unable through no fault of their own to have without explanation any real understanding of the purport of a particular document, whether that be from defective education, illness or innate incapacity.

'But that does not excuse them from taking such precautions as they reasonably can. The matter generally arises where an innocent third party has relied on a signed document in ignorance of the circumstances in which it was signed, and where he will suffer loss if the maker of the document is allowed to have it declared a nullity. So there must be a heavy burden of proof on the person who seeks to invoke this remedy. He must prove all the circumstances necessary to justify its being granted to him, and that necessarily involves him proving that he took all reasonable precautions in the circumstances. I do not say that the remedy can never be available to a man of full capacity. But that could only be in very exceptional circumstances; certainly not where his reason for not scrutinizing the document before signing it was that he was too busy or too lazy. In general I do not think that he can be heard to say that he signed in reliance on someone he trusted. But particularly when he was led to believe that the document which he signed was not one which affected his legal rights, there may be cases where this plea can properly be applied in favour of a man of full capacity.

'The plea cannot be available to anyone who was content to sign without taking the trouble to try to find out at least the general effect of the document. Many people do frequently sign documents put before them for signature by their solicitor or other trusted advisors without making any enquiry as to their purpose or effect. But the essence of the plea *non est factum* is that the person signing believed that the document he signed had one character or one effect whereas in fact its character or effect was quite different. He could not have such a belief unless he had taken steps or been given information which gave him some grounds for his belief. The amount of information he must have and the sufficiency of the particularity of his belief must depend on the circumstances of each case. Further the plea cannot be available to a person whose mistake was really a mistake as to the legal effect of the document, whether that was his own mistake or that of his advisor.'

Thoroughgood's Case (1584): An illiterate woman was induced to execute a deed in the belief that it was concerned with arrears of rent. In fact, the document was a deed releasing another from claims which the woman had against him. HELD: The deed was a nullity.

Foster v. *Mackinnon* (1869): A senile gentleman was induced to sign a bill of exchange in the belief that it was a guarantee. HELD: No liability was incurred by the signature.

Carlisle and Cumberland Banking Co. v. *Bragg* (1911): B was fraudulently induced to sign a guarantee in the belief that it was a document concerning insurance. HELD: The guarantee was not binding.

Muskham Finance v. *Howard* (1963): K, who had entered a hire-purchase agreement with the finance company, obtained the company's permission to sell the car which was the subject-matter of the agreement. At this time, K still owed the company £197. K arranged for T to sell the car for him. T then arranged for H to enter into a hire-purchase agreement with the company. The company required T to have an indemnity form signed by a person willing to indemnify them with respect to their agreement with H. T asked K to sign this form, saying, 'Could you sign this paper, which is a release note?' The heading 'Indemnity Form' was hidden by papers on the desk, and T pointed to the document and said, 'Just sign there and that will clear you with the vehicle.' K thereupon signed. H subsequently defaulted on his payments to the company, who then brought this action against H and K to enforce the indemnity. K pleaded *non est factum*. HELD by the Court of Appeal: The document signed by K was different in class and character from that which he thought he was signing. The mistake was induced by a trick. The indemnity was not enforceable against K.

Howatson v. *Webb* (1908): W, who held certain land as nominee only, was asked to sign documents which he was told were 'deeds for transferring the BEdmonton property'. When the mortgagee sued W for sums due, he pleaded *non est factum*. HELD by the Court of Appeal: The plea must fail because W was misled only as to the contents of the documents and not as to their character and class. He knew that they concerned the property held by him as nominee.

Saunders v. *Anglia Building Society* (1971): The plaintiff was an elderly widow who had made a will leaving all her possessions to her nephew, Walter Parkin. Her house was leasehold with more than 900 years to go. She gave the deeds of the house to Parkin because she had left it to him in her will and she knew that he wanted to raise money on it. She was content to allow him to do this provided she was able to remain in the house during her lifetime.

When Parkin told his friend, the first defendant, that the plaintiff had left the house to him in her will, they came to an arrangement by which the first defendant, who was heavily in debt, could raise some money. According to the arrangement, a document was drawn up by solicitors by which the plaintiff was to sell the house to the first defendant for £3,000. The understanding between Parkin and the first defendant was that after signature by the plaintiff, no purchase price would be paid over, and the first defendant would then mortgage the property to raise money. The first defendant took the document to the plaintiff, who at that time was 78 years old, to get her signature. She did not read the document because she had broken her spectacles. She asked him what it was for, and he replied, 'It is a deed of gift for Wally (Parkin) for the house.' She thought at the time that Parkin was going to borrow money on the deeds and that the first defendant was arranging this for him.

After the plaintiff had signed the document no money was paid to her, although the document provided that she acknowledged receipt of £3,000 paid by the first defendant. The first defendant then obtained a loan of £2,000 from the second defendant, a building society, on the security of the deeds. For this purpose, Parkin gave a reference to the building society, falsely stating that he was a reliable person. Subsequently the first defendant defaulted in the instalment payments to the building society, which then sought to recover possession of the house. The plaintiff then brought this action, contending that she was not bound by the assignment on the grounds that it was not her deed. Stamp J held that the assignment was not her deed and ordered the building society to deliver up the title deed to the plaintiff. It is noteworthy that, had matters been allowed to rest at this decision, the only person to benefit would be Parkin, for the building society had given an undertaking to allow the plaintiff to remain in the house for the rest of her life.

The building society appealed to the Court of Appeal. It was held by the Court of Appeal that the plea of *non est factum* could not be supported and that the appeal must be allowed. The executrix of the plaintiff's estate appealed to the House of Lords. HELD by the House of Lords: The plaintiff fell very short of making the clear and satisfactory case which is required of those who seek to have a legal act declared void and of establishing a sufficient discrepancy between her intentions and her act. The pleas of *non est factum* failed.

In *Lloyds Bank* v. *Waterhouse* (1990) an illiterate signed a bank guarantee in reliance on the bank's negligent misrepresentations as to its nature. He did not tell the bank that he could not read. It was held by the Court of Appeal that he was entitled to rely on the defence of *non est factum* and also to claim in respect of the negligent misrepresentations by the bank.

12. Unilateral mistake as to the identity of the person contracted with: voidable title to goods

It must first be said that this kind of mistake does not logically belong with the above examples of operative mistake. Under this heading we are not concerned with the question whether a contract is void but rather whether a voidable title to goods has passed under a sale to a fraudulent buyer. Where a fraudulent person conceals his true identity in order to gain possession of goods without payment the question of title to the goods will arise if he resells them. To whom do the goods then belong? Do they belong to the original seller who was defrauded? Or do they belong to the subsequent purchaser?

The rogue who concealed his true identity obtains a voidable title to the goods in his possession. The resale is thus governed by s. 23 of the Sale of Goods Act 1979 (previously s. 23 of the 1893 Act). This section provides that: 'When the seller of goods has a voidable title thereto, but his title has not been avoided at the time of the sale, the buyer acquires a good title to the goods, provided he buys them in good faith and without notice of the seller's defect in title.' The vital question then is whether the subsequent buyer bought in good faith and without notice of the seller's defective title. This means that the circumstances must be such that he had no reason to suspect that his seller had obtained the goods by fraud. He must be a bona fide purchaser for value of the goods: if not, he gets no title and the original seller remains the true owner.

The leading case is *Lewis* v. *Averay* (1972) in which previous inconsistencies were clarified. The judgment of Lord Denning MR in this case should be read carefully.

Where the original seller is seeking to recover the goods (or their value) from the ultimate buyer, he usually tries to show:

(a) that he intended to deal with a person other than the rogue;
(b) that at the time of the contract the identity of the other party was crucial; and
(c) that he took steps reasonable in the circumstances to check the proffered identity.

But he cannot succeed against a bona fide purchaser for value even if he proves all three points: *see* Sale of Goods Act 1979, s. 23, below.

Ingram v. *Little* (1960) is now regarded as being of doubtful authority and must be read in the light of *Lewis* v. *Averay*, in which the standing of the earlier cases of *King's Norton Metal Co.* v. *Edridge, Merrett & Co.* (1897) and *Phillips* v. *Brooks* (1919) was restored.

Phillips v. *Brooks* (1919): The plaintiff was a jeweller. One North entered his shop and asked to see some jewellery. He chose a pearl necklace, price £2,250, and a ring, price £450. He then took out his cheque-book and wrote out a cheque for £3,000. As he signed the cheque, he said, 'You see who I am, I am Sir George Bullough', and gave a London address, which the jeweller checked in a directory. The jeweller then asked whether he would like to take the articles with him, to

which North replied that he would like to take the ring.
North promptly pledged the ring with the defendant, a
pawnbroker, for £350. The cheque was dishonoured and
the jeweller claimed to recover the ring from the
pawnbroker. HELD: The jeweller intended to contract with
the person present in front of him, whoever he was, i.e. the
mistake as to identity of the man North did not affect the
formation of the contract. North got a voidable title to the
ring, and since it was not avoided at the time of pledging it,
the pawnbroker got a good title.

In this case, North's title to the ring was voidable because of
the fraudulent misrepresentation, but at the time of the pledge,
his title was still good, since by then the jeweller had done nothing
to avoid his title. Section 23 of the Sale of Goods Act 1979 provides
that when the seller of goods has a voidable title to them, but his
title has not been avoided at the time of the sale, the buyer acquires
a good title to the goods, provided he buys them in good faith and
without notice of the seller's defect of title.

Cundy v. *Lindsay* (1878): Alfred Blenkarn ordered certain
goods from the respondents, signing the order in such a
way as to make it appear to have come from Blenkiron &
Co., a respectable firm. The goods were delivered to
Blenkarn but he did not pay for them. Blenkarn sold the
goods to the appellants. The respondents claimed the
recovery of the goods, or their value from the appellant.
HELD by the House of Lords: The respondents knew
nothing of Blenkarn, intending to deal with Blenkiron &
Co., a fact which was known to Blenkarn, therefore there
was no common intention which could lead to a contract
between these parties: it followed that the property in the
goods remained in the respondents and no title passed to
the appellants.

Lewis v. *Averay* (1972): The plaintiff put an advertisement in
a newspaper, offering to sell his car for £450. In reply to the
advertisement, a man (who turned out to be a rogue)
telephoned and asked if he could see the car. That evening,
he came to see the car, tested it and said that he liked it.
The rogue and the plaintiff then went to the flat of the

plaintiff's fiancée, where the rogue introduced himself as
Richard Greene, making the plaintiff and his fiancée
believe that he was the well-known film actor of that name.
The rogue wrote a cheque for the agreed sum of £450, but
the plaintiff was, at first, not prepared to let him take the
car until the cheque was cleared. When the rogue pressed to
be allowed to take the car with him, the plaintiff asked:
'Have you anything to prove that you are Mr Richard A.
Greene?' Whereupon, the rogue produced a special pass of
admission to Pinewood Studios, bearing the name of
Richard A. Greene and a photograph, which was clearly of
the man claiming to be Richard Greene. The plaintiff was
satisfied that the man was really Mr Richard Greene, the
film actor. He let the rogue take the car in return for the
cheque. A few days later, the plaintiff discovered that the
cheque was from a stolen book and that it was worthless. In
the meantime, the rogue sold the car to the defendant, who
paid £200 for it in entire good faith. The rogue then
disappeared. The plaintiff brought this action against the
defendant, claiming damages for conversion. The county
court judge found in favour of the plaintiff. The defendant
appealed. On the essential question whether there was a
contract of sale by which property in the car passed from
the plaintiff to the rogue, HELD by the Court of Appeal: the
fraud rendered the contract between the plaintiff and the
rogue voidable (and not void) and, accordingly, the
defendant obtained good title since he bought in good faith
and without notice of the fraud, the plaintiff having failed to
avoid the contract in time.

In *Lewis* v. *Averay* Lord Denning said:

'There are two cases in our books which cannot, to my mind,
be reconciled the one with the other. One of them is *Phillips* v.
Brooks, where a jeweller had a ring for sale. The other is *Ingram* v.
Little where two ladies had a car for sale. In each case the story is
very similar to the present. A plausible rogue comes along. The
rogue says that he likes the ring, or the car, as the case may be. He
asks the price. The seller names it. The rogue says that he is
prepared to buy it at that price. He pulls out a cheque-book. He
writes, or prepares to write, a cheque for the price. The seller

hesitates. He has never met this man before. He does not want to hand over the ring or the car not knowing whether the cheque will be met. The rogue notices the seller's hesitation. He is quick with his next move. He says to the jeweller, in *Phillips* v. *Brooks*: "I am Sir George Bullough of 11 St James' Square"; or to the ladies in *Ingram* v. *Little* : "I am P.G.M. Hutchinson of Stanstead House, Stanstead Road, Caterham"; or to Mr Lewis in the present case: "I am Richard Greene, the film actor of the Robin Hood series". Each seller checks up the information. The jeweller looks up the directory and finds there is a Sir George Bullough at 11 St James' Square. The ladies check up too. They look up the telephone directory and find there is a "P.G.M. Hutchinson of Stanstead House, Stanstead Road, Caterham". Mr Lewis checks up too. He examines the official pass to the Pinewood Studios with this man's photograph on it.

'In each case the seller feels that this is sufficient confirmation of the man's identity. So he accepts the cheque signed by the rogue and lets him have the ring, in one case, and the car and log book in the other two cases. The rogue goes off and sells the goods to a third person who buys them in entire good faith and pays the price to the rogue. The rogue disappears. The original seller presents the cheque. It is dishonoured. Who is entitled to the goods? The original seller or the ultimate buyer? The courts have given different answers. In *Phillips* v. *Brooks* the ultimate buyer was held to be entitled to the ring. In *Ingram* v. *Little* the original seller was held to be entitled to the car. In the present case the deputy county court judge has held the original seller entitled. It seems to me that the material facts in each case are quite indistinguishable the one from the other. In each case there was, to all outward appearance, a contract; but there was a mistake by the seller as to the identity of the buyer. This mistake was fundamental. In each case it has led to the handing over of the goods. Without it the seller would not have parted with them.

'This case therefore raises the question: What is the effect of a mistake by one party as to the identity of the other? It has sometimes been said that, if a party makes a mistake as to the identity of the person with whom he is contracting, there is no contract, or if there is a contract, it is a nullity and void, so that no property can pass under it. This has been supported by a reference to the French jurist Pothier; but I have said before, and I repeat now, his statement is no part of English law . . . . But the statement by Pothier has given rise to such refinements that it is time it was dead and buried altogether . . . As I listened to the argument in this case, I felt it wrong that an innocent purchaser (who knew nothing of what passed between the seller and the rogue) should have his title depend on such refinements. After all, he has acted with complete circumspection and in entire good faith; whereas it was the seller who let the rogue have the goods and thus enabled him to commit the fraud. I do not, therefore, accept the theory that mistake as to identity renders a contract void. I think the true principle is that which underlies the decision of this court in *King's Norton Metal Co.* v. *Edridge, Merrett & Co.* and of Horridge J, in *Phillips* v. *Brooks*, which has stood for these last 50 years. It is this: when two parties have come to a contract — or what appears, on the face of it, to be a contract — the fact that one party is mistaken as to the identity of the other does not mean that there is no contract, or that the contract is a nullity and void from the beginning. It only means that the contract is voidable, that is, liable to be set aside at the instance of the mistaken person, so long as he does so before the third parties have in good faith acquired a right under it.'

> *Ingram* v. *Little* (1960): Two ladies, the joint owners of a car, advertised for its sale. A swindler called at their home and agreed to buy the car for £717. He offered a cheque in payment and this was refused. The swindler attempted to convince the ladies that he was a Mr Hutchinson of Stanstead Road, Caterham. One of the ladies checked this name and address in the telephone directory. The ladies then decided to accept the cheque in payment. The cheque was dishonoured and the swindler disappeared (he was not Mr Hutchinson). The swindler had sold the car to L, who bought it in good faith. The ladies sought to recover the possession of the car from L. HELD by the Court of Appeal: The offer to sell, with payment to be made by cheque, was made to Hutchinson only. As the swindler knew this, the offer was not one which he could accept. Therefore, there was no contract for the sale of the car, and the plaintiffs were entitled to its return.

Where a person who was not an offeree purports to accept the offer the case is quite different from those discussed above. This situation is governed by the general rule of offer and acceptance to the effect that only an offeree is capable of accepting an offer. Any purported acceptance by a person other than the offeree will not bring about a contract: *Boulton* v. *Jones* (1857). (*See* 2:8.)

Mistake in equity

13. Equitable relief for mistake

Where a person had entered a contract under a misapprehension, and the contract is good at common law (i.e. the court has not declared it void for operative mistake), the mistaken party may, in proper circumstances, obtain equitable relief from his contractual obligations. The relief afforded by equity is of three kinds:

(a) rescission on terms;
(b) refusal of specific performance;
(c) rectifications.

14. Rescission on terms

In order to get rescission on terms, the claimant must show the court that it would be against good conscience for the other party to take full advantage of his contractual rights. In these circumstances, the court has powers to attach terms to the order that the contract be set aside. In effect, the original contractual rights and obligations are dissolved and replaced by fresh rights and obligations based on what the court thinks fair and just. But the court will not grant rescission if to do so would cause injustice to third parties. Nor will the court rescind a contract where the unilateral mistake has in no way been caused by the conduct of the non-mistaken party: *Riverlate Properties* v. *Paul* (1975). It seems that rescission on terms is available only where there has been a mistake common to both parties, and that it is not available in cases of mutual or unilateral mistake.

Cooper v. *Phibbs* (1867): An appeal from the Chancery Court to the House of Lords. The appellant had taken a three-year lease of a salmon fishery from the respondent. At the time of the agreement, both parties believed that the fishery belonged to the respondent: indeed, he had spent a considerable amount of money on improvements to the property. It was subsequently discovered that the fishery was the property of the appellant, who now sought to be relieved of the obligations he had incurred under the lease. HELD by the House of Lords: The appellant was entitled to have the lease rescinded on terms that the respondent would have lien on the property to the extent of the money spent on improvements.

Solle v. *Butcher* (1950): This was a dispute between landlord and tenant. The landlord had acquired a long lease of a war-damaged house, which had been let off in flats, subject to the Rent Restriction Acts. The landlord carried out repairs and considerable improvements to the house, and, in particular, to the flat which was the subject of this action. This flat was let to the tenant for £250 a year. Both parties were under the impression that the flat was no longer subject to the Rent Restriction Acts. Both parties knew that the controlled rent under the Acts would have been £140 a year. The landlord could have taken steps to have the controlled rent raised to £250 before entering into an agreement with any tenant, but he could not do this while an agreement was afoot. The tenant paid the agreed rent (£250) for more than a year, but then took proceedings in the County Court for a declaration that the flat was still subject to a controlled rent of £140 a year. The landlord contended that the dwelling had undergone a change of identity due to the bomb damage and the subsequent restoration and improvements, and that, accordingly, the Acts did not apply. He contended further that the lease should be rescinded on the grounds of mistake. The county court judge held that the rent was controlled by the Acts at £140, and that the tenant was entitled to recover the sum overpaid. The landlord appealed. HELD by the Court of Appeal: (a) The structural improvements had not altered the identity of the flat so as to render it free from the provisions of the Rent Restriction Acts. (b) The parties were under a common mistake of fact in believing that the flat was no longer subject to the Acts. (c) The landlord was entitled to rescission on terms directed by the court, the terms being that he allow the tenant to enter a new lease at £250 a year.

Grist v. *Bailey* (1966): B entered in a written agreement with G for the sale of a house for £850. The agreement expressed the sale of the house to be 'subject to the existing tenancy thereof'. Both parties believed the house to be in the occupation of a statutory tenant but, unknown to them, the statutory tenant had died and the house was occupied by the tenant's son who did not wish to claim statutory tenancy. On discovering that there was no statutory tenancy and that the house was consequently worth about £2,250, B refused to complete. G brought this action for specific performance of the contract and B counterclaimed for rescission on the grounds of common mistake. HELD: B was not at fault in not knowing that the statutory tenant had died. There was common mistake such as to entitle B to equitable relief. Specific performance was refused and the contract rescinded on terms that B should enter a fresh contract with G at a proper vacant possession price.

Magee v. *Pennine Insurance Co.* (1969): An insurance contract was concluded on the strength of a proposal form signed by the plaintiff. This insurance proposal form included a number of misrepresentations made without fraud. The insurance was renewed from year to year. In 1964 it was transferred to another car. In 1965 the insured car was damaged and the plaintiff made a claim against the company. The company made an offer to pay £385 in settlement of the claim and the plaintiff accepted orally. The company then discovered the misrepresentations in the original proposal form and, in consequence, refused to the agreed £385. HELD by the Court of Appeal (Winn LJ dissenting): The company could set the £385 agreement aside: **(a)** per Lord Denning MR, a common mistake, even on a most fundamental matter, does not make a contract void at law; but it makes it voidable in equity; **(b)** per Fenton Atkinson LJ when the agreement relied on by the plaintiff was made it was made on the basis of a particular and essential contractual assumption, namely, that there was in existence a valid and enforceable policy of insurance, and that assumption was not true.

15. Refusal of specific performance

Specific performance is a discretionary remedy and is not awarded as of right. The court will not usually award specific performance where the defendant entered the contract under some material misapprehension and

(a) it would be unduly harsh to force the defendant to comply specifically with the terms of the contract, or
(b) the mistake was caused by the misrepresentation of the plaintiff, or
(c) the plaintiff knew of the defendant's mistake.

If none of these conditions is satisfied, mistake is no defence to an action for specific performance.

Tamplin v. *James* (1880): An inn and an adjoining shop were put up for auction. Accurate plans showing the extent of the property were displayed in the auction room. The property was knocked down to J, who had not looked at the plans, and who wrongly thought that the lot included some gardens at the back of the inn. (J knew that the tenants of the inn had enjoyed the use of the gardens and, for this reason, thought they were included in the sale.) The vendor sought to have the contract specifically enforced against J. HELD: There was no excuse for the mistake and the contract should be specifically performed.

Webster v. *Cecil* (1861): W offered to buy certain land from C for £2,000, but C rejected the offer. Then C wrote to W offering to sell the land for £1,250, and W accepted by return of post. C immediately gave notice to W that he had written £1,250 in error for £2,250. Nevertheless, W claimed specific performance. HELD: W must have known of the mistake in the expression of C's offer. Specific performance refused.

Where specific performance is refused the defendant may remain liable in damages for breach of contract. But where rescission is granted together with refusal of specific performance (*Grist* v. *Bailey*), there is no liability for breach.

16. Rectification

Where a written contract does not accurately express the agreement actually reached between the parties, the court will rectify the written document so as to bring it into conformity with the actual agreement reached. Where the mistake in setting out the written document is due to the negligence of the plaintiff or of his legal adviser, this, of itself, is no bar to rectification: *Weeds* v. *Blaney* (1976). A party claiming rectification must prove:

(a) that a complete and certain agreement was reached between the parties, and

(b) that the agreement was unchanged at the time it was put into writing, and the writing did not correspond with the agreement reached, i.e. there was a mistake in expressing the terms of the agreement.

> *Craddock Bros.* v. *Hunt* (1923): C agreed orally to sell a house, exclusive of an adjoining yard, to H. The agreement was subsequently expressed in writing but, by mistake, the yard was included. Moreover, when the deed of conveyance was drawn up, it included the same mistake, and the deed was executed. When C discovered the mistake, he asked for rectification of **(a)** the written contract and **(b)** the deed of conveyance. HELD by the Court of Appeal: There had been a complete oral agreement between the parties, and this agreement was not correctly expressed in the written contract, nor in the deed of conveyance. C was entitled to have the contract and the deed rectified to correspond with the oral agreement.

Note
_____

Rectification is never available where the written contract is identical to the antecedent oral agreement, even though one of the parties was under a misapprehension at the time of making the oral agreement.
_____

Rectification is not available to a plaintiff whose careless failure to read the terms of the agreement results in his being unilaterally mistaken as to those terms: *Agip* v. *Navigazione Alta Italia* (1984) CA.

> *Frederick E. Rose* v. *Wm. H. Pim & Co* (1953): In this sale of goods case the buyers had received an enquiry from X for *'horsebeans described here as feveroles'*. The buyers then asked the sellers what feveroles were. The sellers duly informed the buyers that feveroles and horsebeans were one and the same (in fact, feveroles are a special kind of horsebean). Suffering from this misapprehension, the parties entered into an oral agreement for the sale of 500 tons of horsebeans. The oral agreement was subsequently expressed accurately in writing. When the buyers discovered the mistake as to the nature of feveroles, they sought to have the written agreement rectified to read 'horsebeans, feveroles'. HELD by the Court of Appeal: The written contract correctly expressed the oral agreement. Therefore, the contract could not be rectified.

Note

The ultimate aim of the buyers in *Rose* v. *Pim* was that, if they had succeeded in getting rectification, the sellers would then have been in breach of contract (as rectified) and would thus have been liable to pay damages.

> *W. Higgins* v. *Northampton Corporation* (1927): H submitted a tender to the Corporation for the building of certain houses. Due to faulty calculating, H stated the wrong price for the work in his tender. The tender was accepted without knowledge of the mistake. HELD: The contract could not be rectified because there had merely been a mistake by one party only in expressing his intention.

> *Joscelyne* v. *Nissen* (1970) CA: This case concerned an agreement between a father and his daughter. The father lived in a house from where he carried on a car-hire business. In 1960 he received notice to quit and the daughter then, in order to help her father, bought the house with the help of a mortgage. The daughter moved into the first floor with her husband and her parents occupied the ground floor. In 1963 the father ran into

difficulties with his business with the result that the parties
devised a scheme by which the daughter would take over
the business on certain conditions. In 1964, there was a
written contract by which the father transferred his business
to his daughter and the daughter promised, *inter alia*, to
permit her father to reside in the ground floor of the house
'free of all rent and outgoings of every kind in any event'.
At first the daughter paid for the father's gas, electricity and
coal and for his home help. When, later, the daughter
refused to pay for these items, contending that she was not
bound to do so under the contract, the father brought this
action for rectification. HELD: The written contract did not
express the accord between the parties that the daughter
should pay all the outgoings of the house; since this was the
agreement between the parties up to the time they executed
the written contract, the court had jurisdiction to rectify the
contract. It made no difference that there was no concluded
and binding contract between the parties until the written
contract was executed.

Progress test 7

1. Distinguish between common mistake, mutual mistake and
unilateral mistake.

2. What is operative mistake? Give examples.

3. What kind of mistake does not affect the contract at common
law?

4. Explain fully how mistaken identity may affect a contract.

5. In what circumstances may the defence of *non est factum* be
pleaded?

6. Distinguish between mistake at law, and mistake in equity.

7. What do you understand by 'rescission on terms'? Do you consider that an order of rescission on terms is likely to achieve a more just result than a declaration that a contract is void *ab initio*?

8. 'Rectification is concerned with contracts and documents, not with intentions. In order to get rectification, it is necessary to show that the parties were in complete agreement on the terms of their contract, but by an error wrote them down wrongly.' Denning LJ (as he then was) in *Rose* v. *Pim* (1953). Comment on this statement.

9. There was a contract of sale between A, the seller, and B, the buyer, for 1,000 Japanese cameras, described to be lying in A's warehouse in London. Immediately before the agreement, the cameras were destroyed in a fire in A's warehouse. A did not know about the fire until after the agreement. B, who had planned to make a large profit on a re-sale of the cameras, wishes now to claim damages from A for breach of contract. Advise B.

10. C and D thought they were married, but, unknown to them, their 'marriage' was void. While they were under this misapprehension, they entered into a separation agreement under which C promised to make an allowance of £500 a year to D. C has now discovered that he was never married to D, and wishes to know whether he is bound by his agreement to pay the allowance. Advise him.

11. E agrees to buy F's horse Dobbin. At the time of the agreement, F intends to sell his grey horse called Dobbin. He does not know that E thinks he is buying F's white horse, which is also called Dobbin. Is there a binding contract between the parties?

12. G advertises in a newspaper for the sale of his motor car. H calls at G's house in response to the advertisement, introducing himself falsely as 'Henry Jones'. G agrees to sell his car to H and to take a cheque as payment. H drives off in the car, and the cheque is subsequently dishonoured. He sells the car to J, and then disappears. What must G prove in order to be able to recover the car from J?

13. K agrees orally with L that he will guarantee L's bank overdraft up to the sum of £100. K goes to L's bank and signs a form of guarantee, but he does not notice that the amount guaranteed, according to the form, is £1,000. L then becomes overdrawn to the extent of £960. Advise the bank as to K's liability.

14. M attended the auction sale of a farm. He did not bother to examine the accurate plans exhibited at the sale, for he thought he knew the extent of the farm. M made the highest bid and the farm was knocked down to him. He subsequently discovered that the property sold did not include a certain field which he had always thought of as belonging to the farm. The vendor has asked for an order of specific performance, and M wishes to resist this as he no longer wants the property. Advise him as to whether his mistake was of such a nature as to cause the court to refuse the specific performance to the vendor.

15. N, a senior manager, is offered by his employer early retirement with a generous lump sum payment and a pension for himself and his wife in the event of her outliving him. N accepts. After the payment of the lump sum, the employer discovers that N had been in serious breach of contract for which he could have been summarily dismissed. Advise N and his wife of their legal position.

8
Misrepresentation

Representations distinguished from express terms

1. Material statements during negotiations

Businessmen often refer to statements made during negotiations as 'representations'. When a lawyer uses the word 'representation' he usually intends a stricter and narrower meaning. The material statements made during the negotiations leading to a contract can be divided into two classes:

(a) Representations by which the parties intended to be bound. Such statements form the express terms of the contract and are not usually called 'representations' by lawyers. These statements are either warranties or conditions.

(b) Representations by which the parties did not intend to be bound but which, nevertheless, helped to induce the contract. These statements are known as *representations* (using the word in its legal sense) or *mere representations*. The *'mere'* leaves no doubt as to the meaning intended.

2. Misrepresentation

Where a mere representation is a false statement there is misrepresentation. The word 'misrepresentation' has two meanings. First, it means the false statement itself; second, it means the act of making the false statement. In order to arrive at a more complete definition of misrepresentation it is convenient to start by defining a mere representation. The various elements of the definition are considered in the next five paragraphs.

A mere representation is a statement

(a) of material fact;

(b) made by one party to another;

(c) during the negotiations leading to the agreement;

(d) which was intended to operate, and did operate, as an inducement to enter the contract;

(e) but was not intended to be a binding contractual term.

Where a statement of this class proves to be false, there is misrepresentation.

3. Statement of material fact

A misrepresentation is an assertion of the truth that a fact exists or did exist. It can, therefore, have no reference to future events or promises. The assertion must be materially connected to the contract. 'There is a clear difference between a representation of fact and a representation that something will be done in the future. A representation that something will be done in the future cannot be true or false at the moment it is made; and although you may call it a representation, if anything it is a contract or promise': *Beatty* v. *Ebury* (1872), per Mellish LJ.

Points to note are:

(a) A promise to do something relates to the future. If it is material to the agreement, it will be a term and not a mere representation.

(b) A statement as to the state of a man's mind may be a statement of fact. In *Edgington* v. *Fitzmaurice* (1885), Bowen LJ said, 'The state of a man's mind is as much a fact as the state of his digestion.' It is true that it is very difficult to prove what is the state of a man's mind at a particular time but, if it can be substantiated, it is as much a fact as anything else. A misstatement of the state of a man's mind is misrepresentation of fact. A statement as to state of mind may be made with reference to intention or opinion.

  (*i*) An expression of intention may be a statement of fact.

  (*ii*) An expression of opinion may be a statement of fact. If it is proved that the expressed opinion was not actually held, there is a misrepresentation. But if the expressed opinion was actually held there is no misrepresentation — even where the opinion was mistakenly held.

Bisset v. *Wilkinson* (1927): The vendor of a piece of land in New Zealand told a prospective purchaser that, in his opinion, the land would carry 2,000 sheep. In fact, the land would not carry that number of sheep. HELD by the Privy Council: There was no misrepresentation, for the statement was one of opinion which was honestly held.

(c) The question whether or not any misrepresentation would have induced a reasonable person to enter the contract related only to the question of onus of proof: *Museprime Properties Ltd* v. *Adhill Properties* (1990).

(d) *Simplex commendatio non obligat* (a simple commendation does not bind). The law allows a trader a good deal of latitude in his choice of language when commending his wares. Mere advertisement puff is not misrepresentation. The 'desirable residence' advertised by the estate agent may leave much to be desired, but there is, nevertheless, no misrepresentation. However, statements of a specific nature will usually be either terms or representations.

(e) A statement of law must be distinguished from a statement of fact. If a legal principle is wrongly stated there is no misrepresentation: but a false statement as to the existence of a legal right may be a misrepresentation.

Note

A false statement as to the existence of an Act of Parliament is a misrepresentation of fact: *West London Commercial Bank* v. *Kitson* (1884).

---

4. Statement by one party to another

A statement made by a person who is not a party to the agreement cannot be a representation unless there is a principal-agent relationship (express or implied) between that person and one of the parties.

5. Statement made in negotiations

Any statement which was not made during the course of negotiations leading to the formation of an agreement cannot be a representation, e.g. a statement made after the agreement has been concluded.

6. Inducement to enter the contract

A statement cannot be a representation unless it was intended to be an inducement to the other party to enter the contract, and, in fact, operated as an inducement. There is no misrepresentation, therefore, where:

(a) the statement was not actually communicated to the other party; or
(b) the statement did not affect the other party's decision to enter the contract; or
(c) the statement was known to be untrue by the other party; or
(d) the other party did not believe the statement to be true.

Where a statement is made during negotiations leading to a contract for the purpose of inducing the other party to act on it, and that other party acts on it by entering the contract, then, prima facie, the statement was intended as a warranty. But the party making the statement can rebut the inference if he can by showing that it would not be reasonable to hold him bound to it.

In *Dick Bentley Productions* v. *Harold Smith (Motors)* (1965), Lord Denning MR said: '[T]he question whether a warranty was intended depends on the conduct of the parties, on their words and behaviour, rather than on their thoughts. If an intelligent bystander would reasonably infer that a warranty was intended, that will suffice.' (*See* 5:**2**.)

7.   No intention to be bound
A mere representation is a statement by which parties did not intend to be bound. Intention is discovered, in cases of dispute, by the application of an objective warranty and not a mere representation: *see Routledge* v. *McKay* (1954), and *Couchman* v. *Hill* (1947). (*See* 5:**2**.)

Misrepresentation may be innocent or fraudulent

8.   Innocent and fraudulent misrepresentation
Misrepresentation may be innocent or fraudulent and it is necessary to be able to distinguish between the two. Fraudulent misrepresentation is a false statement falling within the definition in *Derry* v. *Peek* (1889) and is explained in the next paragraph. Fraudulent misrepresentation is a tort and sometimes known as deceit. A tort is a civil (as opposed to criminal) wrong for which damages is the usual remedy. The parties to an action in tort may

or may not be parties to a contract. Accordingly, a fraudulent misrepresentation may or may not be connected with a contract. Innocent misrepresentation, however, is of legal significance only when connected with a contract.

9. Fraudulent misrepresentation

Where a statement is made fraudulently there is a tort of deceit, and an action for damages will lie at the suit of the person who has been misled.

The classic definition of fraud was made by Lord Herschell in *Derry* v. *Peek* (1889), in the House of Lords. After a review of the authorities, he said, 'First, in order to sustain an action of deceit, there must be proof of fraud, and nothing short of that will suffice. Secondly, fraud is proved when it is shown that a false representation has been made

(a) knowingly, or
(b) without belief in its truth, or
(c) recklessly, careless whether it be true or false.

Although I treated the second and third as distinct cases, I think the third is but an instance of the second, for one who makes a statement under such circumstances can have no real belief in the truth of what he states. To prevent a false statement being fraudulent, there must, I think, always be an honest belief in its truth. And this probably covers the whole ground, for one who knowingly alleges that which is false has obviously no such belief. Thirdly, if fraud be prove, the motive of the person guilty of it is immaterial. It matters not that there was no intention to cheat or injure the person to whom the statement was made.'

> *Derry* v. *Peek* (1889): A tramway company was empowered by a special Act of Parliament to operate certain tramways by using animal power. The Act further provided that, with the consent of the Board of Trade, mechanical power might be used. The directors of the company, wishing to raise more capital, included the following statement in a prospectus: '. . . the company has the right to use steam or mechanical motive power instead of horses, and it is fully expected that by means of this a considerable saving will result. . . .' P, relying on this representation, bought shares.

The company was later wound up because the Board of Trade refused to allow the use of mechanical power over the whole of the company's tramway. P contended that there was fraud. HELD by the House of Lords: The false statement in the prospectus was not fraudulent.

Akerhielm v. *DeMare* (1959): In a prospectus issued by a company formed in Kenya, the following statement appeared: 'About a third of the capital has already been subscribed in Denmark.' This statement was untrue, but directors of the company believed it to be true at the time of the issue of the prospectus. HELD by the Privy Council: The statement was not fraudulent. It was made in an honest belief in its truth.

10. Remedies for fraudulent misrepresentation

A party who has been deceived by fraudulent misrepresentation may sue for damages in tort for deceit, and in addition, he may either

(a) affirm the contract, or
(b) disaffirm the contract and refuse further performance. Where a party disaffirms the contract he may either
  (i) *take no legal action,* and plead fraud as a defence and counterclaim for damages in the event of his being sued for breach of contract by the other party; or
  (ii) *bring an action* for rescission of the contract and/or damages.

Archer v. *Brown* (1985): The defendant had defrauded the plaintiff by selling to him the share capital in a company when he had sold the same shares to other victims. The defendant was imprisoned for these offences. The plaintiff financed the purchase by borrowing some £30,000 from a bank. The plaintiff also entered an agreement by which he was to be joint managing director at a salary of £16,750 per annum. On discovering the fraud, the plaintiff claimed the return of the £30,000, all damages resulting from the deceit including interest of £13,528 on the bank loan and damages for deceit or breach of contract. The defendant contended that the plaintiff was restricted to the remedy of rescission.

HELD: The plaintiff was entitled to damages as well as rescission because the misrepresentation was fraudulent, but even if it had been innocent, the plaintiff would still be entitled to damages under s. 2 of the Misrepresentation Act 1967. A plaintiff may claim under a contract or tort provided he does not duplicate his claim. Although the measure of damages is different in tort and in contract, it makes no difference which measure is applied in this case: the damages are the same. The plaintiff was entitled to recover the bank interest of £13,528 because the defendant knew how the plaintiff proposed to raise the money and that interest would have to be paid. The plaintiff's impecuniosity in this regard did not help the defendant's case because that impecuniosity was caused by the defendant's deceit. The plaintiff was not entitled to damages for loss of prospective earnings with the company but he was entitled to £2,500 for loss of employment and to £1,000 for the expenses incurred in seeking new employment after discovery of the fraud.

11. Innocent misrepresentation

Any misrepresentation which is not caught by the definition of fraud in *Derry* v. *Peek* is an innocent misrepresentation. That is to say, where a misrepresentation is made with an honest belief in its truth, it is innocent. The test of honesty is a subjective one: the usual objective test of intention is not used in this distinction.

12. Remedies for innocent misrepresentation

A party who has suffered a misrepresentation and who is unable or unwilling to prove fraud may seek his remedy **(a)** at common law, **(b)** in equity or **(c)** under the Misrepresentation Act 1967. These various remedies should now be considered separately.

(a) *At common law*. The party misled may affirm the contract and treat it as binding. At common law damages are not awarded for innocent misrepresentation.
(b) *In equity*. The party misled may disaffirm the contract either by notifying the other party to that effect, or by bringing an action (or counterclaim) for rescission. In either case he must be prepared

to restore any money or property which has been transferred to him under the contract. Similarly, he can claim for the recovery of property transferred to the other party, for equity requires mutual restoration. Where, under the contract, the party misled has assumed burdens which otherwise would have been the responsibility of the other party, these must also be taken back. In other words, the party who made the innocent misrepresentation must indemnify the other party for obligations assumed as a *direct result* of the contract. The obligations must have been created by the contract.

> *Whittington* v. *Seale-Hayne* (1900): In an action for rescission of a lease, the lessees claimed an indemnity from the lessors under the following heads: (*i*) value of stock lost, (*ii*) loss of profits, (*iii*) loss of breeding season, (*iv*) rent and removal of stores, (*v*) medical expenses, (*vi*) rates and (*vii*) cost of repairs ordered by the local authority. HELD: Indemnity was payable for heads (*vi*) and (*vii*) only. No indemnity was payable under heads (*i*) to (*v*) because these losses were not related to obligations created directly by the contract.

Where a contract is disaffirmed by giving notice that further performance is refused, the innocent misrepresentation may be raised as a defence to any action for specific performance which the other party may bring.

Rescission is available to a party misled by an innocent misrepresentation notwithstanding that the misrepresentation has become a term of the contract: Misrepresentation Act 1967, s. 1. Thus the Act has preserved the right rescission in cases where the false statement was first made as a mere representation but subsequently became a term of the contract.

A party misled by an innocent misrepresentation is entitled to rescind even where the contract has been performed: Misrepresentation Act 1967, s. 1. This provision abolishes the rule in *Seddon* v. *N.E. Salt Co.* (1905).

Rescission is not open to a party who has affirmed the contract after becoming aware of the innocent misrepresentation. Nor is it open to a party who has delayed unreasonably either in giving notice or in bringing an action for rescission. A party who has lost his right to rescind may be entitled to damages under s. 2(1) of the 1967 Act.

(c) *The Misrepresentation Act 1967*. The common law rule that damages are not awarded for innocent misrepresentation has been amended by the Misrepresentation Act 1967.

Section 2(1) of the Act provides that where a person has entered into a contract after a misrepresentation has been made to him by another party and has thereby suffered loss, then, if the person making the misrepresentation would be liable in damages if the misrepresentation had been fraudulent, he is nevertheless liable in damages unless he proves that he had reasonable ground to believe and did believe up to the time the contract was made that the facts represented were true.

Section 2(2) provides that where a person has entered a contract after an innocent misrepresentation has been made to him giving him the right to rescind, then, if it is claimed that the contract has been rescinded, the court may declare the contract subsisting and award damages in lieu of rescission if it would be equitable to do so. The court must have regard to the nature of the misrepresentation, the loss that would be caused if the contract were upheld, and the loss that rescission would cause to the other party.

Section 2(3) relates s. 2(1) and s. 2(2) by providing that damages may be awarded under s. 2(2) whether or not there is liability under s. 2(1). But any award under s. 2(2) must be taken into account in assessing liability under s. 2(1).

Howard Marine and Dredging Co. v. *Ogden* (1978) CA: The defendants were contractors wishing to calculate a price for work involving the dumping of excavated earth out at sea. They invited the plaintiffs to quote a price for the hire of two barges owned by them. The plaintiffs quoted a price and stated that the usable capacity of the barges was 850 cubic metres. The plaintiffs' marine manager later stated that the capacity was about 850 cubic metres and that the payload was 1,600 tonnes. In fact the payload was only 1,055 tonnes. The defendants, who by this time had concluded their excavation contract, had calculated that the barge would carry 1,200 tonnes. The marine manager had based his statement of 1,600 tonnes on his recollection of the deadweight figure of 1,800 tonnes given in Lloyd's Register. That figure was incorrect. The marine manager had at some time previously seen the original shipping documents of the barges which showed that the deadweight was in fact 1,195 tonnes. This figure had not registered in his mind. As a result of the defendants being unable to carry the expected amount of earth in the barges, the excavation work was held up. The defendants refused to pay the hire charges and the plaintiffs brought an action for payment. The defendants counterclaimed for damages under s. 2(1) of the Misrepresentation Act 1967 and for negligence. HELD by the Court of Appeal (Lord Denning MR dissenting): The defendants were entitled to succeed on the counterclaim. The plaintiffs were liable under s. 2(1) of the 1967 Act unless they could prove that the marine manager had had reasonable grounds for believing that his statement was true. There was insufficient evidence to show that he had had an objectively reasonable ground for disregarding the deadweight capacity given in the ships' documents and preferring the figure (wrong as it happened) given in Lloyd's Register.

The measure of damages for an innocent misrepresentation giving rise to an action under s. 2(1) of the Misrepresentation Act is the measure of damages in tort for fraudulent misrepresentation. This assertion is based on the provision in s. 2(1) that a person making an innocent misrepresentation which induced another person to enter into a contract as a result of which that other person suffered a loss should be so liable to pay damages as if the innocent party is entitled to recover any loss flowing from the misrepresentation even where the loss could not have been foreseen: *see Royscott Trust* v. *Rogerson* (1991) CA.

13. The equitable remedy of rescission
A party who has been misled by a misrepresentation, fraudulent or innocent, may initiate proceedings for rescission of the contract. The object of this action is to obtain from the court an order that the contract is cancelled.

The remedy is equitable and is given (or withheld) entirely in the discretion of the court: it is not awarded as of right as in the case of damages at common law. Generally, rescission will be awarded only where *restitutio in integrum* (restoration to the original position) is still possible: *Lagunas Nitrate Co.* v. *Lagunas Syndicate* (1899). Thus the order will not be made if third parties have obtained rights in the subject-matter of the contract: *White* v. *Garden* (1851). Restitution involves the mutual restoration of all property transferred between the parties and also, where appropriate, an indemnity against obligations necessarily created by the rescinded contract: *Whittington* v. *Seale-Hayne* (1900). An action for rescission must be brought promptly, for delay defeats the equities.

Leaf v. *International Galleries* (1950): L bought a painting of Salisbury Cathedral, described by the sellers as a genuine Constable. Five years later, L discovered that the painting was not a genuine Constable and he brought this action for rescission on the grounds of innocent misrepresentation. HELD by the Court of Appeal: L's claim must fail. There can be no rescission of a contract of sale of goods after the buyer has taken possession, or at least within a reasonable time thereafter: five years is more than a reasonable time. (When this case was before the county court, L's counsel asked for leave to amend by claiming damages for breach of warranty, but this request was refused. If L had originally asked for damages instead of rescission, he would probably have succeeded.)

Lagunas Nitrate Co. v. *Lagunas Syndicate* (1899): The Syndicate induced the Nitrate Company by means of an innocent misrepresentation to purchase nitrate grounds from it. The Nitrate Company worked the property vigorously as soon as it could and called upon the Syndicate to make large outlays on it. For a time the Nitrate Company made large profits from working the nitrate grounds until the market price of nitrate fell permanently. The Nitrate Company then brought this action to rescind the contract of sale of the nitrate grounds. HELD by the Court of Appeal: Rescission could not be granted because it was impossible to restore the parties to their original position.

14. Exemption clauses

If a contract contains an exemption clause purporting to

protect a party from liability for misrepresentation or purporting to exclude or restrict any remedy available to the other party, the clause will be of no effect except in so far as it satisfies the requirement of reasonableness: Misrepresentation Act 1967, s. 3 as substituted by s. 8 of the Unfair Contract Terms Act 1977.

15. Exceptions to the common law 'no damages' rule

The common law rule that no damages will be awarded for an innocent misrepresentation has now been almost eaten away by exceptions. The most important of these is the provision contained in s. 2 of the Misrepresentation Act 1967, which has already been considered. There are, in addition, the following exceptions:

(a) *Company prospectus.* Where the innocent misrepresentation is included in a prospectus inviting the public to buy shares in a company, *compensation* is payable: Companies Act 1985, ss. 67–69.

(b) *Estoppel.* Where the innocent misrepresentation is made in such a way as to give rise to an estoppel. (Estoppel is a rule of evidence which precludes, i.e. estops, a person from denying the truth of a representation made by him where another person has changed his position on the faith of the representation.)

> *Silver* v. *Ocean Steamship Co.* (1929): Goods were loaded on to a ship and the master signed the bill of lading to the effect that the goods were 'in apparent good order and condition'. The goods were, in fact, seriously damaged. The master was estopped from denying the truth of the representation that the goods were in good order and condition when loaded on to the ship.

> *Holland* v. *Manchester & Liverpool District Banking Co.* (1909): A bank represented to one of its customers that he had a credit balance of £70 when, in fact, he was only entitled to a credit balance of £10. On the faith of this representation, he drew a cheque for £65 which was dishonoured. The customer sued for wrongful dishonour of the cheque. HELD: The bank was estopped from denying that there were sufficient funds to meet the cheque.

(c) *Negligent misstatement.* Where, in the ordinary course of business, a person seeks information or advice from another person who is not under a contractual or fiduciary obligation to give that information or advice, in circumstances where a reasonable man would know that he was being trusted or that his skill or judgment was being relied upon, the giving of the information or advice involves a duty of care. Failure to exercise care in giving the information or advice amounts to negligence and the person misled by the advice or information may claim damages in tort for any loss he has suffered by relying on it. It is a good defence, however, for the person giving the advice or information to show that he qualified his statement by saying that he does not accept legal responsibility for it: *Hedley Byrne & Co.* v. *Heller & Partners* (1963). Where a negligent misstatement of a present or past fact has been made by a party in negotiations leading to a contract, any action against him will more conveniently be brought under the provisions of s. 2 of the Misrepresentation Act 1967. Where, however, there is a negligent misstatement as to a future state of affairs, which induces a party to enter a loss-making contract, then an action for damages under the principle in *Hedley Byrne* will lie.

> *Esso Petroleum Co.* v. *Mardon* (1976): In 1961 Esso acquired a site on a busy street for development as a filling station. Esso had estimated that the annual throughput of petrol at the station would reach 200,000 gallons in the third year of operation. But after the site had been acquired, the local planning authority required the forecourt and pumps to be placed at the back of the site which faced only on to a side street, and which was out of sight of the main road at the front of the site. As a result of this change, the throughput of petrol would be greatly diminished but Esso did not revise their original estimate of 200,000 gallons.
>
> Subsequently, Esso entered negotiations with M for the tenancy of the station and told him in good faith that the throughput was estimated to reach 200,000 gallons after three years. The tenancy contract between M and Esso was entered in April 1963. The business proved to be disastrous and M lost a great deal of money in trying to make it a success. Throughput could never be more than 70,000 gallons annually. Eventually, M was unable to pay Esso for petrol supplied. Esso then brought this action to recover the money due for petrol and also for possession of the station.

In March 1967 M gave up possession of the station, having lost all his capital and having incurred a considerable overdraft as a result of his efforts with the station. By his defence and counterclaim, M contended **(a)** that Esso's statement as to potential throughput amounted to a warranty, the breach of which entitled M to damages, and **(b)** that it also amounted to negligent misrepresentation in breach of Esso's duty of care in advising him as to estimated throughput.

HELD by the Court of Appeal: **(a)** Where one of the parties to pre-contract negotiations, with special knowledge and expertise, makes a forecast based on that knowledge and expertise with the intention of inducing the other party to enter the contract and the other party, in reliance on that forecast, enters the contract, it is open to the court to construe the forecast as a warranty. Esso's estimate had been based on their wide experience in the petrol trade and had induced M to enter the contract. The forecast was, therefore, to be construed as a warranty and Esso were liable for the breach of it. **(b)** In the circumstances, the relationship between Esso and M was such as to give rise to the duty of care because Esso had a special knowledge and skill in estimating throughput. The forecast was made negligently and, therefore, Esso were also liable to M in negligence (*Hedley Byrne* v. *Heller* applied). **(c)** The measure of damages was the loss suffered by M in having been induced to enter the contract.

Where non-disclosure constitutes misrepresentation

16. No general duty to disclose

There is no general duty to disclose material facts during negotiations leading to a contract. Thus, in the case of contracts of sale of goods, the common law rule is a *caveat emptor*. In *Bell* v. *Lever Bros.* (*see* 7:8), the House of Lords held that Bell was under no duty to disclose to Lever Bros. his misconduct in making the secret profit through private trading. In that case, Lord Atkin said, 'Ordinarily the failure to disclose a material fact which might influence the mind of a prudent contractor does not give the right to avoid the contract. The principle of *caveat emptor* applies outside contracts of sale.' Lord Atkin then went on to mention the main exception to this general rule. He said, 'There are certain contracts, expressed by the law to be contracts of the utmost good faith, where material facts must be disclosed; if not the contract is voidable. Apart from special fiduciary relationships contracts for partnership and contracts of insurance are the leading instances. In such cases the duty does not arise out of contract; the duty of a person proposing an insurance arises before a contract is made, so of an intending partner.'

> *Hands* v. *Simpson, Fawcett & Co.* (1928): A commercial traveller applied for, and obtained, a post without informing his new employer that he was disqualified from driving a car. The employer regarded driving as an essential part of the traveller's duties, and he brought this action, contending that his silence about the driving disqualification amounted to misrepresentation. HELD: The traveller was under no duty to volunteer information about his driving disqualification. Mere silence cannot be a misrepresentation where there is no duty to speak.

17. Where there is a duty to disclose

In the following circumstances the withholding of a material fact may constitute misrepresentation.

(a) Contracts *uberimmae fidei*.

(b) Contracts affected by the *uberimma fides* principle.

(c) Where a part-truth amounts to a falsehood.

(d) Where there is a fiduciary element in the relationship between the contracting parties.

There is also a duty of disclosure in the following circumstances:

(e) Where a statement, true at the time it was made, becomes untrue during the course of negotiations: *Davies* v. *London and Provincial Marine Insurance Co.* (1878).

(f) Where a party who made a statement in the belief that it was true subsequently discovers that it was false: *With* v. *O'Flanagan* (1936).

18. *Uberrima fides* **(utmost good faith)**
In contracts of insurance of all kinds, disclosure of all material facts must be made to the insurer. A fact is material if it would affect the judgment of a prudent insurer in deciding whether to accept the risk or in deciding what shall be the premium. It has been held that there was a duty to disclose in the following cases:

(a) Where the insured goods were carried on the deck of a ship instead of in the hold: *Hood* v. *West End Motor Car Packing Co.* (1917).

(b) Where it is not disclosed that a proposal has been refused by another insurance company: *Locker and Woolf* v. *Western Australian Insurance Co.* (1936).

(c) Where a ship was insured and it was not disclosed that her cargo was insured at a value exceeding the real value: *Ionides* v. *Pender* (1874).

Where there has been a material non-disclosure, the insurer may avoid the contract.

19. Contracts affected by the *uberrima fides* **principle**
There are also the following classes of contract in which the principle of *uberrima fides* operates:

(a) *Contracts for sale of land.* The vendor of an estate or interest in land is under a duty to the purchaser to show good title to the estate or interest he has contracted to sell. All defects in *title* must, therefore, be disclosed. This duty does not extend to physical defects in the property itself.

(b) *Family arrangements* are agreements or arrangements between members of a family for the protection or distribution of family property. If any member of the family has withheld material information, the agreement or arrangement may be set aside: *Gordon* v. *Gordon* (1821); *Greenwood* v. *Greenwood* (1863).

(c) *A confidential relationship* between the contracting parties gives rise to a duty to disclose material facts. This rule is sometimes known as the equitable doctrine of constructive fraud, and is closely connected with undue influence.

> *Tate* v. *Williamson* (1866): A, who was a young man heavily in debt, sought the advice of B. B advised A to sell certain land in order to raise money to repay his debts. B then

offered to buy the land for half its real value. Certain facts which were material to the value of the land were known to B and he did not disclose them to A. HELD: The contract could be set aside for constructive fraud.

(d) *Suretyship and partnership contracts.* Contracts of suretyship (guarantee) and contracts of partnership do not require *uberrima fides*: but they do create a relationship between the parties which requires a measure of good faith (i.e. disclosure of material facts) in their dealings after the contract has been made.

Progress test 8

1. Define carefully a 'mere representation', distinguishing it from a contractual term.

2. 'The state of a man's mind is as much a fact as the state of his digestion.' Comment of this statement.

3. How do the courts distinguish between innocent misrepresentation and fraudulent misrepresentation?

4. What are the remedies for:
   (a) innocent misrepresentation, and
   (b) fraudulent misrepresentation?

5. In what circumstances will damages be awarded for an innocent misrepresentation?

6. Is there a general duty to disclose material facts during negotiations preceding a contract?

7. What kinds of contracts are affected by the *uberrima fides* principle?

8. A, the vendor of a small general store, told B, the purchaser, that he thought the trade would double within 12 months because four large blocks of council flats were nearing completion and would soon be occupied. A year after the contract, the trade in B's store had not increased at all. B wishes to know whether he has any claim against A with respect to his statement that trade would double within 12 months. Advise him.

9. Eight years ago, C bought a painting from D, a dealer. D had described the painting as a genuine Picasso, and C paid a high price accordingly. C has just discovered that the painting is not a Picasso, and is almost worthless. There is no evidence that D's false statement was fraudulent. What steps would you advise D to take?

10. E went to his bank and asked what was the state of his current account. The cashier made enquiries and then gave E a slip of paper on which was written, 'Current account credit balance — £210.55'. In fact, there was a clerical error, and the correct balance should have been £120.55. However, on the strength of the information, E drew a cheque for £160, which was dishonoured in due course. E has decided to sue the bank for wrongful dishonour of the cheque. Will he succeed? If so, on what grounds? If not, why not?

11. Compare the tactical position of the plaintiff seeking damages for fraudulent misrepresentation with that of a plaintiff bringing an action under the Misrepresentation Act.

9
Duress and undue influence

1. Coercion

Where a person has been coerced into a contract so that he did not enter it of his own free will he may apply to the court to have the contract avoided or set aside. He will seek his remedy either at common law or in equity, according to whether the coercion amounts to duress or undue influence. If he can prove duress, the contract will be avoided as a matter of right: but if he proves undue influence, the contract will be set aside at the discretion of the court. The remedies for duress, on the one hand, and undue influence, on the other, are distinct. The one is at common law and the other is in equity. Where there is doubt as to whether any particular act of coercion is duress or undue influence, the plaintiff should bring his action to have the contract avoided for duress and, in the alternative, to have the contract set aside for undue influence. If the plaintiff follows this procedure and proves duress, the contract will be avoided and the court does not have to consider whether to exercise its equitable jurisdiction to set the contract aside. If, however, the plaintiff fails to prove duress, the court will consider whether there has been undue influence and whether the circumstances warrant the exercise of the equitable jurisdiction to set the contract aside.

Duress

2. What constitutes duress

Duress at common law occurs where a party enters a contract under violence or threatened violence to himself or to his immediate family; or where he is threatened with false imprisonment; or where he is threatened with the dishonour of a member of his family. Coercion of this kind is legal duress when it is exercised by another party to the contract, or by the agent of another party, or by any person to the knowledge of another party.

Note
_____
Duress is exercised against persons only, and not goods.
_____

3.   Legal effect of duress
A person who has entered into a contract under duress has not done so under his own free will and may either affirm or avoid the contract after the duress has ceased: affirmation may be implied where a party makes no attempt to set the contract aside within a reasonable period of the cessation of the duress: *North Ocean Shipping Co.* v. *Hyundai Construction Co.* (1979).

> *Cumming* v. *Ince* (1847): An inmate of a private lunatic asylum agreed to make certain arrangements as to her property in return for the suspension of the commission of lunacy which was being held on her. HELD: The agreement was not binding as the consent was not freely given.

> *Kaufman* v. *Gerson* (1904): G had taken money which K had entrusted with him. K threatened to prosecute G, unless G's wife made good the loss out of her own property. G's wife agreed to do so, in order to save her husband's honour. HELD: G's wife was not bound by her promise. She was entitled to avoid the contract which she had entered under duress.

Undue influence

4.   What constitutes undue influence
Undue influence in equity occurs where a party enters a contract under any kind of influence which prevents him from exercising a free and independent judgment. Where a plaintiff claims that a contract is voidable for undue influence, he must show that the influence was exerted by the other contracting party, his servant or agent. If the plaintiff entered into the contract under the influence of a third party — a stranger to the contract — the

contract is not voidable: *Goldunell* v. *Gallon* (1985) CA. The courts have always taken care not to define undue influence, for a definition would cramp their equitable jurisdiction in this connection. 'As no court has ever attempted to define fraud, so no court has ever attempted to define undue influence, which includes one of the many varieties': per Lindley LJ in *Allcard* v. *Skinner* (1887). Where undue influence is alleged, the court regards itself as a court of conscience with full discretion to make its findings accordingly. There is a rebuttable presumption of undue influence where a fiduciary or confidential relationship exists between contracting parties: in all other cases, the onus is on the party alleging undue influence to prove it.

5. Legal effect of undue influence

A contract (or gift under seal) may be set aside at the suit of a party who contracted under influence. This relief is equitable and, therefore, discretionary. It may be disallowed where the plaintiff has delayed making his claim, for *delay defeats the equities*: *Allcard* v. *Skinner*. Also, it may be disallowed where the plaintiff's conduct has been tricky, for *he who comes to equity must come with clean hands*.

6. Presumed influence

Where the relationship between contracting parties is such that one is entitled to rely upon the confidential advice of the other, and is, accordingly, in a position to dominate that other, undue influence is presumed to have been exercised.

The presumption arises, for example, where the contracting parties are in any of the following relationships: solicitor and client, trustee and *cestui que trust*, doctor and patient, parent and child, guardian and ward, religious adviser and person over whom religious influence is exercised. It is not clear whether the presumption arises in the cased of engaged couples and it does not normally arise in the case of husband and wife. Evidence required to rebut the presumption will vary according to the circumstances, but it is usually necessary to show

(a) that the consideration moving from the dominant party was at least adequate;
(b) that the plaintiff had the benefit of competent, independent advice, in the light of a full disclosure of all material facts;

(c) that, in the case of a gift by deed, the gift was made spontaneously.

Allcard v. *Skinner* (1887): In 1868 the plaintiff, an unmarried woman, was introduced to a Church of England sisterhood. In 1870 she became a novice and in 1871 she was admitted a full member of the sisterhood, embracing the vows of poverty, obedience and chastity. The plaintiff, without independent advice, made gifts of money and stock to the defendant, who was the lady superior of the sisterhood. In 1879 the plaintiff left the sisterhood and became a member of the Church of Rome. Soon afterwards, she spoke to her brother about getting back her money and he told her that it would be better to leave it alone. She was similarly advised by a Roman Catholic priest. Then, in 1880, her solicitor advised her that the sum was too large to leave with the sisterhood without asking for its return, but she replied that she preferred not to bother about it.

In 1884 the plaintiff heard that one of the sisters had left the sisterhood and that her money had been returned to her at her request. As a result of this news, the plaintiff decided to make an attempt to get her money back from the sisterhood. In the same year, 1884, the plaintiff asked for her money. The lady superior refused to return it and the plaintiff brought this action against her for its recovery in 1885. The plaintiff claimed to recover the entire capital sum which she had given to the lady superior, but the trial judge gave judgment for the defendant. The plaintiff appealed, limiting her appeal to certain railway stock which was transferred to the lady superior and was still standing in the lady superior's name. HELD by the Court of Appeal: **(a)** The lady superior's equitable title was imperfect because, at the time of the gift, the plaintiff was bound by her vows, and the rules of the sisterhood, to make absolute submission to the defendant as lady superior; but **(b)** the plaintiff was not entitled to recover the funds because of the delay in making her claim.

In *Allcard* v. *Skinner* Lindley LJ said: 'It would obviously be to encourage folly, recklessness, extravagance and vice if persons could get back property made away with, whether by giving it to charitable institutions, or by bestowing it on less worthy objects. On the other hand, to protect people from being forced, tricked, or misled, in any way by others into parting with their property, is one of the most legitimate objects of all laws; and the equitable doctrine of undue influence has grown out of and been developed by the necessity of grappling with insidious forms of spiritual tyranny and with the infinite varieties of fraud. As no court has ever attempted to define fraud, so no court has ever attempted to define undue influence, which includes one of the many varieties.

'The undue influence which courts of equity endeavour to defeat is the undue influence of one person over another; not the influence of enthusiasm or the enthusiast who is carried away by it, unless indeed such enthusiasm is itself the result of external undue influence. But the influence of one mind over another is very subtle, and of all influences religious influence is the most dangerous and the most powerful. To counteract it courts of equity have gone very far. They have not shrunk from setting aside gifts made to persons in a position to exercise undue influence over the donors, although there has been no proof of the actual exercise of such influence; and the courts have done this on the avowed ground of the necessity of going to this length in order to protect persons from the exercise of such influence under circumstances which render proof of it impossible. The courts have required proof of its non-exercise, and, failing that proof, have set aside gifts otherwise unimpeachable.'

The principle in *Allcard* v. *Skinner* (1887) CA was applied by the Court of Appeal in *Goldsworthy* v. *Brickell* (1987) where it was held that the presumption that a gift or transaction had been procured by the undue influence of another would be raised if the gift was so large, or the transaction so improvident, that it would not be reasonably accounted for on the ground of friendship, relationship, charity or other motives on which ordinary men acted and if the person effecting it had reposed in the other such a degree of trust and confidence as to place the other in a position to influence him into effecting this. It was not necessary, in order to raise the presumption of undue influence, to show that the person in whom the trust and confidence had been reposed had assumed a role of dominating influence over the person who had effected the gift or transaction.

Inche Noriah v. *Shaik Alli Bin Omar* (1928): A nephew was managing the affairs of his aged aunt and he persuaded her to give him property by deed of gift. The lawyer who drew up the deed of gift explained to the aunt that it was irrevocable and asked whether she was signing it voluntarily. He did not know that the gift constituted practically the whole of her property, nor did he advise her that she could have left the property to her nephew by will instead of making the gift. HELD by the Privy Council: The nephew was unable to rebut the presumption of undue influence and the gift should be set aside.

Lancashire Loans v. *Black* (1933): A daughter who was of full age, married and living in her own home, was persuaded by her mother to enter into an agreement with a moneylender. The agreement was in the mother's interest but against the daughter's interest. The mother was also a party to the agreement. The daughter did not have independent legal advice nor did she understand her obligations under the transaction. The money-lender sued for money due under the agreement, but the daughter contended that the agreement should be set aside for undue influence. HELD by the Court of Appeal: The marriage of the daughter and her departure from the parental home did not necessarily put an end to the parental influence. It is impossible to lay down any hard and fast rule in the matter. In the present case, the daughter had the benefit of a presumption that the influence continued after her marriage, and since the presumption was not rebutted, she was entitled to have the contract set aside.

Lloyds Bank v. *Bundy* (1975): The defendant was an elderly farmer. His home was his farmhouse which had belonged to his family for several generations. It was his only asset. The defendant, his son, and a company formed by his son were all customers of the same branch of the plaintiff's bank. The company ran into difficulties and the defendant guaranteed the company's overdraft for £1,500 and charged his farmhouse to the bank to secure the sum. The company ran into further difficulties and the defendant executed a further guarantee for £5,000 and a further charge for

£6,000. The defendant's solicitor advised that this was the most that he should commit to the son's business, since the house was worth only £10,000. The company's business went from bad to worse and the son went to the bank for more money. The bank's new assistant manager and the son went to see the defendant, the assistant manager taking with him a form of guarantee and a form of charge for up to £11,000 already prepared for the defendant's signature. The assistant manager realized that the defendant relied on him to advise on the transaction 'as bank manager'. He knew that the defendant's farmhouse was his only asset. The defendant, to help his son, executed the guarantee and the charge which the bank's manager had produced.

About five months later a receiving order was made against the son. The bank then attempted to enforce the guarantee and charge against the defendant, bringing this action for possession of the farmhouse. HELD by the Court of Appeal: There was a confidential relationship between the defendant and the bank which imposed on the bank a duty of fiduciary care, i.e. to ensure that the defendant formed an independent and informed judgment on the proposed transaction before committing himself. The bank should have advised the defendant to obtain independent advice on whether the company's affairs had any prospect of becoming viable. The bank was in breach of its fiduciary duty and, accordingly, the guarantee and the charge would be set aside and the action for possession dismissed.

The law governing the presumption of undue influence was summarized by the Court of Appeal in *Midland Bank* v. *Shephard* (1987). It was said:

(a) The confidential relationship between husband and wife did not give rise by itself to a presumption of undue influence.
(b) Even if the relationship between the parties gave rise to a presumption of undue influence, the transaction would not be set aside unless it was to the manifest disadvantage of the person influenced.
(c) The court should examine the facts to see whether the relevant transaction had been or should be presumed to have been procured under undue influence and if so whether the transaction

was so disadvantageous to the person seeking to set it aside as to be unfair.

(d) The court would not enforce a transaction at the suit of a creditor if it could be shown that the creditor entrusted the task of obtaining the alleged debtor's signatures to the relevant document to someone who was to the knowledge of the creditor in a position to influence the debtor by means of undue influence or by means of fraudulent misrepresentation.

7.   Where undue influence must be proved

Where there is no relationship between the parties giving rise to the presumption of undue influence, a party alleging undue influence must prove that the other party had a dominant influence over his mind so that there was no exercise of independent will in entering the contract. Where the existence of the influence is proved, the court will assume that it was exercised, unless the contrary is proved.

> *Williams* v. *Bayley* (1866): B was induced to settle property
> on a bank which had been defrauded by B's son. At the time
> of making the settlement, B thought that if he did not do
> this, his son would be prosecuted, although the bank had
> not actually threatened this. HELD by the House of Lords: At
> the time of making the settlement B was not a free
> voluntary agent, and the settlement must be set aside.

8.   Undue influence in banking transactions

In *Lloyds Bank* v. *Bundy*, Sir Eric Sachs explained the nature of the relationship necessary to give rise to the presumption of undue influence in the context of a banking transaction. He said: 'There remains to mention that counsel for the bank, whilst conceding that the relevant special relationship could arise between banker and customer, urged in somewhat doom-laden terms that a decision taken against the bank on the facts of this particular case would seriously affect banking practice. With all respect to that submission, it seems necessary to point out that nothing in this judgment affects the duties of a bank in the normal case where it obtains a guarantee, and in accordance with standard practice explains to the person about to sign, its legal effect and the sums involved. When, however, a bank, as in the present case, goes further and advises on more general matters germane to the wisdom of the transaction, that indicates that it may — not necessarily must — be crossing the line into the area of confidentiality so that the court may then have to examine all the facts including, of course, the history leading up to the transaction, to ascertain whether or not that line has, as here, been crossed. It would indeed be rather odd if a bank which *vis-à-vis* a customer attained a special relationship in some ways akin to that of a "man of affairs" — something which can be a matter of pride and enhance its local reputation — should not, where a conflict of interest has arisen as between itself and the person advised, be under the resulting duty now under discussion. Once, as was inevitably conceded, it is possible for a bank to be under that duty, it is, as in the present case, simply a case for "meticulous examination" of the particular facts to see whether that duty has arisen. On the special facts here it did arise and it has been broken.' This passage was approved by the House of Lords in *National Westminster Bank plc* v. *Morgan* (1985).

> *National Westminster Bank plc* v. *Morgan* (1985): Husband and wife were joint owners of their home. The husband was unsuccessful in his business venture and was unable to meet the repayments due under a mortgage secured over the home. The then mortgagee commenced proceedings to take possession. The husband tried to save the situation by entering a refinancing arrangement with a bank. The refinancing was secured by a legal charge in favour of the bank. The bank manager made a brief visit to the home so that the wife could execute the charge. The wife made it clear to the bank manager that she had little faith in her husband's business ability and that she did not want the charge to cover his business liabilities. The bank manager assured her that the charge secured only the amount advanced to refinance the mortgage. Nevertheless, it was the bank's intention to treat it as limited to the amount required to refinance the mortgage. This assurance was given in good faith but was incorrect. The terms of the charge were unlimited in extent and extended to all of the husband's liabilities to the bank.
>
> The wife did not receive independent legal advice before

signing the charge. The husband fell into arrears with payments and the bank obtained an order for possession of the home. The husband then died without owing the bank on any business advances. The wife appealed against the order for possession contending that the charge should be set aside as it had been signed as a result of undue influence from the bank. The bank argued that undue influence could be raised only when the transaction was manifestly disadvantageous to the defendant. The bank contended that the refinancing arrangement had averted earlier possession by the previous mortgagee and that this was manifestly advantageous to the wife. The Court of Appeal found in favour of the wife on the grounds that a special relationship had been created which the bank was unable to rebut because of the failure to advise the wife to seek independent legal advice. The bank appealed.

HELD by the House of Lords that a meticulous examination of the facts revealed that the bank manager never 'crossed the line'. Nor was the transaction unfair to the wife. The bank was, therefore, under no duty to ensure that she had independent advice. It was an ordinary banking transaction whereby the wife sought to save her home; and she obtained an honest and truthful explanation of the bank's intention which, notwithstanding the terms of the mortgage deed, was correct; for the bank had not sought to make the wife liable, nor to make the home a security, for any business debt of the husband. Possession of the house granted to the bank.

Midland Bank v. *Shephard* (1987): The bank claimed against Mrs S for the recovery of an overdrawn sum and interest on an account held jointly by Mrs S and her husband. Mrs S contended that the bank could not enforce the joint account mandate against her because she was induced to sign it by the undue influence of her husband who was acting for the purpose of obtaining her signature as the agent of the bank. HELD by the Court of Appeal: The bank should succeed in its claim for the overdue sum and interest.

It was said in this case that the authorities established the following:

(a) The confidential relationship between husband and wife did not give rise by itself to a presumption of undue influence.

(b) Even if the relationship between the parties gave rise to a presumption of undue influence, the transaction would not be set aside unless it was to the manifest disadvantage of the person influenced.

(c) The court should examine the facts to see whether the relevant transaction had been or should have been presumed to have been procured under undue influence and if so whether the transaction was so disadvantageous to the person seeking to set it aside as to be unfair.

(d) The court would not enforce a transaction at the suit of a creditor if it could be shown that the creditor entrusted the task of obtaining the alleged debtor's signature to the relevant document to someone who was to the knowledge of the creditor in a position to influence the debtor and who procured the signature of the debtor by means of undue influence or by means of fraudulent misrepresentation.

9. Inequality of bargaining power

It is an interesting feature of *Lloyds Bank* v. *Bundy* that Lord Denning MR took the opportunity to express his own view that undue influence was merely one category within a wider class which he called 'inequality of bargaining power'. He said: 'There are cases in our book in which the courts will set aside a contract, or a transfer of property, when the parties have not met on equal terms, when the one is so strong in the bargaining power and the other so weak that, as a matter of common fairness, it is not right that the strong should be allowed to push the weak to the wall. Hitherto those exceptional cases have been treated each as a separate category in itself. But I think the time has come when we should seek to find a principle to unite them. I put on one side contracts of transactions which are voidable for fraud or misrepresentation or mistake. All those are governed by settled principles. I go only to those where there has been inequality of bargaining power, such as to merit the intervention of the court.' Lord Denning specified the categories as follows:

(a) duress of goods;
(b) the unconscionable transaction;

(c) undue influence, whether the influence is presumed or not;
(d) undue pressure, e.g. *Williams* v. *Bayley* (1866) and *D. & C. Builders* v. *Rees* (1965); and
(e) salvage agreements, where, for example, a rescuer might refuse to help unless he is promised an exorbitant sum of money as the price.

Lord Denning stated what he regarded as the general principle governing all these categories: 'Gathering all together, I would suggest that through all these instances there runs a single thread. They rest on "inequality of bargaining power". By virtue of it, the English law gives relief to one who, without independent advice, enters into a contract on terms which are very unfair or transfers property for a consideration which is grossly inadequate, when his bargaining power is grievously impaired by reason of his own needs or desires, or by his own ignorance or infirmity, coupled with undue influences or pressures brought to bear on him by or for the benefit of the other. When I use the word "undue" I do not mean to suggest that the principle depends on proof of any wrongdoing. The one who stipulates for an unfair advantage may be moved solely by his own self-interest, unconscious of the distress he is bringing to the other. I have also avoided any reference to the will of the one being "dominated" or "overcome" by the other. One who is in extreme need may knowingly consent to a most improvident bargain, solely to relieve the straits in which he finds himself. Again, I do not mean to suggest that every transaction is saved by independent advice. But the absence of it may be fatal. With these explanations, I hope this principle will be found to reconcile the cases.'

It should be noted that Lord Denning avoided reference to the need to show the domination of one person's will by another. The majority of the court did not follow him, preferring to base the decision on *Allcard* v. *Skinner*.

An example of an unconscionable bargain is given by *Watkin* v. *Watson-Smith* (1986). In this case a frail 80-year-old man agreed to sell his bungalow for £2,950 rather than £29,500 by mistake. It was held that even though the mistake prevented the formation of a contract, in any event, the transaction would be set aside as an unconscionable bargain.

10. Economic duress

Although there has been no separate development of a doctrine of 'economic duress' as in the USA, nevertheless, economic duress may be regarded as falling within the recent development of undue influence in English law. In any case of economic duress, the test must be the usual test in all cases of alleged undue influence, namely that there was the exercise of a dominant influence by one party which negatived the independent will of the other. Lord Scarman stated the position of economic duress in English law in the Privy Council case *Pao On* v. *Lau Yiu Long* (1980) when he said that: 'there is nothing contrary to principle in recognizing economic duress as a factor which may render a contract voidable, provided always that the basis of such recognition is that it must always amount to a coercion of will which vitiates consent.' This dictum was applied in *Atlas Express Ltd* v. *Kafco Ltd* (1989) where it was held by Tucker J that where a party was forced by the other contracting party to renegotiate the terms of the contract to his disadvantage, with no alternative but to accept the new terms, the apparent consent to the new terms was vitiated by economic duress. In *North Ocean Shipping Co.* v. *Hyundai Construction Co.* (1979), Mocatta J recognized a sufficiently powerful coercive force for the case to be one of economic duress but the plaintiffs had lost their right to have the contract set aside because they had affirmed it.

A plaintiff will fail to show economic duress if he cannot establish

(a) that he entered into the transaction unwillingly with no real alternative but to submit to the defendant's demand, or
(b) that his apparent consent to the transaction was exacted by the defendant's coercive acts, or
(c) that he repudiated the transaction as soon as the pressure on him was relaxed: *Alex Lobb Garages Ltd* v. *Total Oil GB* (1985).

> *North Ocean Shipping Co.* v. *Hyundai Construction Co.* (1979):
> Shipbuilders agreed to build a tanker for the shipping
> company for $US30,950,000 payable in five instalments.
> The contract required the builder to open a letter of credit
> for the repayment of instalments in the event of their
> default in performance. After the payment of the first
> instalment, the builders claimed an increase of 10 per cent

on the remaining instalments. There was no legal basis for this claim and the shipping company rejected it, but later agreed to pay the extra 10 per cent in return for which the builders agreed to increase their letter of credit correspondingly. All further instalments were paid as agreed. There was no protest over the additional 10 per cent until six months after delivery of the ship was accepted. The shipping company brought this action to recover the additional 10 per cent. They argued that the agreement to pay the additional money was void for lack of consideration and that the 10 per cent was recoverable as money had been received or, alternatively, that the agreement to pay it was made under economic duress and, accordingly, voidable. HELD: The agreement to pay the additional 10 per cent was binding since it was supported by the builders' promise to increase the letter of credit. Further, although the agreement to pay the additional money might have been voidable for economic duress, the failure on the part of the shipping company to protest against the requirement until more than six months after delivery amounted to an affirmation of the agreement. The shipping company was not, therefore, entitled to the return of the additional 10 per cent.

Not only may economic duress render a contract voidable, but also, it may enable the recovery of money paid under duress during the course of a contract.

B & S Contracts and Design v. *Victor Green* (1984): The plaintiffs contracted to erect stands at Olympia for the defendant. The plaintiffs' workers refused to work unless they were paid £9,000. There was no entitlement to this payment. The plaintiffs offered £4,500 but this was rejected. The plaintiffs then told the defendants that unless they (the defendants) paid an additional £4,500, the contract would be cancelled. The plaintiffs made it clear that the amount to be paid was to be in addition to the contract price. The defendants paid the amount demanded by the plaintiffs so as to get the contract performed: the cancellation of the contract would have caused serious damage to the defendants' economic interests. When the contract was completed the defendants deducted £4,500 from the contract price before payment. The plaintiffs sued to recover this amount. HELD by the Court of Appeal: As the cancellation of the contract would have caused serious damage to the defendants' economic interests they had no choice but to pay the sum demanded by the plaintiffs and so it was paid under duress and the defendants had been entitled to recover it.

Progress test 9

1. Explain carefully what you understand by duress at common law. Mention whether or not duress may be exercised against goods.

2. What constitutes undue influence? In what circumstances is undue influence presumed?

3. What is the legal effect where a contract has been entered into (a) under duress, and (b) under undue influence?

4. Examine and explain the scope of Lord Denning's concept of inequality of power.

5. Is there a separate doctrine of economic duress in English law?

6. A suspects that B's son has taken some money from him. He threatens B that he will prosecute unless B promises to pay the sum taken. If B promises to pay this, will he be bound by the promise?

7. Upon recovering from a serious illness, C, by deed of gift, transferred certain valuable property to D, his medical adviser. The motive for the gift was gratitude. C now regrets his generosity, and wishes to know whether the deed of gift is binding on him. Advise him (a) on the footing that the gift was made 12 years ago, and (b) on the footing that the deed of gift was made eight months ago.

8.   E is a solicitor and he wishes to buy a Georgian house from F, one of his clients. Would you advise E to arrange for F to be independently advised before the sale?

10
Capacity

Contractual capacity

1. Capacity and persons

In law, persons may be natural or artificial. Natural persons are human beings; artificial persons are corporations. Contractual capacity (or the lack of it) is an incident of personality. It is not possible for contractual capacity to attach to animals or inanimate objects.

(a) *Natural persons.* The general rule is that all natural persons have full contractual capacity. But there are exceptions in the case of minors, drunken persons, insane persons and enemy aliens.

(b) *Corporations.* The contractual capacity of a corporation depends on the manner in which it was created.

2. Capacity and rights and obligations

In order to benefit from a contractual right, or to incur a contractual obligation, a contracting party must have the appropriate capacity. Rights and obligations may, therefore, affect the apparent rights and obligations created by a contract.

Minors as contracting parties

3. Definition

By s. 1 of the Family Law Reform Act 1969, the age of capacity for the purpose of any rule of law is 18 years. Section 9 provides further that a person will be deemed to attain the age of 18 at the commencement of the eighteenth anniversary of his birth. A person below the age of capacity may be referred to as an infant or as a minor.

At common law the age of majority was 21 years.

4. Contracts made by minors

The general rule at common law is that a contract entered into between a minor and a person of full age is enforceable against that person by the minor but is not enforceable against the minor. A contract of this kind will become binding on the minor if he ratifies it on or after reaching full age, i.e. 18 years. Ratification is a unilateral act by the minor and does not require a fresh agreement or consideration.

Although the vast majority of minors' contracts will fall into this unenforceable category, there are certain important exceptions to consider. These are

(a) contracts of continuing obligation, which are voidable by the minor, and

(b) contracts for necessaries and contracts for the minor's benefit, which are binding on the minor.

5. Minors' voidable contracts

Where a minor enters a contract of continuing obligation, the contract is voidable at the option of the infant before, or within a reasonable time after, reaching his majority.

Contracts in this class include tenancy agreements, marriage settlements, partnership agreements and agreements to take shares which are not fully paid up. Where an infant repudiates a contract during infancy, he may cancel his repudiation and treat it as binding on reaching the age of 18.

Edwards v. *Carter* (1893): An infant covenanted by a marriage settlement, dated 16 October 1883, to settle after-acquired property. The infant came of age on 19 November 1883. In 1887 the infant became entitled under his father's will to a large sum of money to which the covenant in the marriage settlement should have applied. But in July 1888 the infant repudiated the settlement. The trustees of the settlement brought this action to enforce the covenant to settle after-acquired property. It was held by the Court of Appeal (reversing a decision of Romer J) that an infant must repudiate, if at all, within a reasonable time after he attains his majority, and what is a reasonable time is a question of fact to be determined in the light of all the circumstances, and in the circumstances of the present case, four and a half years was not a reasonable time. The respondent then appealed to the House of Lords. HELD by the House of Lords: The law gives an infant the privilege of repudiating obligations undertaken during minority within a reasonable time after coming of age. The law lays no obligation upon the infant, it merely confers upon him a privilege which he might or might not avail himself of as he chooses. If he chooses to be inactive his opportunity is lost, if he chooses to be active the law comes to his assistance. In the present case the period of four years and eight months which the infant permitted to elapse before he took any steps in the matter could not possibly be regarded as a reasonable time and, therefore, the covenant was binding.

In *Edwards* v. *Carter* Lord Herschell said: 'It is said that in considering whether a reasonable time has elapsed you must take into account the fact that he did not know what were the terms of the settlement and that it contained this particular covenant. He knew that he had executed a deed — he must be taken to have known that the deed though binding upon him could be repudiated when he came of age, and it seems to me that in measuring a reasonable time whether in point of fact he had or had not acquainted himself with the nature of the obligations which he had undertaken is wholly immaterial — the time must be measured in precisely the same way whether he had so made himself acquainted or not. I do not say that he was under any obligation to make himself acquainted with the nature of the deed, which, having executed it as an infant, he might or might not at his pleasure repudiate when he came of age — all I say is this, that he cannot maintain that the reasonable time when measured must be a longer time because he has chosen not to make himself acquainted with the nature of the deed which he has executed.'

6. Effect of repudiation

The general rule is that where a minor repudiates a contract of continuing obligation, he can recover money paid or property transferred only where there has been a total failure of consideration. Total failure of consideration occurs where the party relying on the failure has not received any part of what he bargained for: *Films Rover International* v. *Cannon Film Sales* (1988) CA. Where the minor has received any benefit at all, he cannot recover. In the case of partnership agreements, however, a minor can claim to recover his share of the partnership assets after the payment of partnership debts, i.e. he will have to share in the payment of partnership debts.

> *Steinberg* v. *Scala (Leeds)* (1923): A minor who had bought partly paid up shares in a company sought to repudiate the contract and recover her money. HELD: **(a)** She was entitled to repudiate and have her name removed from the register of members; and **(b)** since the shares had some value, there was no total failure of consideration, and she could not recover money paid.

Note

In *Steinberg* v. *Scala*, the minor was entitled to repudiate her obligation to pay further calls.

7. Restitution

Section 3 of the Minors' Contracts Act 1987 confers on the court a new power to order restitution against minors who unjustly or unfairly acquire property under an unenforceable or voidable contract. This section provides that where 'a person (the plaintiff) has after the commencement of this Act entered into a contract with another (the defendant), and that the contract is unenforceable against the defendant (or he repudiates it) because he was a minor when the contract was made, the court may, if it is just and equitable to do so, require the defendant to transfer to the plaintiff any property acquired by the defendant under the contract or any property representing it.'

The 1987 Act came into force on 9 June 1987.

These new statutory rules of restitution will not be taken to prejudice any other remedy available to the plaintiff: s. 3(2) of the 1987 Act.

8. Contracts binding the minor

Minors are bound when they enter contracts of the following kinds:

(a) contracts for *necessaries*;
(b) contracts of *education*, training or beneficial service.

9. Contracts for necessaries

A minor is liable to pay for necessaries that have been supplied to him. At common law, the concept of 'necessaries' includes goods and services necessary to the infant and his dependant according to his position in life: *Peters* v. *Fleming* (1840); *Chapple* v. *Cooper* (1844). Articles of mere luxury are always excluded though luxurious articles of utility may be allowed according to the infant's station in life: *Chapple* v. *Cooper* (1844). 'Necessaries' would accordingly include such things as medical attendance, lodgings and food for the minor and also for any wife and children of the infant.

The Sale of Goods Act of 1893 and 1979 both define 'necessaries' as goods suitable to the condition in life of the infant and suitable to his actual requirements at the time of sale and delivery. The Acts provide further that where necessaries are sold and delivered to an infant he must pay a reasonable price. The infant's liability under either Act to pay a reasonable price for necessaries is quasi-contractual. He is not liable on an executory contract for necessaries, such liability being excluded by the use of the words 'sale or delivery' and 'sold and delivered' in both Acts.

Where a person sues a minor under the Sale of Goods Act 1979, for the recovery of a reasonable price for goods sold and delivered, he must prove

(a) that the goods were suitable to the condition in life of the minor, and
(b) that the goods were suitable to the minor's actual requirements at the time of sale and delivery.

This is exactly what was necessary under the 1893 Act.

Nash v. *Inman* (1908): The plaintiff had supplied to the defendant clothing to the value of £145 10*s* 3*d* at a time when the defendant was a Cambridge undergraduate. The clothes supplied by the plaintiff included 11 fancy waistcoats. The defendant raised the defence of infancy at the time the goods were supplied and that the goods were not 'necessaries'. The defendant's father had amply supplied the defendant with proper clothes according to his condition in life. It was held by Ridley J that there was no evidence that the goods were 'necessaries' and entered judgment for the defendant. The plaintiff appealed. HELD by the Court of Appeal: There was no evidence that the goods supplied were necessary to the defendant's requirements. On the contrary, the defendant was amply supplied with suitable and necessary clothes.

It has been held that where a person provides an infant with money to buy necessaries, that person may recover the amount from the infant: *Martin* v. *Gale* (1876).

10. Contracts of education, training or beneficial service

A minor is bound by the terms of a contract under which he obtains education, or training for a trade for a profession, or beneficial experience in a trade or profession unless the terms are onerous and unreasonable: *De Francesco* v. *Barnum* (1890). He is bound to pay a reasonable price for training where a price is agreed. The following contracts have been held to be beneficial:

(a) A contract by which an infant boxer undertook to abide by the rules of the British Boxing Board of Control: *Doyle* v. *White City Stadium* (1935).

(b) A contract by which an infant billiards professional undertook to go on tour with a well-known player: *Roberts* v. *Gray* (1913).

(c) A contract between an infant and his wife, on the one part, and a publisher, on the other, by which the publisher agreed to publish the autobiography of the infant. The work was to be written by two journalists based on information provided by the infant and his wife. At the time of contracting, the infant intended to become an author: *Chaplin* v. *Leslie Frewin* (1966).

(d) Apprenticeship agreements.

Note

Where an infant is engaged in trade, an ordinary trading contract is not binding on him, even though it may be for his benefit: *Mercantile Union Guarantee Corporation* v. *Ball* (1937).

11. Disapplication of Infants' Relief Act, etc.

Section 1 of the Minors' Contracts Act 1987 provides that the Infants Relief Act 1874 and s. 5 of the Betting and Loans (Infants) Act 1892 will not apply to any contract made by a minor after the commencement of the 1987 Act, i.e. after 9 June 1987.

By s. 1 of the Infants Relief Act 1874 the following contracts entered into by minors were rendered 'absolutely void':

(a) contracts for the repayment of money lent or to be lent,
(b) contracts for goods supplied or to be supplied (other than contracts for necessaries), and
(c) all accounts stated with minors.

Any such contract entered into after the coming into force of the Minors' Contracts Act 1987 will be unenforceable against the infant by virtue of the common law, but will be subject to the provision for restitution contained in s. 3 of the 1987 Act.

Section 2 of the Infants Relief Act prevented the enforcement of a ratification of a contract when the minor had reached full age. The position now is that any such ratification is binding.

Section 5 of the Betting and Loans (Infants) Act 1892 invalidated contracts entered into by persons of full age to repay any loan contracted during infancy. The position now is that any such agreement is binding.

12. Guarantees

Section 2 of the Minors' Contracts Act 1987 provides that where

'**(a)** a guarantee is given in respect of an obligation of a party to a contract . . ., and
(b) the obligation is unenforceable against him (or he repudiates the contract) because he was a minor when the contract was made,

the guarantee shall not for that reason alone be unenforceable against the guarantor.'

The effect of this provision is that the guarantee of an unenforceable minor's contract or of a voidable minor's contract is as valid and effective as if the minor were a person of full age. Before the Minors' Contracts Act 1987 came into force a person who guaranteed a minor's debt could not be made liable on the guarantee because the contract of loan was rendered 'absolutely void' by the Infants' Relief Act.

Contracts made by insane or drunken persons

13. Incapacity through insanity or drunkenness

Where a person who is drunk or insane, and thus does not understand what he is doing, enters into a contract, the contract is voidable at his option, provided that the other party knew of his condition. Lopes LJ summed up the position in *Imperial Loan Co.* v. *Stone* (1892) as follows: 'A contract made by a person of unsound mind is not voidable at that person's option if the other party to the contract believed at the time he made the contract that the person with whom he was dealing was of sound mind. In order to avoid a fair contract on the ground of insanity the mental incapacity of the one must be known to the other party. A defendant must plead and prove both his insanity and the knowledge of the plaintiff; the burden of proof of both those facts lies on the defendant.'

The validity of a contract entered into by a lunatic who is ostensibly sane is to be judged by the same standards as a contract by a person of sound mind. It will not be voidable by the lunatic by reason of 'unfairness' unless such unfairness amounts to equitable fraud, in which case the complaining party would be able to avoid the contract even if he had been sane: *Hart* v. *O'Connor* (1985) PC.

Note

(a) Mentally unbalanced persons are bound by contracts made during periods of lucidity even if the disability was known to the other party.

(b) Voidable contracts may be ratified and made binding after the period of incapacity has ended.

(c) Insane and drunken persons are bound to pay a reasonable price for necessaries according to the same rules as apply to infants: Sale of Goods Acts 1893 and 1979. This obligation to pay for necessaries arises whether or not the disability was known to the other party.

Progress test 10

1. What do you understand by the expression 'contractual capacity'?

2. State the general rule of common law governing the enforceability of minors' contracts. What exceptions are there?

3. What is the effect of ratification of an unenforceable contract?

4. Which contracts are voidable at the option of the minor? When and how must the minor's option be exercised?

5. Where a minor exercises his option to repudiate a contract, may he recover money paid to the other party?

6. Has the court any power to order restitution of goods obtained by an unscrupulous minor who refuses to pay the price?

7. May the court order a minor to transfer money borrowed by him? Does the power to order restitution apply to goods bought by a minor with money borrowed by him?

8. What are 'necessaries'? To what extent is a minor bound by a contract for necessaries?

9. A minor is bound by a contract for education or training. Explain and illustrate this statement.

10. Comment on the disapplication of the Infants Relief Act and s. 5 of the Betting and Loans (Infants) Act.

11. How has the law governing guarantees been affected by the Minors' Contracts Act?

12. What is the position where a person who is drunk or insane enters into a contract?

13. A, aged 17, is a millionaire pop star. His pocket is picked while he is at a race meeting so he borrows £400 from an adult friend, B. Next day, he quarrels with B and, out of spite, refuses to repay the £400. Advise B.

14. C, aged 17, is married and has one child. He is a commercial traveller earning approximately £180 a week. He receives bills for the following goods which have been delivered to him:

(a) A mink coat for his wife, price £4,000.
(b) A small saloon car, price £5,500.
(c) A pushchair for his child, price £41.
(d) A new suit made for C by a Savile Row tailor, price £750.
(e) Groceries used by his family, price £52.

Advise him as to his liability on each of these transactions.

11
Illegal contracts

The nature of illegality

1. *Ex turpi causa non oritur actio*

It is against the policy of the common law (and, therefore, against public policy) to allow an action on a contract containing an illegal or wrongful element. To allow such an action would be detrimental to the dignity of the court. The maxims giving expression to this policy are:

(a) *Ex turpi causa non oritur actio*: no action arises from a base cause. (Sometimes expressed as *ex dolo malo non oritur actio*.)

(b) *In pari delicto potior est conditio defendentis*: where there is equal fault, the defendant is in the stronger position.

A clear explanation of the two maxims was given by Lord Mansfield CJ in *Holman* v. *Johnson* (1775). He said, 'The objection, that a contract is immoral or illegal as between plaintiff and defendant, sounds at all times very ill in the mouth of the defendant. It is not for his sake, however, that the objection is ever allowed; but it is founded in general principles of policy, which the defendant has the advantage of, contrary to the real justice, as between him and the plaintiff, by accident, if I may say so. The principle of public policy is this: *ex dolo malo non oritur actio*. No court will lend its aid to a man who founds his cause of action upon an immoral or illegal act. If, from the plaintiff's own stating or otherwise, the cause of action appears to arise *ex turpi causa*, or the transgression of a positive law of this country, there the court says he has no right to be assisted. It is upon that ground the court goes; not for the sake of the defendant, but because they will not lend their aid to such a plaintiff.'

Where the plaintiff's cause of action arises from the breach of an illegal contract, the general rule is that the court will refuse its aid and will drive the parties from its presence making no order as to damages or costs. An illegal contract is unenforceable because it is against the policy of the common law to allow an action upon it. It is, therefore, not strictly correct to describe such contracts as void. In *Archbolds* v. *S. Spanglett* (1961), Pearce LJ said, 'If a contract is expressly or by necessary implication forbidden by statute, or if it is *ex facie* illegal, or if both parties know that though *ex facie* it can only be performed by illegality or is intended to be performed illegally, the law will not help the plaintiffs in any way that is a direct or indirect enforcement of rights under the contract; and for this purpose both parties are presumed to know the law.' In the same case Devlin LJ said, 'The effect of illegality on a contract may be threefold. If at the time of making the contract there is an intention to perform it in an unlawful way, the contract, although it remains alive, is unenforceable at the suit of the party having that intent; if the intent is held in common, it is not enforceable at all. Another effect of illegality is to prevent a plaintiff from recovering under a contract if in order to prove his rights under it he has to rely on his own illegal act; he may not do that even though he can show that at the time of making the contract he had no intent to break the law and that at the time of performance he did not know that what he was doing was illegal. The third effect of illegality is to avoid the contract *ab initio*, and that arises if the making of the contract is expressly or impliedly prohibited by statute or is otherwise contrary to public policy.'

2. Examples of illegal contracts

A contract is illegal if it involves the transgression of a rule of law (statutory or otherwise) or where it is base or immoral. Examples are:

(a) contracts prohibited by statute;

(b) contracts to defraud the Revenue;

(c) contracts involving the commission of a crime or tort;

(d) contracts with a sexually immoral element;

(e) contracts against the interests of the United Kingdom or a friendly state;

(f) contracts leading to corruption in public life;

(g) contracts which interfere with the course of justice.

3. Contracts prohibited by statute

To enter into a contract which is expressly prohibited by statute would clearly be a 'transgression of a positive law of this country' — to use Lord Mansfield's terminology. Such a contract would be illegal. Where Parliament seeks to control any aspect of consumer credit, for example, it may do so by providing in an Act that certain specified contracts must not be entered into. The effect is the same where the prohibition is made by statutory instrument. Another example would be where Parliament seeks to control foreign currency exchange with sterling by prohibiting certain currency dealings: *Bigos* v. *Bousted* (1951).

Where a statute does not expressly prohibit a contract, the question sometimes arises whether there is implied prohibition. In such cases the court will decide whether the object of the legislation was to prohibit the contract or whether there was some other object. In *Smith* v. *Mawhood* (1845) a tobacconist failed to take out a licence to sell tobacco as required by a statute which provided for a penalty of £200 for such failure. It was held that a contract by which he purchased tobacco was not thereby made illegal. Parke B explained that, 'the object of the legislation was not to prohibit a contract of sale by dealers who have not taken out a licence . . . but only to impose a penalty upon the party offending for the purposes of the Revenue.'

In *Archbolds* v. *Spanglett* (1961) the defendants undertook to carry goods in a vehicle which was not licensed in accordance with statute. It was argued that such undertakings were prohibited by the statute of implication. This argument failed in the Court of Appeal. Pearce LJ said that the object of the Act 'was not to interfere with the owner of the goods but to control those who provided the transport, with a view to promoting its efficiency.' Thus the Act did not make contracts for the transport of goods illegal. What happened in this case was that a contract which was *ex facie* lawful was carried out in an unlawful manner by one of the parties. The case turned on whether the other party knew of the intention to perform in an illegal manner. *See* also *Ashmore* v. *Dawson* (1973) at **10** below.

In *St John Shipping Corporation* v. *Joseph Rank* (1957) Devlin J refused to hold that a contract for the carriage of goods by sea was made illegal when the ship's master committed an offence during the voyage, namely, loading beyond the loadline. A contract will be declared illegal only if the prohibited act is at the centre of it.

Archbolds v. *Spanglett* (1961): There was a contract between the plaintiffs and the defendants by which the defendants agreed to carry by road certain goods owned by a third party. The vehicle in which the goods were carried had a 'C' licence. The Road and Rail Traffic Act 1933 prohibits the use of goods vehicles on a road except with an 'A' licence. The defendants knew at the time of the contract that a vehicle with the 'C' licence was to be used, but the plaintiffs did not know this. As a result of negligence on the part of the defendants, the goods were stolen in transit. The plaintiff claimed damages for breach of contract and negligence. HELD by the Court of Appeal: The contract was *ex facie* legal. The plaintiffs could succeed in their claim for damages for negligence because they did not know that the vehicle to be used had only a 'C' licence.

4. Contracts to defraud the Revenue

A contract which is designed to defraud the Revenue or a rating authority is illegal.

Napier v. *National Business Agency* (1951): N was employed by the company at a salary plus £6 a week for expenses. As both parties knew, N's expenses were never more than £1 a week. The company dismissed N summarily and he claimed his salary for a period in lieu of notice. HELD by the Court of Appeal: The part of the agreement relating to expenses was tax evasion and illegal: the rest of the agreement was tainted with the illegality and, accordingly, unenforceable.

Alexander v. *Rayson* (1936): In July 1929 the defendant, Mrs Rayson, approached the plaintiff with a view to taking an underlease of a flat at a rent of £1,200 a year, the rent to cover the provision of services. The plaintiff, accordingly, sent to the defendant two documents, the first being a draft sublease of the flat at a rent of £450 a year, the second being a draft agreement for various services in connection with the flat for the payment of an additional sum of £750 a

year. The sublease itself provided for services which were
substantially the same as those in the service agreement
with the exception of the provision and maintenance of a
frigidaire. (The plaintiff had stated to the rating assessment
committee that £450 was the only amount he received for
rent, services and rates. His assessment was then reduced
from £720 to £270. But the committee subsequently
discovered the existence of the agreement and the
assessment of £720 was restored.) The annual sum of
£1,200 was paid by the defendant quarterly up to and
including the instalment due at midsummer 1934. But the
defendant refused to pay the quarterly instalment of the
£750 which fell due in September 1934, contending that the
plaintiff had failed to comply with his obligations in respect
of the services to be rendered under the sublease and under
the agreement. The defendant tendered the sum of £112
10s as the quarterly rent due under the sublease. The
plaintiff refused this tender and brought this action
claiming the sum of £300, being the quarterly instalment
payable under the two documents. The defendant
contended, *inter alia*, that the agreement was void for
illegality and that its enforcement would be contrary to
public policy in that its execution was obtained by the
plaintiff for the purposes of defrauding the Westminster
City Council by deceiving them as to the true rateable value
of the premises and by inducing them to believe that the
true rent received by the plaintiff was £450 and by
concealing from them the terms of the agreement. The trial
judge held that the agreement was not unenforceable for
illegality. The defendant appealed. HELD by the Court of
Appeal: The landlord had intended to use the sublease and
the agreement for an illegal purpose and had, accordingly,
put himself in the same position in law as though he had
intended that the flat, when let, should be used for an illegal
purpose. He was, therefore, not entitled to enforce the
sublease or the agreement. It made no difference that he
had failed to defraud the rating authority and could no
longer use the documents for an illegal purpose.

In *Alexander* v. *Rayson*, Romer LJ in reading the judgment of the court, said: 'It is settled law that an agreement to do an act that is illegal or immoral or contrary to public policy, or to do any act for a consideration that is illegal, immoral or contrary to public policy, is unlawful and therefore void. But it often happens that an agreement which, in itself, is not unlawful, is made with the intention of one or both parties to make use of the subject-matter for an unlawful purpose, that is to say, a purpose that is illegal, immoral or contrary to public policy. The most common instance of this is an agreement for the sale or letting of an object, where the agreement is unobjectionable on the face of it, but where the intention of one or both of the parties is that the object shall be used by the purchaser or hirer for an unlawful purpose. In such a case any party to the agreement who had the unlawful intention is precluded from suing upon it *ex turpi causa non oritur actio*. The action does not lie because the court will not lend its help to such a plaintiff.'

5. Contract claims involving crime or tort

Where the consideration in, or the purpose of, a contract is criminal or tortious, the contract is illegal.

Beresford v. *Royal Insurance Co.* (1938): R shot himself a few minutes before his life insurance policy expired. His personal representatives claimed on the policy. HELD: It would be against public policy to allow a man to benefit his estate by committing a crime. The sum assured was not recoverable.

In *Davitt* v. *Titchcumb* (1990) the defendant claimed a fund which would not have come into being but for his criminal act. He was barred by the rule of public policy from benefiting from his own criminal act. *See* also *Beresford*'s case above. In *Alghussein Establishment* v. *Eton College* (1988) the House of Lords applied the rule of construction that there was a presumption that a party to a contract could not be permitted to take advantage of his own wrong as against the other party. It was held that this rule applied in the absence of an express provision to contradict the presumption. The rule applied as much to a party who sought to obtain a benefit under a continuing contract on account of his breach as it did to a party who relied on his breach to avoid a contract and thereby escape his obligations.

6. Contracts with a sexually immoral element
A contract is illegal for immorality as follows:

(a) Where the consideration is an act of sexual immorality, e.g. an agreement for future illicit co-habitation. (NB: An agreement with respect to *past* illicit co-habitation is not illegal, and is binding if made under seal.)
(b) Where the purpose of the contract is the furtherance of sexual immorality, and both parties know this.

> *Pearce* v. *Brooks* (1866): There was a contract under which a firm of coachbuilders hired out a carriage to a prostitute. It was known that she intended to use the vehicle as part of her display to attract men. The prostitute fell into arrears with the hire payments, and the coachbuilders claimed the sum due. HELD: The contract was illegal and the sum claimed could not be recovered.

7. Contracts against the interest of the state
Any contract which is detrimental to the interests of the United Kingdom is illegal, e.g. a trading contract which would benefit a country at war with the United Kingdom.

The rule also covers agreements which might disturb the friendly relations between the UK and other states. Thus the court once refused to recognize an agreement to export whisky to the USA contrary to the prohibition laws of that country in the 1920s: *Foster* v. *Driscoll* (1929).

8. Contracts leading to corruption in public life
Contracts involving the bribery of officials, or attempts to buy honours, are illegal. Such contracts are void even though no crime has been committed.

> *Parkinson* v. *College of Ambulance* (1925): One Harrison, the second defendant in this case, was the secretary of the defendant company. He fraudulently represented to the plaintiff that he had power to nominate persons to receive titles of honour and that he or the company could arrange for the grant to the plaintiff of a knighthood if the plaintiff would make a donation to the company funds. In response to this false and fraudulent representation, the plaintiff

made a donation of £3,000 to the company. The plaintiff brought this action to recover £3,000 as damages for deceit, or, in the alternative, as money had and received by the defendants to the use of the plaintiff, or, in the further alternative, as damages for breach of warranty of authority. HELD: The contract between the plaintiff and the defendants by which the plaintiff gave the money on the strength of representations that he would receive a knighthood was against public policy and, therefore, illegal; as the parties were *in pari delicto* an action for damages could not be maintained by the plaintiff, nor could he recover the money on the ground that it was had and received by the defendant to his use.

9. Contracts which interfere with the course of justice

Any contract which tends to pervert the course of justice is illegal. A contract not to prosecute, or to compromise, in criminal proceedings is illegal, unless the proceedings could have been initiated in the civil courts for tort. Also, a contract under which an accused person indemnifies a person who has gone bail for him is illegal: *Herman* v. *Jeuchner* (1885).

Kearley v. *Thomson* (1890): A petition in bankruptcy was presented by B against C, a friend of the plaintiff. The plaintiff paid £40 to the defendants, a firm of solicitors, in consideration of an undertaking by them not to appear at C's public examination and not to oppose his discharge. The defendants, in accordance with the agreement, did not appear at the public examination. Before C applied for his order of discharge, the plaintiff brought this action to recover the £40. HELD by the Court of Appeal: The agreement was illegal and the sum could not be recovered. Per Fry LJ: 'The tendency of such an undertaking as that which was given by the defendants is obvious; it tends to pervert the course of justice. The defendants were not bound to appear, but they were bound not to enter an agreement which would fetter their liberty of action as to appearing or not.'

The consequence of illegality

10. Illegal performance

Where a contract is lawful in its inception but it is performed in an illegal manner, any party who participated in the illegal performance will be debarred from claiming damages for breach of contract. A party may not take advantage of his own wrong. This principle was expounded by Atkin LJ in *Anderson* v. *Daniel* (1924) in a passage which was quoted by Devlin J in *St John Shipping Corporation* v. *Joseph Rank* (1957), and approved by Lord Denning in *Ashmore* v. *Dawson* (1973): 'The question of illegality in a contract generally arises in connection with its formation, but it may also arise, as it does here, in connection with its performance. In the former case, where the parties have agreed to do something which is prohibited by Act of Parliament, it is indisputable that the contract is unenforceable by either party. And I think it is equally unenforceable by the offending party where the illegality arises from the fact that the mode of performance adopted by the party performing it is in violation of some statute, even though the contract as agreed upon between the parties was capable of being performed in a perfectly legal manner.' *See* also *Alghussein Establishment* v. *Eton College* (1988).

> *Ashmore* v. *Dawson* (1973): The plaintiffs had manufactured a piece of engineering equipment weighing 25 tons which the defendants, a road haulage company, agreed to carry to a port of shipment. The plaintiffs' transport manager was present when the equipment was loaded on to the defendants' vehicle. He knew that the vehicle provided by the defendants was overloaded contrary to the statutory regulations governing the carrying of loads on motor vehicles. He made no objection to the use of this vehicle, nor did he explain (what he well knew) that the appropriate vehicle for the load in question was a 'low loader'. On its way to the port, the vehicle toppled over and the loaded equipment was damaged. The plaintiffs brought this action for damages contending that there was negligence and/or breach of contract on the defendants' part. HELD by the Court of Appeal: Even if the contract was lawful in its inception, it was performed in an unlawful manner and the

plaintiffs, through their transport manager, had participated in the illegality. Accordingly, the plaintiffs were debarred from claiming damages.

Anderson v. *Daniel* (1924): Sellers of artificial fertilizer are required by statute to provide each buyer with an invoice containing a statement of the proportions of certain chemicals contained in the fertilizer. In this case, the sellers of an artificial fertilizer failed to supply a buyer with the statutory invoice. The contract was *ex facie* lawful but was performed in an unlawful manner by the seller who could not, therefore, recover the price.

11. The general rule

The general rule is that no action can be brought by a party to an illegal contract: *ex turpi causa non oritur actio*. The following points should be noted:

(a) No action will lie for the recovery of money paid or property transferred under an illegal contract: *Parkinson*'s case; *Kearley* v. *Thomson*; *Berg* v. *Sadler & Moore* (1937).

(b) No action will lie for the breach of an illegal contract: *Pearce* v. *Brooks*; *Beresford*'s case.

(c) Where part of an illegal contract would have been lawful by itself, the court will not sever the good from the bad. The whole contract becomes tainted with illegality: *Napier*'s case.

(d) Any contract which is collateral to an illegal contract is also tainted with illegality, and is treated as being illegal, even though it would have been lawful by itself. This rule clearly operates where the parties to the collateral contract are the same as to the original illegal contract. The rule will also apply where a subsequent or collateral contract is made with a third party: *Spector* v. *Ageda* (1971).

Fisher v. *Bridges* (1854): There was an illegal contract under which F agreed to sell certain land to B. B paid the purchase price except for £630, and the land was conveyed to him. By a separate deed B promised to pay £630 to F. HELD: The collateral agreement under seal was tainted with the illegality.

(e) Title of goods may pass under an illegal contract if it is executed. There is no rule that the court will not look at an illegal contract: *Belvoir Finance Co.* v. *Stapleton* (1971).

12. Exceptions to the general rule of no recovery

A party to an illegal contract may sue to recover money paid or property transferred as follows:

(a) Where the parties are not *in pari delicto*, i.e. not equally at fault, the 'innocent' party may recover. This circumstance may arise in a number of ways:

    (*i*) where the contract is prohibited by statute in order to protect the class of person to which the plaintiff belongs: *Amar Singh* v. *Kulubya* (1964);

    (*ii*) where a party has been induced to enter an illegal contract by fraudulent misrepresentation, or where an ignorant man enters an illegal contract under the influence of a cleverer man.

Hughes v. *Liverpool, etc. Friendly Society* (1916): H was induced by the fraudulent misrepresentation of an insurance agent to enter an illegal contract of life insurance. H sought to recover the premiums paid. held by the Court of Appeal: The parties were not *in pari delicto* and the premiums were recoverable.

(b) Where no substantial part of the illegal act has been performed, a party who is truly repentant may recover. In this way, the law encourages repentance. But a party seeking to take advantage of this rule must show that his repentance is genuine, and that he is not repudiating the contract for mere reasons of convenience: *Bigos* v. *Bousted* (1951).

(c) Where a contract is apparently lawful in its actual formation, but there is an illegal purpose known to one party and not to the other, the innocent party may recover: *Cowan* v. *Milbourn* (1967). But a contract which is *ex facie* lawful will be treated as illegal if both parties knew of the illegal purpose: *Pearce* v. *Brooks* (1866).

(d) Where a party to an illegal contract is able to frame his action so as not to depend on contract, he may succeed in recovering property: *Bowmakers* v. *Barnet Instruments* (1944); *Sajan Singh* v. *Sardara Ali* (1960).

(e) A contract is not normally enforceable where it would enable a plaintiff to benefit from his criminal conduct since to do so would be an affront to the public conscience. Nevertheless, where there has been a statutory offence committed by the plaintiff, there are circumstances when it would be wrong to disqualify him from recovering under the contract, for example where the plaintiff committed criminal acts in order to escape danger to his life: *Howard* v. *Shirlstar Container Transport* (1990) CA.

Progress test 11

1. Explain the maxims *ex turpi causa non oritur actio* and *in pari delicto potior est conditio defendentis*. Mention *Holman* v. *Johnson* in your answer.

2. Give some examples of the kinds of contract which are illegal.

3. Explain how a contract may be expressly or implicitly prohibited by statute. What test is applied by the courts?

4. Where a party to a lawful contract performs his side of the agreement in a manner forbidden by statute, is the contract rendered illegal?

5. 'Any contract which is collateral to an illegal contract is tainted with illegality.' Explain this statement and illustrate your answer with a case.

6. The general rule is that there is no recovery of money paid or property transferred under an illegal contract. Give a careful account of the exceptions to this rule.

7. A entered a contract of service with an employer, B. According to the terms of the contract, B agreed to pay A £90 a week salary and £50 a week by way of expenses. The agreement was designed to defraud the Revenue, for it was never envisaged that A should require more than £10 a week as expenses. B has just dismissed A summarily, giving no reason for doing so. A seeks your advice as to whether he can claim three weeks' arrears of salary and expenses. Advise him.

8.   C agrees to let D have the use of C's motor yacht for a week. C knew at the time of the agreement that D intended to use the yacht for smuggling dope into England. D paid C £2,000 deposit before going aboard the yacht, and when he got aboard, he found that C had removed some vital parts of the engine, so that it was impossible to put to sea. Advise D as to whether he can recover the £2,000.

9.   E has cohabited with his mistress, F, for the past five years. E tells F that he wishes to leave her, and then takes her to his solicitor's office, where he makes a promise under seal to pay her £500 per annum for the rest of her life, in consideration for what she has done for him. Advise F as to whether she can enforce E's promise in the event of non-payment.

10.   G is anxious that his dull son, H, shall be admitted into Dotheboys College. G knows that competition is keen and that H has not the intelligence to pass the entrance examination; so he arranges to meet J, the college bursar, privately and agrees to pay him (J) the sum of £2,000 on the understanding that H shall be admitted in the following Michaelmas term. When J received the £2,000 from G, he immediately sent it to his favourite charity. He then wrote to G. telling him that on no account would H be admitted into the college. G now wishes to recover the £2,000. Advise him.

11.   K enters a contract with L for the purchase of 100 packets of cigarettes which he knows that L has recently stolen. K pays £20 to L under the agreement, but when, later, L tries to deliver the cigarettes, K refuses to accept them. K's refusal was due to a sudden fear that the stolen cigarettes would be traced to him. L now refuses to return the £20. Will K be able to recover the money? Would your answer be different if K's refusal had been out of true repentance?

12

Contracts against public policy

Contracts void at common law as being against public policy

1. Contracts offending public policy

Certain contracts which offend against public policy are illegal, and have been dealt with in Chapter 11. There are, however, certain remaining contracts against public policy which have escaped the full stigma of illegality. These contracts are void, but only so far as they are against public policy. They are:

(a) contracts to oust the courts from their jurisdiction;
(b) contracts striking at the institution of marriage;
(c) contracts impeding parental duties;
(d) contracts in restraint of trade.

Note
The following paragraphs of the chapter are concerned with the underlying common law applicable to restrictive agreements. Modern statutory controls over such agreements are outside the scope of this book. However, students of elementary contract law should be aware that the Restrictive Trade Practices Act 1976 provides for the registration and judicial investigation of restrictive agreements. Any agreement found by the Restrictive Practices Court to be contrary to the public interest is void.

2. Contracts to oust the jurisdiction

The court is the final arbiter on questions of law, and this jurisdiction cannot be ousted by any agreement between the parties. Thus, although a party may bind himself to submit to the findings of fact by a competent arbitrator or domestic tribunal, he cannot bind himself to refrain from submitting questions of law to the courts: *Lee* v. *Showmen's Guild* (1952). Similarly, an agreement not to refer disputes as to interpretation to the court is void: *Baker* v. *Jones* (1954). It is not against public policy for an arbitration clause to provide that the award of an arbitrator is a condition precedent to litigation in the courts: *Scott* v. *Avery* (1856).

3. Contracts striking at the institution of marriage

The institution of marriage is protected by the policy of the courts. Contracts in undue restraint of marriage, contracts which impede a party in his marital duties, and marriage brokage contracts are void.

Examples

(a) A contract by which a party undertakes not to marry at all is void. A partial restraint is not necessarily void, e.g. where X contracts not to marry Y, the restraint does not necessarily make the contract void; but where X promises not to marry at all, the contract is void. A contract not to marry for six years has been held to be void.

(b) A contract between husband and wife for a definite or possible future separation is void. But a contract between husband and wife for an immediate separation is valid.

(c) Where a party, whose present spouse is still alive, contracts to marry another, the contract is void, e.g. X, who is married to Y, contracts with Z that he will marry her after the death of Y — the contract is void. But a contract to marry, entered into after a decree nisi and before the decree absolute of divorce, is not void.

4. Contracts impeding parental duties

A contract by which a party deprives himself of the custody of his child is void. But note that a court order to the same effect is binding.

5. Contracts in restraint of trade

A contract in restraint of trade is one whereby a party undertakes to suffer some restriction as to carrying on his trade or profession. There is an agreement in restraint of trade:

(a) where an employee, apprentice or articled clerk undertakes not to set up in business, or enter the service of another, within a specified area;

(b) where the vendor of the goodwill of a business undertakes not to compete with the purchaser;

(c) where merchants or manufacturers or trade associations give mutual undertakings for the regulation of their business relations: e.g. by agreeing

> (*i*) to regulate the output of any commodity,
> (*ii*) to control prices, or
> (*iii*) to regulate the trading use of a particular piece of land.

6. Contracts in restraint of trade are prima facie void

Although a contract in restraint of trade is prima facie void, it will be upheld by the court if it can be shown that the restraint is:

(a) reasonable as between the parties — in particular the restraint must be no wider than is necessary to protect the proper interests of the person whom it is designed to benefit; and also

(b) reasonable as regards the interests of the public, i.e. not injurious to the public.

The essential law on this point was stated by Lord MacNaghten in the *Nordenfelt* case as follows: 'Restraints of trade and interference with individual liberty of action, may be justified by the special circumstances of a particular case. It is sufficient justification, and indeed, it is the only justification, if the restriction is reasonable — reasonable, that is, in reference to the interests of the parties concerned and reasonable in reference to the interests of the public, so framed and so guarded as to afford adequate protection to the party in whose favour it is imposed, while at the same time it is in no way injurious to the public.'

7. Reasonableness in contracts in restraint of trade

The question of whether a restraint is reasonable is decided by the judge. The duty of the jury is to find any facts which are necessary to the judge's decision. The concept of *reasonableness* should be considered separately with reference to restraints in contracts of

(a) employment,
(b) sale of goodwill, and
(c) trading agreements.

In the case of a covenant said to be in restraint of trade, the decision to grant or withhold an injunction for practical purposes is usually decisive because of the very short time limits: *Office Overload Ltd* v. *Gunn* (1977) and *John Michael Design* v. *Cooke* (1987).

8. Reasonableness in contracts of employment

An employer is entitled to the benefit of a restraint clause protecting confidential information or a proprietary interest, e.g. goodwill or trade secrets. Where an employer can show that the restraint is no wider than this, the presumption that the contract is void is rebutted. The test is whether the stipulated restraint exceeds what is necessary for the protection of both parties, taking into account the interest of the public.

A restraint clause which purports to restrict an employee from using his *skill* in competition with his master (after leaving his master's employment) is always void, even where the skill was acquired in that master's service: *Morris* v. *Saxelby* (1916). In deciding whether a restraint is reasonable, the courts will consider all the relevant circumstances, in particular the following:

(a) the nature of the employer's business;
(b) the status of the employee;
(c) the geographical area covered by the restraint clause;
(d) the duration of the restraint clause in time.

Bull v. *Pitney-Bowes* (1967): The employer manufactured postal franking machines. By the terms of the contract of employment, the employee was required to join a pension scheme. Under this scheme it was provided that retired employees would be liable to forfeit their pension rights if they engaged in any activity in competition with the employer. The plaintiff employee retired from the defendant's employment after 26 years. He then became employed by another company in the same business as the defendant. The defendant warned the plaintiff that his pension was in jeopardy and the plaintiff brought this action for a declaration that the provision for forfeiture in the pension scheme was an unreasonable restraint and void. HELD: The pension scheme was part of the plaintiff's contract of employment. The forfeiture provision was to be treated as a covenant in restraint of trade. It was against public policy that the public should be deprived of the plaintiff's skill. The forfeiture provision was, accordingly, void and the plaintiff should not be deprived of his pension.

Mason v. *Provident Clothing and Supply Co.* (1913): A canvasser contracted not to be employed in any business similar to his employer's within 25 miles of London within three years of the termination of his employment. HELD by the House of Lords: the restriction was wider than reasonably necessary and, therefore, void.

Note

An employee can be restrained from using a list of customers made while in the employment of his former master: *Robb* v. *Green* (1895).

Herbert Morris v. *Saxelby* (1916): In his contract of employment with Herbert Morris Ltd S undertook not to be concerned with the sale or manufacture of pulley blocks, overheads runways or overhead travelling cranes during a period of seven years from the date of ceasing to be employed by the company. S left the company's service and the company subsequently brought this action to restrain him from breach of the restrictive undertaking in the contract of employment. HELD by the House of Lords: Having regard to all the circumstances, the undertaking was not reasonable in reference to the interests of the parties and was prejudicial to the interests of the public. The undertaking by S was therefore void and unenforceable by the company. All restraints on trade of themselves, if there is nothing more, are contrary to public policy, and, therefore, void. It is not that such restraints must of themselves necessarily operate to the public injury, but that it is against the policy of the common law to enforce them except in cases where there are special circumstances to justify them. To be valid a restraint must be reasonable in the interests of the contracting parties, and secondly, it must be reasonable in the interests of the public. To be reasonable in the interests of the parties the restraint must afford adequate protection to the party in whose favour it is imposed and be to the advantage of the covenantee who otherwise might lose such advantages as obtaining the best terms on the sale of a business or the possibility of obtaining employment or training under competent employers . . . The only reason for upholding a restraint on an employee is that the employer has some proprietary right, whether in the nature of trade connection or trade secrets, for the protection of which such a restraint is, having regard to the duties of the employee, reasonably necessary.

Fitch v. *Dewes* (1921): The respondent was a solicitor practising in Tamworth in Warwickshire. In 1899 the appellant entered the employment of the respondent as a junior clerk and continued in that employment until 1914. In 1903 the appellant was articled to the respondent. In 1908 there was an agreement between the respondent and the appellant which provided that if the appellant was successful in his final law examination he should serve the respondent as managing clerk. There was a further agreement made in 1912 by which the appellant agreed to serve the respondent as managing clerk for a period of three years from 31 December 1911. This agreement contained the following restraint clause: 'The said Thomas Birch Fitch hereby expressly agrees with the said John Hunt Dewes that he will not on the expiration or sooner determination of the said term of three years or any extended term as herein provided either alone or jointly with any other person or persons directly or indirectly be engaged or manage or concerned in the office, profession or business of a solicitor within a radius of seven miles of the town hall of Tamworth, but nothing herein contained shall at any time prevent the said Thomas Birch Fitch from carrying on the legal business of the North Warwickshire Miners' Association at Tamworth or within the aforesaid radius thereof.'

When the respondent sought to enforce the restraint clause the appellant contended that it was against public policy and void. HELD by the House of Lords: The question whether or not the unlimited restriction as to time was void as being in restraint of trade and so against public policy, depended on (a) whether it was against the public interest and **(b)** whether it exceeded what was required for the respondent's protection. And that, on the facts of this case, the unlimited restriction as to time was not against the public interest and it was reasonable to give the respondent the specified protection.

Home Counties Dairies v. *Skilton* (1970): In June 1963 the respondent became employed as a roundsman in a dairyman's business. The agreement made between employer and employee in July 1964, when the employee had already been employed for one year, contained the following two clauses among others. Clause 12 provided that: 'During his employment hereunder the Employee shall not, without the previous consent of the Employer, enter the service of or be employed in any capacity or for any purpose whatsoever by any person, firm or company carrying on any dairy business.' Clause 15 provided that: 'The Employee expressly agrees not at any time during the period of one year after the determination of his employment under this agreement (whether the same shall have been determined by notice or otherwise) either on his own account or representative or agent of any person or company, to serve or sell milk or dairy produce to, or solicit orders for milk or dairy produce from any person or company, who at any time during the last six months of his employment shall have been a customer of the Employer and served by the Employee in the course of his employment.' In March 1969, the employer sold the goodwill of his business to the appellant company which agreed to take over all employees. At the end of March the employee gave a week's notice to end his employment with the employer. In April, he entered the employment of another dairyman whose business was in the same area and immediately began to serve the same milk round that he had worked during the course of his previous employment. The respondent company then brought this action to enforce clause 15 of the agreement. HELD by the Court of Appeal: The agreement, on its true construction, was an agreement not to serve another employer as a milk roundsman calling on the customers of the old milk round who he had served in the previous six months, and that the restraint contained in clause 15 was not unreasonable and was binding on the respondent.

9. Reasonableness in sale of goodwill

Where the vendor of the goodwill of a business undertakes not to compete with the purchaser, the courts are more likely to uphold the restraint than in the case of the restraint imposed on an employee. Nevertheless, restraints of this class are void unless they protect a definite proprietary interest. When the goodwill of a business is sold, one of the main items will always be the trade connections and the buyer is entitled to the protection of a restraint clause by which the vendor has agreed not to set up in competition with the very business he has sold.

Nordenfelt v. *Maxim Nordenfelt Co.* (1894): N had established a business for the manufacture and sale of guns and ammunition. His dealings were world-wide. He entered a contract by which he sold the business to a company formed for the purpose of buying it. The contract included a restraint clause intended to protect the business in the hands of the company. Two years later, the company transferred the business to the Maxim Nordenfelt Company with the concurrence of N. On the occasion of the transfer, N entered another restraint agreement in substitution for that entered into with the original purchasers. The restraint stipulated was that N should not, during the term of 25 years from the formation of the company, engage in the trade or business of a manufacturer of guns, explosives or ammunition. N subsequently engaged in business contrary to his undertaking to the company, which then brought this action claiming an injunction to restrain him from further breach. N contended in his defence that the undertaking was void as being in restraint of trade and going beyond what was reasonably necessary for the protection of the company's interests. HELD by the House of Lords: N's undertaking was valid because the area supplied by the company was practically unlimited, the customers being states all over the world, and so the restraint was not wider than the protection of the company required.

Deacons v. *Bridge* (1984): The plaintiff firm of Hong Kong
solicitors had 27 partners and 49 assistant solicitors. The
firm was divided into a number of more-or-less
self-contained specialist departments. The intellectual
property and trademarks department dealt with 10 per cent
of the firm's files and billed about 4.5 per cent of the firm's
fees. In 1967 the defendant joined the firm as an assistant
solicitor. He became a salaried partner in 1973 and a full
capital partner in 1974. At this last stage he was given
charge of the intellectual property and trademarks
department where he dealt only with those clients of the
firm who used this department. On first becoming a partner
the defendant became bound by the terms of the
partnership agreement by which he received a 5 per cent
share in the partnership business and its assets, including
goodwill (which was put as purely a nominal amount in the
agreement). The agreement contained a provision that if a
partner ceased to be a partner he must not act as a solicitor
in Hong Kong for a period of five years for any client of the
firm or any person who had been a client in the three years
preceding his departure from the firm.

In 1982 the defendant resigned from the firm and
received payment for his share in the partnership. Of the
sum paid, only a nominal amount was stated to be for
goodwill. Soon after leaving the firm, the defendant set up
in practice on his own account in Hong Kong. In his new
practice, the defendant acted for former clients of the
plaintiff firm which then sought to enforce the restrictive
covenant in the partnership agreement. The defendant
contended that (a) the restraint was unreasonable since it
purported to restrict the plaintiff from acting for 90 per
cent of the firm's clients with whom he had no dealings
while he was with the firm, (b) because the firm had paid
only a nominal amount for the goodwill, it was not entitled
to protect it by the restrictive covenant and (c) that the
duration of the restraint was unreasonable.

HELD by the Privy Council: (a) It was reasonable, as
between the parties, for the firm to protect itself against the
appropriation by the defendant of any part of the firm's

goodwill, notwithstanding the division into self-contained departments, (b) it was irrelevant that the defendant had received only a nominal sum for goodwill when he resigned since his share of the goodwill passed back to the firm not by a sale for a cash consideration, but as part of the partnership contract made in 1974 under which he was charged only a nominal sum for goodwill and (c) having regard to the nature of the firm's business and the defendant's position in it, the scope and duration of the restraint was not unreasonable.

British Reinforced Concrete Co. v. *Schelff* (1921): In 1918, a partnership firm engaged in a small business of supplying steel reinforcements for concrete roads contracted to sell to the plaintiff company a patent, the goodwill of the firm and certain stock. The contract contained a restraint clause to the effect that none of the partners would engage in a similar business until three years after the end of the war. One of the partners took employment with a company as manager of its reinforced materials department. The plaintiff company sought an injunction to restrain this breach of the agreement for the sale of the firm's goodwill. HELD: In an agreement for the sale of the goodwill of a business, the reasonableness of the vendor's restrictive undertaking was to be judged by the extent and circumstances of the *business sold* and its need of protection in the hands of the purchaser and not by the extent or range of any business of the purchaser. The restraint clause in the present case was wider than necessary for the reasonable protection of the transferred business in the hands of the plaintiff company. Injunction refused.

10. Reasonableness in contracts regulating trade

Agreements between merchants, manufacturers and others to regulate trade will not be regarded as reasonable unless each party derives some advantage from it. In *English Hop Growers* v. *Dering* (1928) a member of the growers' association was held to be bound by his agreement to deliver his entire crop of hops to the association for onward sale. The arrangement by which the growers eliminated competition between themselves by putting the marketing and price-fixing in the hands of the association divided the overall benefit or loss in any one year fairly amongst the members.

Where experienced businessmen are contracting on an equal footing, it is unlikely that the court will presume to know their interests better than they do themselves. It is otherwise, however, where the parties are not on an equal footing. For example, in *Schroeder Music Publishing Co.* v. *Macaulay* (1974) there was a contract between a music publisher and a young and unknown composer. By this contract, the world copyright in any composition was assigned; royalties would be payable only on those compositions which were exploited; the publisher did not undertake to exploit all compositions submitted to him; the original five years' contract period was to be extended automatically if royalties reached £5,000 in total; the publishers could terminate the agreement at any time by giving one month's notice; and there was no determination provision in favour of the composer. It was held by the House of Lords that this agreement was in unreasonable restraint of trade because of the lack of balance as between the heavy burdens on the composer as compared with the few obligations of the publisher. The quantum of consideration may, as in this case, affect the question of reasonableness. Where the parties have bargained on an equal footing, the restraints must not only give advantages to both parties, but also must not be grossly in excess of what is reasonably necessary to protect the interests under consideration. In *Kores Manufacturing Co.* v. *Kolok Manufacturing Co.* (1959) there was an agreement between the two companies that neither would take on any employee who had worked for the other during the last five years. The companies manufactured the same kinds of products and the purpose of the agreement was to prevent leakage of trade secrets and other confidential information. It was held that the agreement was unreasonable as between the parties.

Esso Petroleum Co. v. *Harper's Garage (Stourport)* (1968): The respondent garage company had entered into what is known as a solus agreement with the appellants in respect of each of the respondents' two garages. By these agreements, the respondents undertook, *inter alia*, to sell

Esso petrol and no other in each of their garages. The first agreement (the Corner Garage agreement) was expressed to remain in force for a period of 21 years from 1 July 1962. In October 1962 the respondents charged the Corner Garage by way of legal mortgage, covenanting to repay the appellants £7,000 with interest by quarterly instalments over a period of 21 years, and undertaking that they would not be entitled to redeem the mortgage otherwise than by payments over the full period of 21 years. The respondents covenanted by the same deed to sell Esso petrol and no other during the continuance of the mortgage.

The second agreement (the Mustow Green agreement) was expressed to remain in force for a period of four years and five months from 1 July 1963. By this agreement, the respondents undertook, *inter alia*, to keep open at all reasonable hours to sell Esso petrol and not to dispose of the garage except to a person willing to enter into a similar solus agreement with the appellant. The appellants appealed to the House of Lords against the Court of Appeal decision that the doctrine of restraint of trade could apply to covenants in mortgage deeds and that the restrictions in the solus agreements and the mortgage deed were unreasonable and, consequently, void. (At the time of the action, the respondents had tendered repayment of the mortgage.) HELD by the House of Lords: Contracts or covenants regulating the trading use made of a particular piece of land are not necessarily outside the doctrine of restraint of trade and the doctrine may apply to mortgages; the solus agreements and the provisions in the mortgage deed relating to trading were within the scope of the doctrine of restraint of trade and must therefore be justified if they are to be enforceable; a restriction is justified only if it is reasonable; the Mustow Green restrictions were reasonable because the period of four years and five months was reasonable, taking into account the advantages derived by the respondents; the Corner Garage agreement and the restrictive provisions in the mortgage deed were unreasonable because the period of duration, 21 years, was unreasonable, and these provisions were, accordingly, unenforceable.

Consequences where a contract is void as being against public policy

11. General consequences

Contracts to oust the jurisdiction, or which are prejudicial to marriage, or which impede parental duties, or which are in restraint of trade, are not illegal in the full sense: they are merely void in so far as public policy is contravened. Contracts of this kind are binding except as to clauses which do not satisfy public policy. Points to note are:

(a) such contracts are severable;
(b) collateral transactions are not necessarily void;
(c) money paid or property transferred is recoverable.

12. Severance

Although it is said that contracts of this class are severable, there are two different senses in which the expression is used. First, there is severance where a particular provision is declared to be void and, thus, severed from the rest of the contract which remains unaffected. In the second sense there is severance if a restrictive clause contains, in effect, several distinct promises some of which offend against public policy and some of which are reasonable; in such cases, the court will sever the void elements from the reasonable elements, which will then be enforced. In *Attwood* v. *Lamont* (1920), the separate elements in the employee's promise could not be severed because they merely added up to the totality of the employer's business, which he sought to protect as a whole by the restrictive provision. This case should be compared with *Goldsoll* v. *Goldman* (1915), where the question of severance arose at two levels,

(a) as between imitation and real jewellery, and
(b) as between several specified geographical areas.

The Court of Appeal found itself able to order severance in both these respects because:

(a) the promise with respect to real jewellery could be regarded as quite distinct from that with regard to imitation jewellery, and
(b) the promise with regard to the different geographical areas

could be regarded as a set of separated promises, each pertaining to a different area.

Attwood v. *Lamont* (1920): L, who was a tailor's cutter, entered a contract of employment as head of the tailoring department of A's general outfitting shop. Under the contract, L covenanted not to engage in 'the trade of a tailor, dressmaker, general draper, milliner, hatter, haberdasher, gentlemen's, ladies' or children's outfitter at any place within a radius of 10 miles of (A's) place of business'. HELD by the Court of Appeal: **(a)** No part of this clause could be severed because it constituted a single covenant for the protection of A's entire business. It must stand or fall in its unaltered form. **(b)** The clause as a whole was wider than necessary in the circumstances and was void.

Goldsoll v. *Goldman* (1915): The parties had entered a restrictive agreement with the purpose of ending competition between them. The plaintiffs were dealers in jewellery (substantially imitation jewellery) and the defendant undertook that he would not for a period of two years be concerned directly or indirectly in the business of real or imitation jewellery, 'in the county of London, England, Scotland, Ireland, Wales, or any part of the United Kingdom of Great Britain and Ireland and the Isle of Man or in France, the United States of America, Russia or Spain, or within 25 miles of the Potsdamer Strasse, Berlin or St Stefan's Kirche, Vienna'. HELD by the Court of Appeal: **(a)** The area of restraint was unreasonable and should be severed so that it is limited to the United Kingdom and the Isle of Man; **(b)** the restraint with regard to real jewellery was unreasonable and should be severed from the restraint with regard to imitation jewellery, which was reasonable; and **(c)** after severance in these two respects, the restraint covenant, as so limited, was enforceable against the defendant.

13. Collateral transactions
Where a contract is void, in part or in whole, as being against public policy, collateral transactions remain unaffected.

14. Recovery of money

In *Hermann* v. *Charlesworth* (1905) it was held that money paid under a marriage brokage contract was recoverable upon total failure of consideration. It would seem to follow that money paid, or property transferred, under a contract merely void as contravening public policy is always recoverable.

Progress test 12

1. Which kinds of contracts are void at common law as being against public policy?

2. Is it possible for contracting parties to make a binding agreement to refrain from submitting to the courts **(a)** any dispute on a matter of law, or **(b)** any dispute on a matter of the construction of a document?

3. Give some examples of contracts which are considered to strike at the institution of marriage.

4. Into which classes can contracts in restraint of trade be divided?

5. In what circumstances will a contract in restraint of trade be upheld by the court?

6. What is the rule as to consideration in contracts in restraint of trade?

7. Consider the concept of 'reasonableness' in connection with a restraint clause in a contract between employer and employee. Compare this with 'reasonableness' in other types of restraint agreement.

8. Consider the 'reasonableness' of restraint clauses which limit or prevent persons from being employed in a particular kind of work. Mention some decided cases in your answer.

9. Distinguish between the legal consequences of **(a)** a contract which is void as being against public policy, and **(b)** an illegal contract.

10. What do you understand by 'severance' in contracts which contain a void clause?

11. A is about to drive from London to Brighton in a vintage motor car. B bets A that he (A) will not reach Brighton without a breakdown. According to the agreement, if A reaches Brighton without a breakdown, B will pay £100 to B. Is this a wager? Give reasons for your answer.

12. F enters into a written agreement with G. The agreement includes the following clauses:

(a) 'This agreement is binding in honour only and is not intended to give rise to legal rights and obligations.'
(b) 'The contracting parties hereby agree that, in the event of a dispute as to the interpretation of this agreement, no recourse shall be had to any court of law.'

Comment on the validity of these clauses.

13. H, who is married to J, agrees to marry K, if and when he, H, can get a divorce from J. Is the agreement between H and K in any way binding on the parties?

14. L entered into a contract under seal whereby he (L) became articled to M, a chartered accountant. There was a clause in the agreement by which L covenanted not to be concerned in any chartered accountant's business within six miles of M's office during his (L's) lifetime. L wishes to know whether the restraint is binding on him. Advise him.

15. N sold his tobacconist retail shop to Universal Tobaccos Ltd, a company owning a chain of tobacco shops throughout the country. In the agreement of sale, N covenanted not to engage in the trade of tobacconist within 10 miles of any of the branch shops of Universal Tobaccos Ltd. N has opened a new tobacco shop 100 miles from the one he sold to the company, but within ten miles of one of their numerous branches. The company now wish to take action against N to enforce the restraint. Advise the company.

16. O entered a contract under seal by which P, a goldsmith, undertook to teach him the trade of goldsmith during a period of five years. One of the terms of the agreement was that O should not, after the five-year period, engage in the trade of goldsmith or jeweller within 50 miles of P's workshop. One year after the agreement, P dismissed O, claiming that he was not bound to continue to teach O, because the contract was void as being in restraint of trade. Advise O as to whether he had an action against P for breach of contract.

13

Form: contracts of guarantee and sale of land

Contracts of guarantee

1. Statute of Frauds 1677

Section 4 of the Statute of Frauds 1677 provides that, 'No action shall be brought whereby to charge the defendant upon any special promise to answer for the debt, default or miscarriage of another person unless the agreement upon which such action be brought, or some memorandum or note thereof, shall be in writing and signed by the party to be charged therewith or some other person thereunto by him lawfully authorized.'

Section 4 originally governed contracts for the disposition of interests in land, but this part of the section was repealed and replaced by s. 40(1) of the Law of Property Act 1925.

2. Law of Property Act 1925

Section 40(1) of the Law of Property Act 1925 provides that, 'No action shall be brought whereby to charge the defendant upon any special promise to answer for the debt default or miscarriage of another person unless the agreement upon which such action be brought or some memorandum or note thereof, shall be in writing and signed by the party to be charged therewith or some other person thereunto by him lawfully authorized.'

3. Contracts of guarantee

A contract of guarantee is made where one party, the guarantor, promises to answer for the 'debt default, or miscarriage of another person'. The expression 'debt default or miscarriage' covers the guarantee of a contractual liability or a tortious liability. In *Kirkham* v. *Marter* (1819), Abbott CJ said that the word 'miscarriage' seems to mean 'that species of wrongful act for the consequences of which the law would make the party civilly responsible'. In most cases, however, the liability guaranteed is a contractual debt.

The obligation must be that 'of another person'. This predicates the existence of a primary obligation to which the guarantee is secondary. There must, therefore, be three parties involved in the overall transaction. Any promise to undertake a sole liability is outside the statute. *See*, for example, *Birkmyr* v. *Darnell* (1704) and *Mountstephen* v. *Lakeman* (1871).

4. Three parties

In any contract of guarantee, there is a principal creditor, a principal debtor and a guarantor. Thus, where G guarantees D's debt to C, there is a triangular relationship in which three collateral contracts may be distinguished:

(a) As between C and D there is a contract out of which the guaranteed debt arises.

(b) As between G and C there is the contract by which G makes himself secondarily liable to pay D's debt. G promises that he will pay D's debt in the event of D's default.

(c) As between G and D there is always a contract by which D indemnifies G. Thus, if G pays according to the guarantee, then D will be liable to G. This contract is always implied if it is not expressed between the parties.

5. Indemnity

A contract of indemnity must be distinguished from a contract of guarantee. There are the following points of difference:

(a) A guarantor makes himself secondarily liable.

(b) A person giving an indemnity makes himself primarily liable.

The distinction depends entirely upon the intention of the parties.

In *Birkmyr* v. *Darnell* (1704), it was expressed that if two people enter a shop and one buys goods and the other says to the seller: 'Let him have the goods, I will be your paymaster' or 'I will see you paid', then that other buyer is on his own account. The transaction is outside the statute. *Mountstephen* v. *Lakeman* (1871) shows clearly that the statute does not apply unless there is a principal debtor whose debt has been guaranteed. In this case the surveyor of a local authority proposed to a builder that he should construct some drains. The authority itself had not ordered the work. The builder asked how he would be paid and the surveyor replied, 'do the work and I will see you paid'. The builder failed in his action to recover the price of the work from the authority. The authority had not ordered the work. The surveyor's promise was outside the statute.

6. Note or memorandum

Any contract of guarantee, or any contract for the sale or other disposition of land or any interest in land, must be evidenced by a sufficient note or memorandum, or the agreement will be unenforceable. Points to note are:

(a) The memorandum need not be in any special form. It may consist of several documents provided there is evidence to connect them: *Timmins* v. *Moreland Street Property* (1958). The memorandum may have been made at any time after the contract was made.

(b) The memorandum must be signed by the defendant or his agent.

(c) In order that there be a sufficient memorandum there must be a signed admission that there was a contract and a signed admission of what that contract was: *Thirkell* v. *Cambi* (1919). Where a memorandum is expressed to be 'subject to contract', it does not satisfy the requirements of s. 40 because such a memorandum does not contain any recognition or admission of the existence of a contract: *Tiverton Estates* v. *Wearwell* (1975).

(d) The memorandum must contain the material terms of the agreement. Thus included are: (*i*) *the parties*: the parties must be named or described sufficiently in the note; (*ii*) *the subject-matter of the agreement*: e.g. in the case of a lease, the address of the premises, the duration of the lease, the rent to be paid.

Contracts governed by the Law of Property (Miscellaneous Provisions) Act 1989

7. The requirement of writing

A contract for the sale or other disposition of an interest in land can only be made in writing and only by incorporating all the terms which the parties have expressly agreed in one document or, where contracts are exchanged, in each: Law of Property (Miscellaneous Provisions) Act 1989, s. 2(1).

8. Incorporation of terms

The terms may be incorporated either by being set out in that document or by reference to some other document: s. 2(2).

9. The requirement of a signature

The document incorporating the terms or, where contracts are exchanged, one of the documents incorporating them (but not necessarily the same one) must be signed by or on behalf of each party to the contract: s. 2(3).

10. Rectification

Where a contract for the sale or other disposition of an interest in land satisfies the conditions of this section by reason only of the rectification of one or more documents in pursuance of an order of a court, the contract will come into being, or be deemed to have come into being, at such time as may be specified in the order: s. 2(4).

11. Exceptions

Section 2 does not apply to short leases, auction sales and contracts under the Financial Services Act 1986.

Progress test 13

1. Write a note on the Statute of Frauds 1677.

2. What is the difference between a contract of guarantee and a contract of indemnity?

3. What are the proper contents of a 'note or memorandum'?

4. Must a contract for sale of land be made in writing?

5. Which document or documents must be signed by or on behalf of each party to a contract for sale of land?

6. Does the Law of Property (Miscellaneous Provisions) Act 1989 apply to auction sales?

14
Privity of contract

1. The doctrine of privity

A contract creates rights and obligations only between the parties to it. A contract does not confer rights on a stranger, nor does it impose obligations on a stranger. It is a fundamental principle of the common law, therefore, that no person can sue or be sued on a contract unless he is a party to it.

Per Lord Haldane in *Dunlop* v. *Selfridge* (1915): 'Our law knows nothing of a *jus quaesitum tertio* arising by way of contract.' (Third party rights.)

> *Scruttons* v. *Midland Silicones* (1962): There was a contract between X and Y for the carriage of a cargo of goods belonging to Y. There was another contract between X and Z for the unloading of the goods from X's ship. The goods were damaged through Z's negligence during unloading. Y claimed damages from Z. Z relied on an exemption clause in the contract between X and Y. HELD by the House of Lord: Z was a stranger to the contract between X and Y, and could not rely on the exemption clause. Z's defence therefore failed.

2. Rights and benefits compared

Although a contract cannot confer a substantive right upon a stranger, it is possible for a contract to confer a benefit upon him. In these circumstances it has been held that the stranger cannot sue in the event of his not receiving the benefit: *Tweddle* v. *Atkinson* (1861). But the matter is now open to doubt. In *Woodar* v. *Wimpey* (1980) Lord Scarman said that he hoped the House of Lords would have the opportunity to reconsider the 'unjust rule' in *Tweddle* v.

Atkinson. The Law Revision Committee recommended in 1937
(Cmd. 5449) that 'where a contract by its express terms purports
to confer a benefit directly on a third party it shall be enforceable
by the third party in his own name.' In *Beswick* v. *Beswick* (1968),
Lord Denning MR said that 'Where a contract is made for the
benefit of a third person who has a legitimate interest to enforce
it, it can be enforced by the third person in the name of the
contracting party or jointly with him or, if he refuses to join, by
adding him as a defendant.' Accordingly, a person specified to
benefit from a contract to which he is a stranger may have a
procedural right of action, notwithstanding that he has no
substantive rights under the contract. However, when *Beswick* v.
Beswick was heard on appeal to the House of Lords in 1967, their
Lordships declined to deal with the point because it was not
essential in that case. But Lord Reid said that if one had to
contemplate a further long period of parliamentary
procrastination, the House of Lords might have to deal with the
matter.

In *Woodar* v. *Wimpey* (1980) the House of Lords held that a
party who had broken a promise to pay a sum of money to a third
party was liable for nominal damages only.

Dunlop Pneumatic Tyre Co. v. Selfridge & Co. (1915): There
was a contract dated 12 October 1911 by which Dew & Co.
agreed to purchase a quantity of tyres and other goods from
Dunlop. By this contract, Dew & Co. undertook not to sell
at prices below the current list prices except to genuine
trade customers, to whom they could sell at a discount. The
contract provided that such discount would be substantially
less than the discount that Dews themselves were to receive
from Dunlop. Where such sales took place, Dews
undertook, as the agents of Dunlop, to obtain from the
customer a written undertaking that he similarly would
observe the terms so undertaken to be observed by
themselves. On 2 January 1912 Selfridges agreed to
purchase goods made by Dunlop from Dew & Co., and gave
the required undertaking to resell at the current list prices.
Selfridges broke this agreement and Dunlop sued for
breach of contract. HELD by the House of Lords: The
agreement of 2 January 1912 was between Selfridge and

Dew only, and that Dunlop was not a party to that contract because no consideration moved from them to Selfridges.

Note

This case illustrates the general common law rule as to privity of contract but cases of this kind are now governed by statute.

Beswick v. *Beswick* (1968): In March 1962 a coal merchant, Peter Beswick, agreed to sell his business to his nephew John in return for the following undertakings: **(a)** that John should pay to Peter the weekly sum of £6 10s during the rest of Peter's life; **(b)** that, in the event of Peter's wife surviving him, John should pay her an annuity of £5 weekly. Peter died intestate in November 1963 and in 1964 his widow took out letters of administration. After Peter's death, John made one payment of £5 only to the widow, refusing to make any further payments. The widow, who brought this action as administratrix of her husband's estate and also in her personal capacity, claimed arrears of the annuity and specific performance of the contract between Peter and John.

It was held by the Court of Appeal that she was entitled, as administratrix, to specific performance of the contract. Lord Denning and Danckwerts LJ held further that she could succeed under s. 56(1) of the Law of Property Act 1925. (Section 56(1) provides that: 'A person may take an immediate or other interest in land or other property, or the benefit of any condition, right of entry, covenant or agreement over or respecting land or other property, although he may not be named as a party to the conveyance or other instrument.' The Act further provides, by s. 205, that: 'unless the context otherwise requires, the following expressions have the meaning hereby assigned to them respectively, that is to say . . . "Property includes any thing in action, and any interest in real or personal property." ' John appealed to the House of Lords. HELD by the House of Lords: The widow, as administratrix, was entitled to specific performance of the agreement to which her deceased husband was a contracting party; but the statute gave her no right of action in her personal capacity against John.

In *Beswick* v. *Beswick*, Lord Hodson said: 'Section 56 had as long ago as 1937 received consideration by the Law Revision Committee presided over by Lord Wright, then Master of the Rolls, and containing a number of illustrious lawyers. The committee was called on to report specially on consideration including the attitude of the common law towards the *jus quaesitum tertio* . . . By its report (Cmd. 5449) it impliedly rejected the revolutionary view, for it recommended that — "Where a contract by its express terms purports to confer a benefit directly on a third party, it shall be enforceable by the third party in his own name". Like my noble and learned friend, Lord Reid, whose opinion I have had the opportunity of reading, I am of opinion that s. 56, one of the 25 sections of the Act of 1925 appearing under the cross-heading "Conveyances and other instruments", does not have the revolutionary effect claimed for it, appearing as it does in a consolidation Act. I think, as he does, that the context does otherwise require a limited meaning to be given to the word "property" in the section.'

The rule that consideration must move from the promisee is closely related to the wider doctrine of privity of contract. The two common law principles combine to produce a rule that no person can sue on a simple contract unless **(a)** he is a party, and **(b)** he gave consideration to the defendant in return for his promise.

3. Exceptions to the privity doctrine

Although the doctrine of privity of contract has been regarded as fundamental to the English law of contract, there are, nevertheless, circumstances where there is conflict with other principles. This gives rise to certain exceptions:

(a) *Law of Property Act 1925*. Section 56(1) of the Act provides that, 'A person may take an immediate or other interest in land or other property or the benefit of any condition, right of entry, covenant or agreement over or respecting land or other property although he may not be named as a party to the conveyance or other instrument', and by s. 205, 'property' includes 'anything in action, and any interest in real or personal property'. Although the plain meaning of the words used in these two sections appears to restore the common law rule prevailing before *Tweddle* v. *Atkinson* (1861), dicta and decisions show that this is not the effect of the provision: *Re Sinclair's Life Policy* (1938); *Re Millers Agreement, Uniacke* v. *A.-G.* (1947) and *Beswick* v. *Beswick* (1968).

(b) *The law of agency*. Where the relationship of principal and agent exists, the principal is bound by contracts entered into by the agent with third parties. Moreover, where an agent contracts without authority on behalf of a named principal, the person named as principal may ratify the contract so that it becomes binding as between himself and the third party. Also, where an agent contracts with a third party, without disclosing the existence of his principal, a contract is created between the principal and the third party.

(c) *Trusts*. Where, as a result of a binding contract, a person agrees to act as a trustee, the beneficiaries under the trust (not being parties to the contract) will have an action against the trustee in the event of a breach of trust. This is merely an apparent exception to the *common law* doctrine of privity, because the rights of the beneficiaries are equitable.

Where a contract confers a mere benefit upon a stranger, the courts are reluctant to imply a trust unless there is a clear intention to create a trust; thus, the doctrine of constructive trusts does not generally operate as a method of evading the privity rule.

(d) *Negotiable instruments*. In the event of the dishonour of a bill of exchange, the holder in due course may sue any prior party to the bill who has signed as drawer, endorser or acceptor. This right is in addition to the contractual right against the person who transferred the bill to him for value: e.g. where X sells goods to Y and takes a bill of exchange as conditional payment, if the bill is dishonoured, X may either sue Y or any prior party to the bill, or he may sue Y for the price of the goods, i.e. he may either sue on the bill or sue in contract. *See* Chapter 15.

(e) *Restrictive covenants*. A restrictive covenant is a promise under seal made between neighbouring landowners by which the promiser binds himself not to use his land in some stipulated manner. A restrictive covenant is enforceable as follows:

> (*i*) At common law a restrictive covenant is enforceable as between the covenantee and covenantor in the same way as any specialty contract.
>
> (*ii*) In equity the benefit of a restrictive covenant may generally be enforced by an assignee of the covenantee.

(*iii*) In equity the burden of a restrictive covenant may devolve upon an assignee of the covenantor.

Although restrictive covenants may 'run with the land', they do not run with goods. It is unlikely that the Privy Council decisions in the *Strathcona* case (1926), will be followed. (In that case it was held that a purchaser of a ship was bound by the terms of a charter-party between the vendor and a third party.)

(f) *Assignment*. Where A is under a contractual obligation to B, and B assigns his contractual right to C, it may be possible for C to sue A on his promise to B. *See* Chapter 15.

(g) *Guarantor's right of subrogation*. Where a guarantor has paid the principal creditor, he is subrogated to the rights of the principal creditor against the debtor, i.e. the guarantor 'stands in the principal creditor's shoes'.

4. The duty of care

Where a contracting party owes a duty of care to the other contracting party, a breach of contract may also constitute a breach of the duty of care. Where this is the case, the aggrieved party may sue for damages in contract or in tort. *See Hedley Byrne* v. *Heller* (1963) HL and *Esso* v. *Marden* (1976) CA (8:**15**). The question arises whether a person who is not a party to the contract may be owed a duty of care, so that a breach on the part of one of the contracting parties will constitute a breach of the duty of care, giving a third party the right to sue the contracting party for damages in tort.

Damages for tort are not assessed in the same way as they are for breach of contract. The purpose of damages for breach of contract is to put the claimant into the position in which he would have been had there been no breach: the purpose of damages for tort is to put the claimant into the position in which he was before the tort was committed. The effect of this difference as between contract and tort is that certain kinds of economic or financial loss which may be recoverable for breach of contract are not recoverable in an action in tort: *Muirhead* v. *Industrial Tank Specialities* (1986) CA (*see* **5** below).

5. The *Junior Books* case

This case plays an important part in the development of the law governing third-party claims in negligence.

Junior Books Ltd v. *Veitchi Ltd* (1983) as main contractors: Junior Books Ltd entered into a contract with O Ltd, as main contractors for the construction of a factory. Junior Books Ltd through their architect nominated Veitchi Ltd as specialist subcontractor to lay the flooring in the production area of the factory. Building work was completed and the floor laid by May 1970. In 1972 Junior Books Ltd noticed that cracks had appeared in the flooring and they brought this action against Veitchi Ltd contending that there was bad workmanship in the laying of the flooring and that they were liable in negligence. Junior Books Ltd claimed damages for negligence under the following heads: replacing the flooring, £50,000; storage of books during the replacement works, £1,000; movement of machinery, £2,000; loss of profit due to closure of premises, £45,000; non-productive wages paid, £30,000; overheads, £16,000; and cost of investigatory work, £3,000. HELD by the House of Lords: **(a)** There was between Veitchi Ltd and Junior Books Ltd (building owner and nominated subcontractor) a sufficient proximity of relationship as to give rise to a duty of care owed by Veitchi Ltd, the nominated subcontractors, to Junior Books Ltd, the building owners; and **(b)** the duty of care included the avoidance of causing economic loss arising from defects in the work. There was nothing to reduce or limit the duty of care to avoid causing physical loss only.

The *Junior Books* decision is now regarded as unsatisfactory on the question of proximity and also with regard to recovery of financial loss. Lord Fraser said in *Junior Books*, 'The proximity between the parties is extremely close, falling only just short of a direct contractual relationship. The injury to Juniors Books was direct and foreseeable result of negligence by Veitchi. Junior Books, through their architect, nominated Veitchi as specialist subcontractors and they must therefore have relied upon their skill and knowledge.'

The question regarding economic loss was expressed by Lord Russell as whether the law 'extends the duty of care beyond a duty to prevent harm being done by faulty work to a duty to avoid such faults being present in the work itself.'

For reasons which do not appear, Veitchi did not claim for breach of contract against the main contractor.

The *Junior Books* decision has been much criticized in regard to both questions arising, namely, proximity and economic loss.

In *D. & F. Estates* v. *Church Commissioners for England* (1989) HL it was said that the factual circumstances relating to proximity and duty of care were 'unique', and that the decision in *Junior Books* on this point has no general application in tort and should not affect the further development of the law. In the *D. & F. Estates* case the House of Lords firmly stated their preference for the principles state by Lord Brandon in his dissenting speech in *Junior Books*. *See* also *Van Oppen* v. *Clerk to the Bedford Charity Trustees* (1990) and *Murphy* v. *Brentwood District Council* (1990).

It is quite clear from the above authorities that any party wishing to claim to recover pure economic or financial loss must do so in a claim in contract. There is no such claim available in tort even where the claimant for whatever reason is not able or willing to base his claim in contract. *See* particularly *D. & F. Estates* v. *Church Commissioners for England* (1988) HL.

In *Simaan General Contracting Co.* v. *Pilkington Glass Ltd* (No. 2) (1988), the defendants were nominated suppliers of special glass to be installed into a building to be constructed by the plaintiff main contractor. Accordingly, the special glass was sold and delivered to one of the plaintiff's subcontractors, who had undertaken to install it. There was no contract between the plaintiff and the defendant. When the glass was delivered, it was found not to be of the colour specified in the main contract and in the contract of sale to the subcontractor. As a result, the building owner refused payment to the plaintiff main contractor, causing a financial loss to the plaintiff. It was held by the Court of Appeal that the defendant's breach of contract did not give the plaintiffs a right to recover their economic loss in an action of tort.

A further example of restriction on the scope of *Junior Books* is to be found in *Muirhead* v. *Industrial Tank Specialities Ltd* (1986) CA in which the plaintiff was a wholesale fish merchant. He wished to expand his business by the purchase of lobsters in the summer, storing them alive in a large tank and selling them on the Christmas market when prices were higher. In the furtherance of this scheme, the plaintiff entered into a contract for the purchase of pumps. The pumps failed because their electric motors were defective. The plaintiff could not succeed against the manufacturer of electric motors in contracts, for there was no contract between them. It was held by the Court of Appeal that a manufacturer of defective goods could be liable in negligence for the economic loss suffered by an ultimate purchaser if there was a very close proximity of relationship between the parties and the ultimate purchaser had placed real reliance on the manufacturer. However, in the present case there was no such proximity and reliance by the plaintiff on the manufacturer. The manufacturer was, accordingly, not liable for the economic loss suffered by the plaintiff. It was further held that whether damages were recoverable in tort for the loss of the stock of lobsters depended on whether damage *of that type* was reasonably foreseeable by the manufacturers. The plaintiff succeeded in his claim in tort with regard to the physical damage done, namely the value of the lobsters which had died in the tank, and also financial loss which was suffered in consequence of the physical damage. This covered loss of profits which would have been earned upon the sale of those lobsters. A further claim for the whole economic loss suffered by the plaintiff, namely for loss of profits that he would have made had the installation not been defective, was rejected by the Court of Appeal.

Progress test 14

1. 'Our law knows nothing of a *jus quaesitum tertio* arising by way of contract.' Comment on this statement.

2. State in simple terms the doctrine of privity of contract.

3. Distinguish between a right and a benefit conferred by a contract on a stranger.

4. Mention some exceptions to the doctrine of privity of contract.

5. In what circumstances is a restrictive covenant enforceable?

6.   How has the court interpreted s. 56(1) of the Law of Property Act 1925?

7.   Explain the significance of the *Junior Books* case to the doctrine of privity of contract.

8.   A contract was made between A and B. One of the terms of the contract was that B should pay £100 to C. B now refuses to pay C, and A declines to sue B. Advise C as to whether he can claim against B.

9.   E enters a contract with F. E contracted, with full authority, as G's agent, but he did not inform F that he was an agent. F has now broken his agreement. Can G sue F for breach of contract?

15
Assignment

Assignment of contractual rights

1. Contractual rights as a form of property

A right under a contract has a certain economic value and may, therefore, be regarded as a personal right of property. In property law, contractual rights belong to a class known as choses in action or things in action.

2. Choses in action

'Chose in action' has been defined as 'an expression used to describe all personal rights of property which can only be claimed or enforced by action, and not by taking physical possession': per Channell J in *Torkington* v. *Magee* (1903). Choses in action may be legal or equitable, according to whether they are founded on legal or equitable rules.

(a) Legal choses in action include debts and other contractual rights, company shares, insurance policies, bills of lading, patents, and copyrights.
(b) Equitable choses in action include rights under a trust and legacies.

3. Assignment of choses in action

A valid assignment of a chose in action may take place in one of three ways:

(a) statutory (or legal) assignment;
(b) equitable assignment;
(c) assignment by operation of the law.

Note
The doctrine of privity of contract prevents any assignment at common law of a contractual right.

Statutory assignment

4. Law of Property Act 1925, s. 136
A statutory assignment is one which complies with the provisions of s. 136 of the LPA 1925. Statutory assignments are sometimes called legal assignments. Section 136 provides that:

'Any absolute assignment by writing under the hand of the assignor (not purporting to be by way of charge only) of any debt or other legal thing in action, of which express notice in writing has been given to the debtor, trustee or other person from whom the assignor would have been entitled to claim such debt or thing in action, is effectual in law (subject to equities having priority over the right of the assignee) to pass and transfer from the date of such notice:

(a) the legal right to such debt or thing in action;
(b) the legal and other remedies for the same; and
(c) the power to give a good discharge for the same without the concurrence of the assignor.'

5. Analysis of s. 136
In order to comply with s. 136, the assignment must

(a) be in writing;
(b) be signed by the assignor;
(c) be absolute, i.e. the entire chose must be assigned and not merely a part of it;
(d) not purport to be by way of charge only; and
(e) be accompanied or followed by express notice in writing to the debtor or other person from whom the assignor would have been entitled to claim the chose in action.

Further points to note are:

(a) The expression legal thing in action in its context in s. 136, means lawful thing in action. Thus, the section applies to equitable as well as to legal choses in action.

(b) It is not necessary that the assignee should have given consideration to the assignor.

(c) The assignment takes effect from the date when written notice was given to the debtor.

(d) Statutory assignments are subject to the equities (as indeed are equitable assignments). This means that:

    (*i*) any defence or counter-claim which would have been available to the debtor against the assignor at the time of notice of the assignment is available against the assignee;

    (*ii*) if there have been two or more assignments of the same chose in action, the rights of the second and subsequent assignees are postponed to the first.

Equitable assignment

6. Equity looks to the intent rather than to the form

If, in any transaction, there was an intent to assign a chose in action, but s. 136 was not complied with, there may be a valid assignment in equity.

Note ─────────────────────────────────

There is no statutory assignment, e.g. where the assignment is not in writing, or where the assignment is not signed by the assignor, or where the assignment is of part only of a chose of action, or where no written notice was given to the debtor. In all these circumstances there may be a valid equitable assignment.

7. Equitable assignments of equitable choses in action

Equity has always allowed the assignment of equitable choses in action so that the assignee can bring an action in his own name without joining the assignor. Note that:

(a) The assignment is subject to the equities. Thus, although notice to the person liable is not essential, it is highly desirable, for where there are two or more assignees, they take priority each according to the date on which notice was given.

(b) Consideration is necessary unless the assignment is complete and perfect, i.e. unless all necessary formalities are completed according to the nature of the equitable right assigned.

8. Equitable assignments of legal choses in action

Provided the assignee can show that there was an intention to assign a legal chose in action, there may be a good equitable assignment. Points to note are:

(a) The assignment is subject to the equities.

(b) The assignee must join the assignor in any action he takes against the debtor. (If the assignor refuses to be co-plaintiff, he will be made a co-defendant.)

(c) The assignee must show that he gave consideration to the assignor.

Note
_____

These rules do not apply where title has passed to the assignee.

_____

Assignment by operation of law

9. Automatic assignment

An involuntary assignment of choses in action will take place automatically on the death or bankruptcy of the owner.

10. Assignment on death

The general rule is that all contractual rights and obligations pass to the personal representatives of a party who dies. Thus, the personal representatives may sue or be sued on a contract to which the deceased party was privy. The rule does not, however, apply to contracts of personal services.

11. Assignment on bankruptcy

The principal aim of bankruptcy law is to provide for a fair distribution of the debtor's property between the creditors. By s. 306 of the Insolvency Act 1986, a bankrupt's estate will vest in the trustee of that estate immediately on his appointment taking effect or, in the case of the official receiver, on his becoming trustee.

Assignment of contractual obligations

12. Obligations cannot be assigned

There can be no effective assignment at common law or in equity of contractual obligations without the creditor's consent. The need for the creditor's consent means, in effect, that the assignment may be achieved only through a new contract. This process is known as *novation*.

For example, a partner in a firm will usually wish to assign his liabilities to the firm as newly constituted on his retirement. Any such assignment of a liability is ineffective unless the creditor is a party. Novation is a tri-partite agreement.

13. Vicarious performance

Where A is under a contractual obligation to perform services of a personal nature for B, A cannot be discharged if the services are vicariously performed by C. B is entitled to the personal performance by A.

> *Robson and Sharpe* v. *Drummond* (1831): A coachbuilder contracted to hire out, maintain and repaint a carriage. He purported to assign this contractual obligation. HELD: There could be no vicarious performance of this obligation. The other party was entitled to the taste and judgment of the coachbuilder.

Where, however, the obligation does not involve a personal element, the law permits vicarious performance on the principle that *qui facit per alium facit per se* (he who does anything by another does it himself): *British Waggon Co.* v. *Lea & Co.* (1880).

Note

Where a party arranges for his obligations to be vicariously performed, he is not thereby discharged. He remains liable until the vicarious performance is complete. For example, where X is under an obligation to Y, and X arranges with Z for Z to perform the obligation, X is not discharged merely because Z has promised performance. He remains liable until Z's performance is complete.

Negotiable instruments

14. Negotiability

Negotiability is a characteristic which should be distinguished from assignability. It is a characteristic which has been conferred on certain instruments, mainly bills of exchange and promissory notes.

A cheque is a particular kind of bill of exchange.

15. Definitions

The following definitions are taken from the Bills of Exchange Act 1882:

(a) 'A bill of exchange is an unconditional order in writing, addressed by one person to another, signed by the person giving it, requiring the person to whom it is addressed to pay on demand or at a fixed or determinable future time a sum certain in money to or to the order of a specified person, or to bearer': s. 3(1).

(b) 'A cheque is a bill of exchange drawn on a banker payable on demand': s. 73.

(c) 'A promissory note is an unconditional promise in writing made by one person to another signed by the maker, engaging to pay, on demand or at a fixed or determinable future time, a sum certain in money, to, or to the order of, a specified person or to bearer': s. 83(1).

16. Meaning of negotiability

The special legal qualities of a negotiable instrument are as follows:

(a) *Transfer of ownership.* The rights of ownership of the instrument are transferred thus:

    (*i*) where the instrument is drawn payable to order, or is specially endorsed, ownership is transferred by endorsement and delivery to the transferee;

    (*ii*) where the instrument is payable to bearer or endorsed in blank, ownership is transferred by mere delivery.

(b) *Free from the equities.* Where an instrument is negotiated, the transferee takes the rights of ownership free from the equities, provided he is a holder in due course.

(c) *Holder may sue in own name.* The holder of a negotiable instrument may, in the event of dishonour, sue all prior parties to the instrument, i.e. the drawer, the acceptor and all persons who transferred the instrument by endorsement and delivery.

17. Holder in due course

'A holder in due course is a holder who has taken the bill, complete and regular on the face of it, under the following conditions, namely:

(a) that he became the holder of it before it was overdue, and without notice that it had been previously dishonoured, if such was the fact;

(b) that he took the bill in good faith and for value, and that at any time the bill was negotiated to him he had no notice of any defect in the title of the person who negotiated it': Bills of Exchange Act 1882, s. 29(1).

Progress test 15

1. What is a chose in action?

2. On what grounds does the common law forbid an assignment of a chose in action?

3. What are the requirements of a statutory assignment of a contractual right? Is consideration necessary?

4. How may an equitable assignment of a chose in action take place?

5. Is it possible to assign a contractual obligation?

6. Define a bill of exchange.

7. What are the main characteristics of a negotiable instrument?

8. What is a holder in due course?

9. A owes B the sum of £50. B owes A the sum of £20. B assigns his right to the £50 to C, and the assignment satisfies the requirements of s. 136 of the Law of Property Act 1925. Comment on C's rights against A.

10. D owes E the sum of £100. E assigns his rights against D to F by way of gift. The assignment is in writing, but E has not signed it. Written notice has been given to D. F wishes to know whether he can claim against D for the £100. Advise him.

16
Discharge

The end of a contract

1. Discharge of obligations

Every contractual obligation gives rise to a corresponding contractual right. Thus, where the obligation of one party is discharged, the corresponding right of the other party is extinguished. Where all obilgations which arose under a contract are discharged — and all rights are thus extinguished — the contract is said to be discharged.

2. Ways in which a contract may be discharged

A contract may be discharged in any of the following ways:

(a) performance;
(b) agreement;
(c) acceptance of breach;
(d) frustration.

Discharge by performance

3. Performance must be complete

A contractual obligation is discharged by a complete performance of the undertaking. The promisee is entitled to the benefit of complete performance exactly according to the promisor's undertaking. Where the promisor is unable or unwilling to give more than a partial performance, the general rule is that there is no discharge.

The practical effect of this rule is that where a contract provides for payment by one party after performance by the other, no action to recover payment may be maintained until the performance is complete. Nor will an action for a proportional payment be available on the basis of *quantum meruit*.

Cutter v. *Powell* (1795): The plaintiff sued as administratrix of her deceased husband's estate. The defendant had, in Jamaica, subscribed and delivered to T. Cutter, the intestate, a note as follows: 'Ten days after the ship *Governor Parry*, myself master, arrives at Liverpool, I promise to pay to Mr T. Cutter the sum of 30 guineas, provided he proceeds, continues and does his duty as second mate in the said ship from hence to the port of Liverpool, Kingston, 31 July 1793.' The *Governor Parry* sailed from Kingston on 2 August 1793 and arrived in Liverpool on 9 October. But T. Cutter died on 20 September, until which date he did his duty as second mate. The plaintiff claimed payment on a *quantum meruit*. HELD: According to the express terms of the contract, the sum of 30 guineas was payable only on completion of the whole voyage. A term to the effect that proportional payments should be made in a case of partial performance could not be implied. The plaintiff could not, therefore, succeed in her claim on a *quantum meruit*. Per Ashurst J: 'Here the intestate was by the terms of his contract to perform a given duty before he could call upon the defendant to pay him any thing; it was a condition precedent, without performing which the defendant is not liable. And it seems to me to conclude the question: the intestate did not perform the contract on his part; he was not indeed to blame for not doing it; but still as this was a condition precedent, and as he did not perform it, his representative is not entitled to recover.'

Sumpter v. *Hedges* (1898): S agreed to erect certain buildings on H's land in consideration of a stipulated sum. When the buildings were only half finished, S ran out of money and could not complete them. H refused to pay S at all and S brought this action to recover on a *quantum meruit*. HELD by the Court of Appeal: The claim must fail. Where there is a contract to do certain work for a lump sum, the person who is to do the work cannot sue for the lump sum until he has completed that which he agreed to do. The plaintiff's claim to recover something of a *quantum meruit* fails because he showed no evidence of a fresh contract by which the defendant agreed to pay for the work that had been done.

Bolton v. *Mahadeva* (1972): By a contract with the defendant, the plaintiff undertook to install a central heating system in the defendant's house. The system did not work and the defendant refused to pay any money. HELD by the Court of Appeal: The plaintiff was not entitled to recover any of the £800 agreed.

4. Exceptions to the rule in *Cutter* v. *Powell*

The following exceptions exist to the rule that performance must be complete and total:

(a) *Divisible contracts.* Where the parties are deemed to have intended their contract to be divided into two or more separate contracts, then each separated contract is discharged separately, e.g. where there is a contract for the delivery of goods by instalments, payment is due from the buyer upon the delivery of each instalment. The buyer cannot defer payment until all instalments have been delivered unless there is a term of the contract to that effect: *Ebbw Vale Steel Co.* v. *Blaina Iron Co.* (1901).

Note _____

The question as to whether a contract is divisible or entire, depends upon the intention of the parties. Divisible contracts are sometimes called severable contracts.

_____

(b) *Substantial performance.* According to the doctrine of substantial performance, a promisor who has substantially done what he promised to do can sue on the contract. His right to sue will be subject to a claim for damages by the promisee in respect of that part of the contract remaining unperformed. This doctrine does not apply where entire performance is a condition precedent.

H. Dakin & Co. v. *Lee* (1916): There was a contract by which a builder undertook to carry out substantial repairs to a building. He completed the entire contract work but some of it was carried out carelessly and with bad workmanship. The building owner refused to pay the balance due on the contract contending that there was no liability because the contractor's performance was not complete. The builder brought this action to recover the balance due. HELD by the Court of Appeal: The builders were entitled to recover the balance of the contract price, less the value of the defective work. Per Lord Cozens-Hardy MR: 'I regard the present case as one of negligence and bad workmanship, and not as a case where there has been an omission of any one of the items in the specification. The builders thought, apparently, that they had done all that was intended to be done in reference to the contract; and I suppose the defects are due to carelessness on the part of some of the workmen or of the foremen: but the existence of these defects does not amount to a refusal by them to perform part of the contract; it simply showed negligence in the way in which they have done the work.'

Hoenig v. *Isaacs* (1952): The plaintiff, an interior decorator and designer of furniture, entered into a contract to decorate and furnish a one-roomed flat belonging to the defendant. The agreed price was the sum of £750 to be paid 'net cash, as the work proceeds, and balance on completion'. While the work was in progress, the defendant paid two instalments of £150, and when the plaintiff claimed to have finished he asked for the balance of £450. At this point the defendant complained of faulty design and bad workmanship, paid a further instalment of £100 to the plaintiff and entered into occupation of the flat, using the furniture provided under the contract. The plaintiff sued for the balance of £350, and the Official Referee held that there was substantial compliance with the contract and that the defendant was liable to pay the sum due under the contract less the cost of remedying the defects. The defendant appealed from this decision.

HELD by the Court of Appeal: In a contract for work and labour for a lump sum payable on completion, the employer cannot repudiate liability on the ground that the work, when substantially performed, is in some respects not in accordance with the contract. In these circumstances the employer is liable for the balance due under the contract less the cost of making good the defects or omissions. And where the employer takes the benefit of the work by using chattels made under the contract, he cannot treat entire performance as a condition precedent to payment, for the condition is waived by his taking the benefit of the work.

Per Denning LJ: 'In determining this issue the first question is whether, on the true construction of the contract, entire performance was a condition precedent to payment. It was a lump sum contract, but that does not mean that entire performance was a condition precedent to payment. When a contract provides for a specific sum to be paid on completion of specified work, the courts lean against a construction of the contract which would deprive the contractor of any payment at all simply because there are some defects or omissions. The promise to complete the work is therefore construed as a term of the contract, but not as a condition. It is not every breach of that term which absolves the employer from his promise to pay the price, but only a breach which goes to the root of the contract, such as an abandonment of the work when it is only half done. Unless the breach goes to the root of the matter, the employer cannot resist payment of the price. He must pay it and bring a cross claim for the defects and omissions, or, alternatively, set them up in diminution of the price. The measure is the amount by which the work is worth less by reason of the defects and omissions and is usually calculated by the cost of making them good.'

Note

In contracts of sale of goods which are governed by s. 13 of the Sale of Goods Act 1979, the courts apply the maxim *de minimis non curat lex* (the law does not concern itself with trifles). Section 13 provides that where there is a contract for the sale of goods by description, there is an implied condition that the goods shall correspond with the description. Where goods do not correspond exactly with description there is a breach of this implied condition unless the discrepancy is minute. In *Wilensko* v. *Fenwick* (1938), a discrepancy of about one per cent constituted a breach of the implied condition as to correspondence with description.

(c) *Prevention of performance.* Where a party is prevented from completing his undertaking because of some act or omission of the other party, it would be unjust to apply the rule in *Cutter* v. *Powell*. In these circumstances, the party who has been prevented from performance may sue either for damages or on a *quantum meruit* (as much as he has earned).

5. Tender of performance

In an action for breach of contract, it is a good defence for the defendant to prove that he tendered performance, i.e. that he offered to perform his side of the bargain, and that the plaintiff refused to accept this. In these circumstances, the defendant is discharged from all liability under the contract.

But the following points should be noted:

(a) The tender of performance must be exactly in accordance with the terms of the contract.

(b) Where tender of performance took the form of an offer to make a money payment:

> (*i*) the amount tendered must have been the exact amount due, and in the form required by the Coinage Act 1971, and the Currency and Bank Notes Act 1954; and
>
> (*ii*) the defence of tender must be accompanied by payment into court of the amount due.

Discharge by agreement

6. Discharge by agreement

On the principle that a thing may be destroyed in the same manner in which it is constituted, a contractual obligation may be discharged by agreement. Discharge by agreement may occur in either of two ways:

(a) A contractual obligation may be discharged by a subsequent binding contract between the parties.

(b) A contractual obligation may be discharged by the operation of one of the terms of the contract itself.

7. Discharge by subsequent binding contract

Discharge by subsequent agreement (which must be binding) may occur in any of the following ways:

(a) Where the contract is wholly executory, i.e. where neither party has completed his undertaking:

    (*i*) *Waiver*. A contract may be discharged by mutual waiver. In effect, there is a new contract under which each party agrees to waive his rights under the old contract in consideration of being released from his obligations under the old contract. *See*, for example, *Hannah Blumenthal* (1983).

    (*ii*) *Waiver plus new rights and obligations*. A subsequent agreement between the parties may be to waive the old agreement and substitute an entirely new contract.

(b) Where the contract is partially executory, i.e. where one party only has completed his undertaking, and something remains to be done by the other party:

    (*i*) *Release*. The party to whom the obligation is owed may release the other party by a subsequent agreement under seal. (NB: Such a promise must be under seal because it is given for no consideration.)

    (*ii*) *Accord and satisfaction*. The party to whom the obligation is owed may agree with the other party to accept something different in place of the former obligation. The subsequent agreement is the accord, and the new consideration is the satisfaction. Where there has been accord and satisfaction, the former obligation is discharged. But where the subsequent agreement by which one party consents to accept something different in place of the original obligation is under a threat that he will otherwise get nothing at all, there is no true accord and, consequently, the original obligation remains undischarged. The essential point is that unless there is a new consideration there can be no satisfaction, i.e. there can be no discharge of the previous agreement and no formation of an agreement in new terms. In *Pinnel*'s case (1602), 'It was resolved by the whole court that payment of a lesser sum on the day in satisfaction of a greater, cannot be any satisfaction for the whole, because it

appears to the Judges that by no possibility, a lesser sum
can be a satisfaction to the plaintiff for a greater sum: but
the gift of a horse, hawk or robe, etc., in satisfaction is
good. For it shall be intended that a horse, hawk or robe
etc., might be more beneficial to the plaintiff than the
money, in respect of some circumstances, or otherwise the
plaintiff would not have accepted of it in satisfaction.'

D. & C. Builders v. *Rees* (1965): In July 1964 the defendant
owed £482 13s 1d to the plaintiffs for work done by them as
a jobbing builders. In August and again in October the
plaintiffs wrote to the defendant asking for payment. In
November 1964 the defendant's wife telephoned the
plaintiffs and said, 'My husband will offer £300 in
settlement. That is all you'll get. It is to be in satisfaction.'
The plaintiffs then discussed the problem between
themselves. The company was a small one and it was in
desperate financial straits; for this reason the plaintiffs
decided to accept the £300. The plaintiffs then telephoned
the defendant's wife, telling her that '£300 will not even
clear our commitments on the job. We will accept £300 and
give you a year to find the balance.' She replied, 'No, we
will never have enough money to pay the balance. £300 is
better than nothing.'

When she was told by the plaintiffs that they had no
choice but to accept, she said, 'Would you like the money by
cash or by cheque. If it is cash, you can have it on Monday.
If by cheque, you can have it tomorrow (Saturday).' The
next day, the defendant's wife gave the plaintiffs a cheque
for £300, asking for a receipt, and insisting on the words 'in
completion of account'. So the wording of the receipt was as
follows: 'Received the sum of £300 from Mr Rees in
completion of the account. Paid, M. Casey.' In evidence, Mr
Casey explained why he gave a receipt in those terms: 'If I
did not have the £300 the company would have gone
bankrupt. The only reason we took it was to save the
company. She knew the position we were in.' The plaintiffs
brought this action to recover the balance of £182 13s 1d.
On a preliminary point whether there was accord and
satisfaction, it was held by the county court judge that the

taking of the cheque for £300 did not discharge the debt of
£482 13*s* 1*d*. The defendant appealed. HELD by the Court of
Appeal: There was no accord and satisfaction and the
plaintiff was entitled to recover the balance. Per
Danckwerts LJ: 'The giving of a cheque of the debtor for a
smaller amount than the sum due is very different from
"the gift of a horse, hawk, or robe, etc." mentioned in
Pinnel's Case. I accept that the cheque of some other person
than the debtor, in appropriate circumstances, may be the
basis of an accord and satisfaction, but I cannot see how in
the year 1965 the debtor's own cheque for a smaller sum
can be better than payment of the whole amount of the debt
in cash. The cheque is only conditional payment, it may be
difficult to cash, or it may be returned by the bank with the
letters "R.D." on it . . . I agree also that, in the
circumstances of the present case, there was no true accord.
Mr and Mrs Rees really behaved very badly. They knew the
plaintiffs' financial difficulties and used their awkward
situation to intimidate them.'

The courts had to consider the principle of discharge by
agreement in cases where the contracting parties have referred
dispute to an arbitrator and then have allowed proceedings to
become moribund as a result of years of inactivity and neglect. It
is clear that, by ordinary contract principles, the parties to an
arbitration agreement may by express mutual waiver abandon
their arbitration process. The question has arisen whether the
arbitration agreement and process can be abandoned through
inferring an agreement to abandon. In *The Hannah Blumenthal*
(1983), the House of Lords made it clear that the doctrine of
abandonment of arbitration depended on the formation of a
contract of abandonment to which the normal rules of contract
applied. *The Hannah Blumenthal* concerned the sale of a ship and it
was the sellers' contention that there was a tacit but binding
abandonment of the arbitration agreement by both parties. The
sellers failed in their claim.

Lord Brightman said: 'The basis of "tacit abandonment by
both parties", to use the phraseology of the sellers' case, is that the
primary facts are such that it ought to be inferred that the contract
to arbitrate the particular dispute was rescinded by mutual

agreement of the parties. To entitle the sellers to rely on abandonment, they must show that the buyers so conducted themselves as to entitle the sellers to assume, *and that the sellers did assume*, that the contract was agreed to be abandoned *sub silentio*. The evidence which is relevant to that inquiry will consist of or include:

(a) what the buyers did or omitted to do *to the knowledge of the sellers*. Excluded from consideration will be that acts of which the sellers were ignorant, because those acts will have signalled nothing on the part of the sellers;

(b) what the seller did or omitted to do, *whether or not to the knowledge of the buyers*. These facts evidence the state of mind of the sellers, and therefore the validity of the assertion by the sellers that they assumed that the contract was agreed to be abandoned. The state of mind of the buyers is irrelevant to a consideration of what the sellers were entitled to assume. The state of mind of the sellers is vital to what the sellers in fact assumed.'

On the evidence, the House of Lords decided that the sellers were unable to show that the buyer's conduct was such as to induce in the minds of the sellers a reasonable belief that the buyers had abandoned the arbitration agreement or that the sellers had acted on any such belief.

The principle enunciated by Lord Brightman in *The Hannah Blumenthal* was applied by the Court of Appeal in *The Leonidas* (1985), in which absolutely nothing happened between the parties for five and a half years after the appointment of the arbitrators.

8. Waiver unsupported by consideration

The cases show that equity has been more successful than the common law in the enforcement of a waiver or promise of forebearance. In *Birmingham and District Land Co.* v. *London & North Western Railway* (1888) Bowen LJ explained the position as follows: 'If persons who have contractual rights against others induce by their conduct those against whom they have such rights to believe that such rights will either not be enforced or will be kept in suspense or abeyance for some particular time, those persons will not be allowed by a court of equity to enforce the rights until such time has elapsed, without at all events placing the parties in the same position as they were in before.' Although the principle is not entirely clear, it seems that a concession, waiver, variation or forebearance promised by one party to the other will be enforced in equity subject to proper notice being given to the other party of the resumption of the strict contract provisions. Proper notice will involve the honouring of any time period contained in the original concession, otherwise, equity will insist on a reasonable period of notice. *See Rickards* v. *Oppenheim* (1950) CA and *Brikom Investments* v. *Carr* (1979) CA.

> *Brikom Investments* v. *Carr* (1979): The landlords of certain flats offered leases to their sitting tenants. By the leases the landlords undertook to maintain the structure of the blocks and the tenants undertook to contribute to the cost. Before the leases were executed the landlords stated orally to the tenants' association and to some individual tenants that they would repair the roofs at their own expense. At this time the roofs were in need of repair. The landlords carried out the repairs and claimed payment according to the terms of the leases. The first defendant was an original lessee who admitted that she would have taken the lease regardless of the landlords' statement. The second and third defendants were assignees from original lessees. HELD by the Court of Appeal: **(a)** Per Lord Denning MR, the claim against the first defendant failed because the principle of promissory estoppel applied to all cases where a party to whom a representation or promise had been made had in fact relied on it, e.g. by going ahead with a transaction under discussion; **(b)** per Lord Denning MR, the claim against the second and third defendants failed because the estoppel raised against the landlords was an equity intended to be for the benefit of those from time to time holding the leases; and **(c)** per Roskill and Cumming-Bruce LJJ, Lord Denning concurring, the claim against all three defendants failed because the landlords had waived their right to claim the cost of repairs from the tenants and their assignees. In the case of the first defendant, there was a collateral contract since she had given consideration for the landlords' promise by entering the lease in reliance on that promise.

9. **Discharge by the operation of a term in the contract**
   There is no reason why a contract should not contain a term

providing for the discharge of obligations arising from the contracts. Such a term may be either a condition precedent or a condition subsequent, or it may be a term giving one or both parties the right to end the agreement by giving notice to the other party.

(a) *A condition precedent* is a condition which must be satisfied before any rights come into existence. Where the coming into existence of a contract is subject to the occurrence of a specific event, the contract is said to be subject to a condition precedent. The contract is suspended until the condition is satisfied. Where a condition precedent is not fulfilled, there is no true discharge because the rights and obligations under the contract were contingent upon an event which did not occur, i.e. the rights and obligations never came into existence: *Pym* v. *Campbell* (1856).

(b) *A condition subsequent* is a term providing for the discharge of obligations outstanding under the contract, in the event of a specified occurrence: *Head* v. *Tattersall* (1871).

(c) *Determination clauses.* It is usual in commercial contracts of certain types (particularly building and civil engineering contracts) to include clauses which enable one of the parties to bring the contract to an end before completion. Such clauses usually allow one party to determine the contract on the serious default of the other. Some government contracts allow the government department to determine without showing fault and without giving compensation. Apart from commercial contracts, contracts of employment generally contain clauses providing for the termination of employment by notice given by either party.

There is no presumption that a commercial contract with no express power of determination is intended to be perpetual. In appropriate cases the court will imply a term to empower a party to determine the contract on giving reasonable notice to the other party: *see Beverley Corporation* v. *Richard Hodgson & Sons* (1972).

Discharge by acceptance of breach

10. Breach of contract

The usual remedy for breach of contract is the award of damages, i.e. monetary compensation: but, in certain special circumstances, a plaintiff may treat the contract as having been repudiated by the breach. In such cases, the plaintiff is discharged from further liability under the contract and he may sue for damages.

At this stage, students may find it helpful to consider the analysis into primary and secondary obligations as put forward by Lord Diplock in the *Photo Productions* case. The express and implied terms of contract are a source of primary obligations. These are the promises given by the one party to the other. Where a party fails to do what he promised to do he has failed to fulfil his own primary obligation. Apart from those comparatively rare cases in which the court is able to enforce a primary obligation by decreeing specific performance of it, breaches of primary obligations give rise to substituted secondary obligations on the part of the party in default. The failure to perform a primary obligation is a breach of contract. The secondary obligations to which it gives rise is to pay monetary compensation for the loss sustained (by the party not in default) in consequence of the breach. Lord Diplock called this secondary obligation to pay compensation (damages) for non-performance of primary obligations the 'general secondary obligation'. The general rule is that, where there is a breach of primary obligation, the primary obligation of both parties, so far as they have not been fully performed, remain unchanged. To this general rule there are two important exceptions:

(a) *Fundamental breach.* Where the event resulting from the failure by one party to perform a primary obligation has the effect of depriving the other party of substantially the whole benefit which it was the intention of the parties that he should obtain from the contract, the party not in default may elect to put an end to all primary obligations of both parties remaining unperformed.

(b) *Breach of condition.* Where the contracting parties have agreed, whether by express words or by implication of law, that *any* failure by one party to perform a particular primary obligation (condition), irrespective of the gravity of the event that has in fact resulted from the breach, shall entitle the other party to elect to put an end to all primary obligations remaining unperformed.

Where an election is made under either of the principles (a) or (b) above, the consequences are twofold. First, there is substituted by implication of law for the primary obligations of the party in default which remain unperformed a secondary obligation to pay monetary compensation to the other party for the loss sustained by him in consequence of their non-performance in the future. This secondary obligation is additional to the general secondary obligation and is called by Lord Diplock 'the anticipatory secondary obligation'. Secondly, the unperformed primary obligations of the other party are discharged.

11. The right of election

In the event of a fundamental breach or a breach of condition, the aggrieved party has a right to elect whether to affirm or to rescind the contract. A contract is discharged in this manner only if the aggrieved party makes the election to treat the breach as a repudiation, putting an end to all unperformed primary obligations. The point was made strikingly by Asquith LJ in *Howard* v. *Pickford Tool Co.* (1951) when he observed that: 'An unaccepted repudiation is a thing writ in water and of no value to anybody: it confers no legal rights of any sort or kind.' Where the breach is neither fundamental nor a breach of condition (going to the root of the contract), the aggrieved party's remedy sounds in damages only and there is no right of election: it has been held that if, in such a case, the aggrieved party wrongfully gives notice of his election to put an end to the contract, that notice of itself will be a serious breach of contract and may be accepted by the other party as a repudiation: *Decro-Wall International SA* v. *Practitioners Marketing* (1971). Where, however, such a notice is sent in good faith, it does not necessarily constitute a 'repudiatory breach': the effect will depend on the circumstances and the party's conduct as a whole: *Woodar Investment Development* v. *Wimpey Construction UK* (1980). *See* also *Telephone Rentals* v. *Burgess Salmon* (1987).

If a party having a right of election decides to sue for specific performance he has not, in so doing, irrevocably affirmed the contract: *Johnson* v. *Agnew* (1980) HL.

In a case of repudiation of contract occurring before the due date for performance, the aggrieved party may immediately accept the repudiation if he so wishes: he does not have to wait until the due date for performance: *Hochster* v. *De la Tour* (1853). This kind of repudiation is usually referred to as 'anticipatory breach'.

Where a person has a right to elect whether to affirm or to rescind, he will not be bound by the course he takes unless in deciding upon that course he was aware not only of the facts giving rise to the right to elect, but also that that right existed: *Peyman* v. *Lanjani* (1984) CA.

It is, for example, a fundamental breach for the buyer in a c.i.f. contract to refuse to pay the price on presentation of the shipping documents and if the seller accepts such breach, the contract is discharged and the seller's obligations, so that the buyer thereafter has no right to reject the goods as not conforming to contract description: *Berger & Co.* v. *Gill & Duffus* (1984) HL.

Failure to make punctual payment is not, of itself, a repudiation of contract: but where it is expressly provided that punctual payment is of the essence of the agreement, any breach of the payment provision will entitle the other party to treat the contract as repudiated: *Lombard North Central* v. *Butterworth* (1987).

White and Carter (Councils) v. *McGregor* (1962): a Scottish appeal. The appellant company's business was the supply of litter bins to local authorities in urban areas. It was the company's practice to attach advertisement plates to the bins, for which the advertisers would pay according to the terms of a standard form of contract. The respondent, who carried on a garage business, entered into a contract through his sales manager by which the company undertook to prepare and exhibit plates advertising McGregor's business for a period of three years. The contract form was headed by a notice that it was not to be cancelled by the advertiser and one of the express conditions provided to the same effect. Immediately after this contract was signed, the following letter was sent to the company: 'We regret that our Mr Ward signed an order today continuing the lamp post advertisements for a further period of three years. He was unaware that our proprietor Mr McGregor does not wish to continue this form of advertisement. Please therefore cancel the order.' The appellant company did not accept the attempted cancellation and displayed the advertisements during the ensuing three years. The respondents refused to pay and the appellant sought to recover the sum due under the

contract. HELD by the House of Lords: The contract
remained unaffected by the unaccepted repudiation and the
appellant company was entitled to recover the sums due
under the contract. Per Lord Hodson: 'It is settled as a
fundamental rule of the law of contract, that repudiation by
one of the parties to a contract does not itself discharge it. . .
It follows that, if, as here, there was no acceptance [of the
breach], the contract remains alive for the benefit of both
parties and the party who has repudiated can change his
mind but it does not follow that the party at the receiving
end of the proffered repudiation is bound to accept it before
the time for performance and is left to his remedy in
damages for breach.'

Ellen v. *Topp* (1851): T was apprentice to E to learn three
trades, namely auctioneer, appraiser and corn factor.
During the contract period, E gave up trading as a corn
factor, T refused further performances. HELD: T was
discharged from further liability on the contract of
apprenticeship because E's act had rendered the real
purpose of the contract unattainable.

Hong Kong Fir Shipping Co. v. *Kawasaki Kisen Kaisha* (1962):
The owners of a ship undertook by charter-party to let it to
the charterers for a period of 24 months. They undertook
that the ship was fitted in every way for ordinary cargo
service and that they would maintain her in a thoroughly
efficient state in both hull and machinery. It was agreed that
no payment should become due for time lost exceeding 24
hours in carrying out repairs to the vessel and that such
off-hire periods might, at the option of the charterers, be
added to the charter time. The charterers took delivery of
the vessel at Liverpool on 13 February 1957, when she
sailed in ballast for Newport News, USA, where it was
intended that she should pick up a cargo of coal and then
proceed to Osaka via the Panama Canal. Between Liverpool
and Osaka, the ship was at sea for eight and a half weeks,
and for five weeks she was off-hire for repairs.

When the ship arrived at Osaka on 15 May, it was
discovered that her engines were in bad condition and that
major repairs were necessary. The bad state of the engines

on arrival at Osaka was due in part to the incompetence of the engine-room staff. On 15 September, the ship was once more ready to put to sea and the engine-room staff was by then adequate and efficient. In the meantime, the charterers wrote to the owners on 6 June, 27 July and 11 September, repudiating the charter-party and claiming for breach of contract. On each occasion, the owners replied that they would treat the contract as wrongfully repudiated and that they would claim damages accordingly. On 13 September, the owners formally accepted the charterers' repudiation and subsequently brought this action for damages for wrongful repudiation of the charter-party. The charterers counter-claimed for damages for breach of the charter-party.

The owners succeeded before Salmon J and the charterers appealed. HELD by the Court of Appeal: Neither the unseaworthiness by itself nor the delay caused by the owners' breach of contract entitled the charterers to repudiate the charter-party.

General Billposting Co. v. *Atkinson* (1909): The defendant, a billposter, entered into a contract of employment with the plaintiff company, the contract being subject to termination by either party giving 12 months notice in writing. By the contract, the defendant undertook that he would not, within two years of leaving the plaintiff company's employment, engage as a billposter within a radius of 50 miles of the company's registered office. The company dismissed him without giving the agreed 12 months' notice. He then set himself up as a billposter within 50 miles of the company's registered office.

The company brought this action against him, claiming damages and an injunction to restrain him from working as a billposter within the range of 50 miles as agreed in the contract of employment. The action came before Neville J who gave judgment for the plaintiff company. The defendant appealed and it was held by the Court of Appeal that the company, by dismissing the employee without the agreed period of notice, had completely and totally repudiated the contract of employment and that,

accordingly, the employee was entitled to accept the
repudiation and regard himself as no longer bound by any
of its terms. The company appealed to the House of Lords.

HELD by the House of Lords: The employers dismissed
the defendant in deliberate disregard of the terms of the
contract, and the defendant was thereupon justified in
rescinding the contract and treating himself as resolved
from further performance of it on his part. Per Lord
Robertson: 'The respondent's position in entering into the
contract is a very intelligible one. He says: "I am a
billposter, and I desire occupation, either on my own
account or in the service of others. If I enter the
employment of others, I am willing to give up the right to
trade on my own account to the extent specified in this
agreement. I do not desire to have it both ways." The claim
of the appellants, on the other hand, as now put forward, is
taking him at his word, as expressed in the contract, and
getting his services, they are to be entitled both to deprive
him (against the contract) of the right to serve them and
also of the right to serve himself. It seems to me that the
covenant not to set up business is not only germane but
ancillary to the contract of service, and that, once the
contract of service is rescinded, the other falls with it.'

Decro-Wall International SA v. *Practitioners in Marketing*
(1971): An oral agreement was made in March 1967
between the plaintiffs, a French manufacturing company,
and the defendants, a marketing company. By this
agreement, the plaintiffs undertook **(a)** not to sell their
goods in the United Kingdom to anyone other than the
defendants, **(b)** to ship any goods ordered by the defendants
with reasonable despatch, and **(c)** to supply the defendants
with advertising material. In return for these undertakings,
the defendants promised as part of the oral agreement **(a)**
not to sell goods competing with the plaintiffs' goods, **(b)** to
pay for the goods by means of bills of exchange due 90 days
from the date of invoice and **(c)** to use their best endeavours
to create and develop a market for the plaintiffs' goods.
(The agreement made no express provision defining its
duration and it was conceded by both parties at the trial that

the agreement was terminable by reasonable notice on either side.)

The defendants succeeded in developing a market for the goods which, by April 1970, constituted 83 per cent of the defendants' business. The defendants were consistently late in payment, the delay in each instance varied from 2 to 20 days. At the beginning of April 1970, without warning the defendants, the plaintiffs appointed another company to be their sole concessionaires in the UK. On 9 April the plaintiffs wrote to the defendants contending that the delays in payment constituted a repudiation of contract and that they accepted the repudiation and that the contract was, accordingly, at an end. The plaintiffs brought this action **(a)** for moneys due under the contract, and **(b)** for a declaration that the defendants had ceased to be their sole concessionaires in the UK from 10 April 1970.

HELD by the Court of Appeal: **(a)** The failure to pay promptly and the likelihood of delays in the future did not constitute a repudiation of the agreement as time of payment was not expressed to be of the essence of the contract and the delays did not, therefore, go to the root of the contract. **(b)** The plaintiffs' breach by appointing another concessionaire and their repudiation was not accepted by the defendants. **(c)** In the circumstances, 12 months was the reasonable period of notice required for termination of the agreement. **(d)** The plaintiffs' letter of 9 April wrongfully purported to accept the defendants' alleged repudiation of the agreement, and constituted a repudiation of the agreement by the plaintiffs. **(e)** The plaintiffs should be released from their positive undertakings to supply goods to the defendants but they should remain bound by their undertaking not to sell goods to anyone in the UK other than the defendants, for otherwise it would enable the plaintiff to inflict a ruinous blow to the defendants' business for which damages could not provide full compensation.

Woodar Investment Development v. *Wimpey Construction UK* (1980) HL: The vendors agreed to sell and purchasers agreed to buy 14 acres of land for development. Wimpey were the purchasers and Woodar the vendors. The price was £850,000 with a provision of a further payment on completion of £150,000 to a third party. The contract contained a provision (condition E) by which Wimpey could rescind the contract 'if prior to the date of completion any Authority having a statutory power of compulsory acquisition shall have commenced to negotiate for the acquisition by agreement or shall have commenced the procedure required by law for the compulsory acquisition of the property or any part thereof'.

In good faith Wimpey sent to Woodar a notice purporting to rescind under this condition citing a compulsory acquisition process which both parties now accept was not caught by the condition. Woodar contended that, by invoking condition E, Wimpey must be taken to have repudiated the contract. Woodar further contended that they accepted the repudiation and were entitled to sue for damages. HELD by a majority: that Wimpey's notice did not amount to a repudiatory breach. Unjustified rescission of a contract does not always amount to repudiation. It is necessary to consider the circumstances and the party's conduct as a whole. Wimpey's attempt at rescission was in fact a reliance (albeit mistaken) on the contract condition E rather than a refusal to be bound by the contract. The erroneous and unsuccessful notice of rescission did not amount to repudiation.

Johnson v. *Agnew* (1980) HL: By a contract dated 1 November 1973 the vendors agreed to sell a house and some grazing land. The properties were separately mortgaged. The purchase price exceeded what was required to pay off the mortgages and also a bank loan obtained by the vendors in order to purchase another property. Completion date was stated to be 6 December. The purchaser paid part of the deposit but failed to complete by that date. On 21 December the vendors served notice on the purchaser making time of the essence of the contract and requiring completion by 21 January 1974. The purchaser failed to complete.

On 8 March the vendors brought an action claiming

specific performance. At this point it is clear that they could have brought the contract to an end for breach of condition by the purchaser. Specific performance was granted on 27 June 1974 but by this date the mortgagees of the house and those of the grazing land had sold these properties after exercising their rights to possession. The vendors then sought leave to sue for damages. The purchaser contended that the election to proceed for specific performance was irrevocable. HELD by the House of Lords: In electing to sue for specific performance, a vendor merely elected for a course which might or might not lead to the implementation of the contract. He was not electing for an eternal or unconditional affirmation of the contract. The non-completion was the fault of the purchaser and the vendors were entitled to **(a)** an order discharging the specific performance order and **(b)** to damages at common law for breach of contract.

Federal Commerce and Navigation Co. v. *Molena Alpha Inc.* (1979) HL: The owners of three ships chartered them to charterers for a period of six years. Because of slow steaming, the charterers deducted $47,122 from the hire due on one of the vessels. In retaliation, the owners instructed the masters of the three ships **(a)** to withdraw all authority to the charterers to sign bills of lading, **(b)** to refuse to sign any bill of lading endorsed 'freight pre-paid' and **(c)** to insist that all bills of lading should be endorsed with the charter-party terms. The charterers were informed of these instructions. The owners knew that the carrying out of these instructions would result in serious difficulties to the charterers whose sub-charterers would blacklist the vessels. The owners, having taken legal advice, mistakenly but honestly believed that they were entitled to act in this way. The charterers claimed that the owners had repudiated the contract. HELD by the House of Lords: The breach of contract by owners threatened to deprive the charterers of substantially the whole benefit of the contract, and had gone to the root of the contract since the charter-parties would have become useless for the purpose for which they had been entered: the breach was, therefore, such as to entitle the charterers to terminate them. Per Lord Wilberforce: 'A threat to commit a breach, having radical consequences, is nonetheless serious because it is disproportionate to the intended effect. It is . . . irrelevant that it was in the owners' real interest to continue the charters rather than put an end to them. If a party's conduct is such as to amount to a threatened repudiatory breach, his subjective desire to maintain the contract cannot prevent the other party from drawing the consequences of his actions.'

12. Contracts of sale of goods

Where there has been a breach of *condition* by the seller of goods, the buyer may treat the contract as repudiated and refuse further performance. But the buyer may elect, or be compelled, to treat the breach of condition as a breach of warranty giving rise to an action for damages only. Where a condition sinks to a level of warranty in this way, the breach is known as a breach of warranty *ex post facto*. These rules apply equally to express conditions and to implied conditions.

The Sale of Goods Act 1979, s. 11, provides that:

'11(2) Where a contract of sale is subject to any condition to be fulfilled by the seller, the buyer may waive the condition or may elect to treat the breach of such condition as a breach of warranty, and not as a ground for treating the contract as repudiated.'

'11(3) Whether a stipulation in a contract of sale is a condition, the breach of which may give rise to a right to treat the contract as repudiated, or a warranty, the breach of which may give rise to a claim for damages but not to a right to reject the goods and treat the contract as repudiated, depends in each case on the construction of the contract. A stipulation may be a condition, though called a warranty in the contract.'

'11(4) Whether a contract of sale is not severable, and the buyer has accepted the goods, or part thereof, or where the contract is for specific goods, the property in which has passed to the buyer, the breach of any condition to be fulfilled by the seller can only be treated as a breach of warranty, and not as a ground for rejecting the goods and treating the contract as repudiated, unless there be a term of the contract, express or implied, to that effect.'

Discharge by frustration

13. Supervening impossibility

It is a basic common law rule that a party is *not* discharged from his contractual obligations merely because performance has become more onerous or impossible owing to some unforeseen event. The general rule is that a contractual obligation is absolute, and if a party wishes to protect himself against subsequent difficulties in performance, he should stipulate for that protection. The doctrine of frustration has, however, developed a number of exceptions to this general rule of absolute contractual liability.

Paradine v. *Jane* (1648): The plaintiff brought this action to recover rent due under a lease and was met with the defence 'that a certain German prince, by name Prince Rupert, an alien born, enemy to the King and kingdom, had invaded the realm with an hostile army of men; and with the same force did enter upon the defendant's possession, and him expelled, and held out of possession from the 19 of July 18 Car, till the feast of the Annunciation, 21 Car, whereby he could not take the profits; . . .'

The court held that 'when the party by his own contract creates a duty notwithstanding any accident by inevitable necessity, because he might have provided against it by his contract . . . Now the rent is a duty created by the parties upon the reservation, and had there been a covenant to pay it, there had been no question but the lessee must have made it good, notwithstanding the interruption by enemies, for the law would not protect him beyond his own agreement, no more than in the case of reparations; this reservation then being a covenant in law, and whereupon an action of covenant hath been maintained (as Roll said) it is all one as if there had been an actual covenant. Another reason was added, that as the lessee is to have the advantage of casual profits, so he must run the hazard of casual losses, and not lay the whole burthen of them upon his lessor; and

> . . . that though the land be surrounded, or gained by sea, or
> made barren by wildfire, yet the lessor should have his
> whole rent: and judgment was given for the plaintiff.'

14. The doctrine of frustration

The strict rule in *Paradine* v. *Jane* was first relaxed so as to allow
the development of the doctrine of frustration in the case of *Taylor*
v. *Caldwell* in 1863. The doctrine will apply where, due to some
event, the fundamental purpose of the contract becomes either
frustrated or rendered impossible of performance, so that any
attempted performance would amount to something quite
different from what must have been contemplated by the parties
when they made their contract. Where such an event occurs, both
parties are discharged from their obligations of further
performance. The doctrine applies to all types of contract,
including leases: *National Carriers* v. *Panalpina (Northern)* (1981).
In *Davis Contractors* v. *Fareham Urban District Council* (1956), Lord
Radcliffe said that 'frustration occurs whenever the law recognizes
that, without default of either party, a contractual obligation has
become incapable of being performed because the circumstances
in which performance is called for would render it a thing radically
different from that which was undertaken by the contract'. He
went on to say that: 'It is for that reason that special importance is
necessarily attached to the occurrence of any unexpected event
that, as it were, changes the face of things. But even so, it is not
hardship or inconvenience or material loss itself which calls the
principle of frustration into play. There must be as well such a
change in the significance of the obligation that the thing
undertaken would, if performed, be a different thing from that
contracted for.'

The doctrine will not apply in the following circumstances:

(a) Where the contract contains an absolute undertaking to be
performed in any event: *Blackburn Bobbin Co.* v. *T.W. Allen & Sons*
(1918).

(b) Where the event is clearly embraced by an express provision
in the contract. (But where the event is more catastrophic than
that envisaged by the contract provisions, the contract may be
frustrated: *Pacific Phosphate Co.* v. *Empire Transport Co.* (1920).)

(c) Where the event is such as the parties must be taken to have regarded as a risk inherent in the contract: *Amalgamated Investment and Property Co.* v. *John Walker & Sons* (1976).

(d) Where the event was induced by one of the parties: *Maritime National Fish* v. *Ocean Trawlers* (1935). If it is alleged that the event was induced by one of the parties, the burden of proof is on the party making the allegation.

> *Joseph Constantine Steamship Line* v. *Imperial Smelting Corporation* (1942): A ship was chartered to load a cargo at Port Pirie in South Australia and to carry it to Europe. While the vessel was anchored in the roads off Pirie and before she became an 'arrived ship', there was a violent explosion near her auxiliary boiler, causing damage and making it impossible to perform the charter-party. The charterers claimed damages, alleging that the owners had broken the charter-party by their failure to load the cargo. The owners contended that the contract was frustrated by the destructive consequences of the explosion. There was no evidence that the explosion was due to the fault of the owners. It was held by the Court of Appeal that the defence raised by the owners, that the charter was frustrated, must fail unless the owners could prove affirmatively that the frustration occurred without their default. The owners appealed. HELD by the House of Lords: The onus of proving default lies upon the party denying frustration. Since there was no evidence that the explosion was attributable to the fault of the owners, the contract was frustrated.

> *J. Lauritzen* v. *Weissmuller, the Superservant Two* (1990) CA: Shipowners contracted to transport a drilling rig using one of two vessels, namely *Superservant One* and *Superservant Two*. One of these vessels was wrecked and became a total loss. The shipowners refused to carry out the contract, contending, *inter alia*, that the loss of the vessel was a supervening event which caused the contract to be frustrated. HELD by the Court of Appeal: The loss of one of the two vessels did not frustrate the contract.

(e) Where the event is onerous but not sufficiently grave to constitute a frustrating event: *Davis Contractors* v. *Fareham UDC* (1956); *National Carriers* v. *Panalpina (Northern)* (1981).

National Carriers v. *Panalpina (Northern)* (1981) HL: A
warehouse was let for a term of ten years. Five years after
the commencement of the lease the local authority closed
the road giving the only access to the warehouse. The
closure was expected to last for about two years. The lessee
stopped paying rent and the lessor brought this action to
recover amounts due under the lease. The lessee raised the
defence that the lease was frustrated by the closure. HELD
by the House of Lords: **(a)** The doctrine of frustration
applied to leases and **(b)** although the lessee's business was
severely disrupted, the closure of access was not sufficiently
grave to amount to a frustrating event since there would be
a further three years of the lease remaining after access was
re-established.

15. The basis of the doctrine of frustration

In the *Joseph Constantine* case, Viscount Simon said: '[I]t is well
to emphasize that, when "frustration" in the legal sense occurs, it
does not merely provide one party with a defence in an action
brought by the other. It kills the contract itself and discharges both
parties automatically. The plaintiff sues for breach at a past date
and the defendant pleads that at that date no contract existed. In
this situation, the plaintiff could only succeed if it were shown that
the determination of the contract were due to the defendant's
"default", and it would be a strange result if the party alleging this
were not the party required to prove it. The doctrine of discharge
from liability by frustration has been explained in various ways,
sometimes by speaking of the disappearance of a foundation which
the parties assumed to be the basis of their contract, sometimes as
deduced from a rule arising from impossibility of performance,
and sometimes as flowing from the inference of an implied term.
Whichever way it is put, the legal consequence is the same. The
most satisfactory basis, I think, upon which the doctrine can be put
is that it depends on an implied term in the contract of the parties.
It has the advantage of bringing out the distinction that there can
be no discharge by supervening impossibility if the expressed
terms of the contract bind the parties to performance
notwithstanding that the supervening event may occur. Every case
in this branch of the law can be stated as turning on the question

of whether, from the express terms of the particular contract, a further term should be implied which, when its conditions are fulfilled, puts an end to the contract. If the matter is to be regarded in this way, the question, therefore, is as to the construction of the contract, taking into consideration its express and implied terms.' The implied condition theory of the basis of the doctrine of frustration is merely an extension of the more general doctrine of the implied term, i.e. that the law will imply a term where necessary to give effect to the unexpressed but presumed intentions of the parties. In *Taylor* v. *Caldwell* (1863), which may, perhaps, be regarded as the origin of the doctrine of frustration, the subject-matter of the contract was destroyed: in holding that the parties were discharged, Blackburn J said that the contract was 'subject to an implied condition that the party shall be excused in case, before breach, performance becomes impossible from the perishing of the thing without default of the contractor'.

The most recent theory of the basis of the doctrine of frustration is that the courts have a power to impose a solution on the parties. In other words, that the courts have a power to impose a condition which will discharge the contract. In a 1944 House of Lords case, in which the parties were in dispute as to whether frustration had occurred, Lord Wright said, 'The data for decision are on the one hand the terms and construction of the contract, read in the light of the then existing circumstances, and on the other hand the events which have occurred. It is the court which has to decide what is the true position between the parties': *Denny, Mott & Dickson* v. *James Fraser & Co.* (1944).

16. Factual circumstances in which a contract may be frustrated
Decisions show that the doctrine of frustration may be invoked in circumstances such as the following:

(a) Where there is a total or partial destruction of some object necessary to the performance of the contract: *Taylor* v. *Caldwell* (1863).
(b) Where a change in the law or state intervention renders any attempted performance illegal. For example, in *Baily* v. *De Crespigny* (1869), statutory powers conferred on a railway company frustrated the performance of a covenant in a lease.

(c) Where death or illness prevents a party from performing an obligation of a personal nature: *Robinson* v. *Davidson* (1871).

(d) Where an event which is fundamental to the contract does not occur: *Krell* v. *Henry* (1903). But there must be an absolute non-occurrence: *Herne Bay Steamboat Co.* v. *Hutton* (1903).

Taylor v. *Caldwell* (1863): The defendants agreed to let the plaintiff have the use of the Surrey Gardens and Music Hall on four specific days for the purpose of giving a series of four concerts and day and night fetes. After the making of this agreement and before the date fixed for the first concert, the Hall was destroyed by fire. The contract contained no express stipulation with reference to fire. The plaintiffs, who had spent money on advertisements and otherwise in preparing for the concerts, brought this action to recover damages. It was contended that, according to the rule in *Paradine* v. *Jane*, the destruction of the premises by fire did exonerate the defendants from performing their part of the agreement. HELD: Both parties were excused from the performance of the contract.

Robinson v. *Davidson* (1871): The plaintiff was a professor of music and a giver of musical entertainments, and the defendant was the husband of a celebrated pianist. The plaintiff entered into a contract with the defendant's wife (as her husband's agent) to perform at a concert he had arranged for a specified evening. A few hours before the concert was due to begin the plaintiff received a letter from the defendant's wife informing him that on account of her illness she could not perform at the concert. The plaintiff brought this action for breach of contract. HELD: The contract was conditional upon the defendant's wife being well enough to perform and, consequently, the defendant was excused. Per Bramwell B: 'This is a contract to perform a service which no deputy could perform and which, in case of death, could not be performed by the executors of the deceased; and I am of the opinion that by virtue of the terms of the original bargain incapacity either of body or mind in the performer, without default on his or her part, is an excuse for non performance. Of course the parties might expressly contract that incapacity should not excuse, and thus preclude the condition of health from being annexed to their agreement. Here they have not done so; and as they have been silent on that point, the contract must in my judgment be taken to have been conditional, and not absolute.'

Krell v. *Henry* (1903): By a written contract, the defendant agreed to hire from the plaintiff a third-floor flat in Pall Mall for 26 and 27 June 1902. The defendant's purpose was to view the coronation processions which had been proclaimed to pass along the street below on those date, but there was no express mention of this in the contract. The agreed price was £75, of which £25 was advanced to the plaintiff at the time the contract was made. The King fell ill and processions did not take place on the days appointed, and the defendant refused to pay the balance of £50 according to the agreement. The defendant denied liability and counter-claimed for the recovery of £25, the amount paid by way of deposit. Darling J, following *Taylor* v. *Caldwell*, gave judgment for the defendant on the claim and on the counter-claim. The plaintiff appealed and the defendant abandoned his counter-claim.

HELD by the Court of Appeal: There was a necessary inference from the circumstances, recognized by both parties, that the coronation procession and the relative position of the rooms was the foundation of the contract; the express terms of the contract to pay for the use of the flat on the days named, though unconditional, were not used with reference to the possibility of the cancellation of the procession, and consequently, the plaintiff was not entitled to recover the balance of £50, the contract being discharged. Per Vaughan Williams LJ: 'I think that the coronation procession was the foundation of this contract, and that the non-happening of it prevented the performance of the contract and, secondly I think that the non-happening of the procession, to use the words of Sir James Hannen in *Baily* v. *De Crespigny*, was an event "of such character that it cannot reasonably be supposed to have been in the contemplation of the contracting party when the contract was made, and that they are not to be held bound by general words which, though large enough to include, were not used with reference to the possibility of the particular contingency which afterwards happened".'

Herne Bay Steamboat Co. v. *Hutton* (1903): The plaintiff steamboat company contracted to place their steamboat *Cynthia* at the disposal of the defendant on 28 June 1902, 'for the purpose of viewing the Naval Review and for a day's cruise round the fleet; also on Sunday 29 June 1902, for a similar purpose'. The *Cynthia* was fitted out for this trip but on 25 June the postponement of the Review was announced. On 26 June the plaintiffs telegraphed the defendant: 'What about *Cynthia*? She is ready to start at six tomorrow. Waiting cash.' There was no reply from the defendant. The plaintiff brought this action for damages for breach of contract. Grantham J gave judgment for the defendant on the claim and on the counter-claim. The plaintiff appealed. HELD by the Court of Appeal: The defendant was not discharged from his obligations under the contract by the postponement of the Naval Review because **(a)** the object in hiring the vessel was the defendant's alone and of no concern to the plaintiff and **(b)** the holding of the Naval Review was not the foundation of the contract.

Davis Contractors v. *Fareham Urban District Council* (1956): The contractors tendered for a contract with the UDC to build 78 houses within a period of eight months. The tender was accompanied by a letter stating that the tender was 'subject to adequate supplies of material and labour being available as and when required to carry out the work within the time specified'. A standard form of contract was executed which contained a clause specifying certain binding contract documents. This clause did not mention the tender, nor was the letter mentioned anywhere in any contract document. The contractor took 22 months instead of eight months to complete the houses, mainly due to a shortage of skilled labour. The UDC paid the price according to the contract and the contractors brought this action claiming a larger sum on the basis of *quantum meruit*. They contended that the contract price was not binding either **(a)** because the contract was subject to an overriding condition (contained in the letter accompanying the tender) that there should be adequate supplies of materials and labour, or **(b)** because the contract had been frustrated owing to the long delay caused by the scarcity of labour. HELD by the House of Lords: **(a)** The letter accompanying the tender was not incorporated into the contract, and **(b)** the fact that the performance of the contract had become more onerous for the contractor did not result in the contract being frustrated.

Amalgamated Investment and Property Co. v. *John Walker & Sons* (1976): The defendants advertised a property as being suitable for redevelopment. The plaintiff negotiated for the purchase of this property and the defendants knew that they intended to redevelop it although it was clear that they would have to get planning permission for this. In their enquiries before the purchase, the plaintiffs asked the defendants whether the building was designated as being of special architectural or historic interest to which they replied in the negative. However, unknown to the parties, officials in the Department of the Environment had included the building in a list which was proposed to be listed under the Town and Country Planning Act 1971, as being of architectural or historic interest. The parties did not know this at the date when they entered their contract, but on the following day, the Department of the Environment informed the defendants that the building had been listed. The property now having no development potential was worth about £1,500,000 less than the contract price of £1,710,000. The plaintiffs brought this action for rescission on the ground of common mistake or, in the alternative, that the contract was frustrated. HELD by the Court of Appeal: **(a)** The doctrine of common mistake did not apply because the mistake did not exist at the date of the contract, the property not being under any fetter until a date after the date of contract. **(b)** Listing was an inherent risk of which every purchaser of property should be aware. It could not therefore be said that the performance of the contract that would be called for would, in consequence of the listing, be radically different from that which had been undertaken by the contract. The contract was, therefore, not frustrated.

17. Payment, retention and recovery of money after frustration

Where a contract is terminated by frustration the parties are under no liability for obligations which would otherwise have accrued after the frustrating event took place. The contract is terminated at that point in time. It is not, however, rendered void by the frustrations. Accordingly, at common law, obligations which accrued before the frustrating event are not affected. And money paid before the frustrating event can be recovered in quasi-contract where there has been a complete failure of consideration.

> *Fibrosa Spolka Akcyjna* v. *Fairbairn Lawson Combe Barbour* (1943), HL: The parties entered a contract in July 1939 by which the vendors undertook to manufacture and deliver certain machinery c.i.f. Gdynia. By the terms of the contract (a) if dispatch was hindered by any cause beyond the vendor's reasonable control, a reasonable extension of time should be granted, and (b) one-third of the purchase price was payable at the time of the order being given. One-third of the purchase price was £1,600, and, of this £1,000 only was paid in July 1939. In September 1939 Gydnia was occupied by the enemy, rendering impossible the lawful delivery of the machinery there. The London agents of the purchasers brought this action to recover the £1,000 paid in advance, contending that the contract was frustrated notwithstanding the provision for reasonable extension. HELD by the House of Lords: The stipulation providing for a reasonable extension referred only to a temporary impossibility and not to the prolonged period of impossibility occasioned by the outbreak of war, and that the contract was, accordingly, frustrated: the buyer was entitled to the recovery of the £1,000 paid in advance as money paid upon a consideration which had wholly failed.

In the *Fibrosa* case Viscount Simon LC said of the decision: 'While this result obviates the harshness with which the previous view in some instances treated the party who had made a prepayment, it cannot be regarded as dealing fairly between the parties in all cases, and must sometimes have the result of leaving the recipient who has to return the money at a grave disadvantage. He may have incurred expenses in connection with the partial carrying out of the contract which are equivalent, or more than equivalent, to the money which he prudently stipulated should be prepaid, but which he now has to return for reasons which are no fault of his. He may have to repay the money, although he has executed almost the whole of the contractual work, which will be left on his hands. These results follow from the fact that the English common law does not undertake to apportion a prepaid sum in such circumstances. It must be for the legislature to decide whether provision should be made for an equitable apportionment of prepaid moneys which have to be returned by the recipient in view of the frustration of the contract in respect of which they were paid.' The legislation envisaged by Viscount Simon was passed very shortly after the *Fibrosa* decision in the form of the Law Reform (Frustrated Contracts) Act 1943. The Act gives the court a statutory power to order payment, retention or recovery of money as it thinks just, having regard to the circumstances of each case.

The Act does not apply to voyage charter-parties, insurance contracts, or to contracts to which the Sale of Goods Act, s. 7 applies (s. 7 of the SGA provides that where there is an agreement to sell specific goods, and subsequently the goods without any fault on the part of the seller or buyer, perish before risk passes to the buyer, the agreement is thereby avoided).

Progress test 16

1. In what ways may a contract be discharged?

2. Explain the rule in *Cutter* v. *Powell*.

3. What exceptions are there to the rule in *Cutter* v. *Powell*?

4. 'In an action for breach of contract, it is a good defence for

the defendant to prove that he tendered performance.'
Comment on this statement.

5. Explain how a contract may be discharged by agreement.

6. Comment on the significance of *Brikon Investments* v. *Carr*
(1979).

7. Explain fully Lord Diplock's analysis of primary and
secondary obligations. What bearing has it on the discharge of
contracts?

8. 'It is a basic common law rule that a party is not discharged
from his contractual obligations merely because performance
has become more onerous or impossible owing to some
unforeseen event.' Explain the doctrine of frustration as an
exception to this rule.

9. What do you consider to be the theoretical basis of the
doctrine of frustration?

10. Explain the effect of the Law Reform (Frustrated Contracts)
Act 1943.

11. A, an American exporter, contracted to sell to B, a British
importer, 5,000 tins of cooked ham, to be packed in cases of 50
tins. When the ham was tendered to B, he discovered that about
a third of the cases contained only 25 tins, but the total
consignment was 5,000 tins. B therefore refused to take
delivery of the ham. A wished to know whether he can claim
against B. Advise him.

12. C agrees to coach D for an examination. Shortly before the
date of that first lesson, C falls seriously ill, and is unable to give
any lessons at all. D cannot find another tutor, and he fails the
examination. Consider the legal position.

13. E, a British manufacturer, contracts to make certain
machinery for F, a Ruritanian importer. F pays to E the sum of
£1,500 by way of deposition. E prepares his factory for the

manufacture of the machinery at a cost of £1,200, but before he can begin production, it becomes illegal to export machinery to Ruritania. F now seeks to recover his deposit of £1,500. Do you think he will succeed?

14. What is the connection between anticipatory breach, repudiation, and fundamental breach?

17
Remedies for breach of contract

Remedies

1. *Ubi jus ibi remedium* (where there is a right, there is a remedy)

A right would be of little value if there were no remedy available in the event of an infringement. A remedy is the means given by law for the enforcement of a right, or for the recovery of pecuniary compensation in lieu of performance. A breach of contract by one party necessarily causes an infringement of the contractual rights of the other party. A breach of contract usually, but not always, causes a loss: in any event, there is a right of action against the contract-breaker.

2. Primary and secondary obligations

It is a characteristic of a contract that the parties promise one another that something will be done, e.g. that goods will be delivered, a building will be constructed or that a ship will be chartered. These are examples of primary obligations undertaken by contracting parties. The detailed descriptions of the primary obligations are contained in the express and implied terms of a contract. Except in the relatively rare cases where specific performance is available, breaches of primary obligations give rise to substituted secondary obligations on the part of the party in default. This secondary obligation is to pay compensation (i.e. damages) for non-performance of primary obligations: *see Photo Productions* v. *Securicor Transport* (1980), per Lord Diplock (16:10).

3. Anticipatory breach

Where a party repudiates his contractual obligations before

the time for performance, a right of action will immediately accrue to the other contracting party. Repudiation before performance is due is known as anticipatory breach. Notice that, in theory, there is no breach, for the time for performance has not arrived, yet a right of action exists as if there were a breach. An anticipatory breach may arise from an express or an implied repudiation of the contractual obligation. For example, if A has contracted to sell Blackacre to B, and he (A) subsequently contracts to sell the same land to C, there is an implied repudiation of A's obligation to B: but if A had said to B, 'I shall not convey Blackacre to you according to our agreement,' there would be an express repudiation.

Where there is a wrongful repudiation by one party which is not accepted by the other party, the contract survives and the rights of the innocent party are preserved. There is no duty on the innocent party to vary the terms of the contract, and he can, accordingly, carry out his own obligations under the contract after the wrongful repudiation, and then sue on the contract for the other party's breach: *White & Carter* v. *McGregor* (1962).

Where a contract has been repudiated by an anticipatory breach and the contract-breaker subsequently becomes entitled under the contract to cancel the contract, the damages awarded will be nominal only.

Maredelanto Compania Naviera SA v. *Bergbau-Handel GmbH* (1970): It was provided by a charter-party dated 25 May 1965 that the *Mihalis Angelos* 'now trading and expected ready to load under this charter about 1 July 1965' would proceed to Haiphong and there load a cargo of apatite. The charter-party also provided that, 'Should the vessel not be ready to load . . . on or before the 20 July 65 Charterers have the option of cancelling this contract'. The ship arrived at Hong Kong on 23 June and discharged its cargo by 23 July. She then underwent a special survey lasting two days. On 17 July the charterers purported to cancel the charter-party on grounds of *force majeure*. The owners accepted the cancellation as a repudiation of the charter and on 29 July they contracted to sell the vessel. On arbitration, it was found (a) that there was no frustration of the charter-party before 17 July, (b) that on 25 May the owners could not reasonably have estimated that the vessel would arrive at Haiphong 'about 1 July 1965', and **(c)** that, had the vessel ultimately proceeded to Haiphong, the charterers would have exercised their contractual right to cancel on grounds of delay. HELD by the Court of Appeal: **(a)** The expected readiness clause was a condition of the contract meaning that the owner honestly expected the vessel to be ready to load on 1 July; there was a breach of this condition and, accordingly, the charterers were entitled to terminate the charter forthwith. **(b)** The charterers could not have relied on the cancellation clause to justify their cancellation on 17 July because the right to cancel was not exercisable before 20 July. **(c)** The owners were entitled to nominal damages only for the wrongful repudiation of the charterers because the charterers could have cancelled as of right on 20 July.

M.S.C. Mediterranean v. *B.R.E. Metro* (1985): The plaintiffs contracted to carry rail waggons for the defendants. Prior to any performance the defendants cancelled the contract. The plaintiffs complained but argued at a meeting that they had accepted the repudiation. At a further meeting in 1978 the plaintiffs stated that they would withdraw their claim if offered a further shipment. In this action the plaintiffs claimed damages. The defendants contended that their breach was anticipatory and had never been accepted or that the plaintiffs' claim had been compromised at the meeting in 1978. HELD: The plaintiffs had accepted the defendants wrongful repudiation and had never abandoned their claim for damages.

4. Remedies for breach of contract

There are various remedies for breach of contract. The usual remedy is monetary compensation in the form of unliquidated damages. The other (less usual) remedies may be available according to the circumstances. In all cases the plaintiff must state in his pleadings the remedy (or remedies) that he desires: he may

(a) sue for unliquidated damages;
(b) sue for liquidated damages;
(c) sue a *quantum meruit*;

(d) sue for a reasonable price for goods where the price is not determined in accordance with s. 8 of the Sale of Goods Act 1979;

(e) sue for a decree of specific performance;

(f) sue for an injunction to restrain the breach of negative term.

These various remedies should each be considered separately.

Note
_____
Where a person has entered into a contract after an innocent misrepresentation has been made to him, and the misrepresentation has become a term of the contract, he may be entitled to the equitable remedy of rescission as an alternative to his remedy for breach of contract. *See* 8:**12**.

_____

Unliquidated damages

5. Compensation, not punishment, is the object

Where a plaintiff claims damages for breach of contract, it is the function of the court to assess the money value of the loss suffered, and to award this sum as damages. In effect, this is an order to the party in breach to pay the sum fixed by the court as compensation to the other party. Notice that damages is a remedy to the injured party: punishment of the contract-breaker is *not* the object of damages. Unliquidated damages may be:

(a) *substantial damages*, i.e. pecuniary compensation intended to put the plaintiff in the position he would have enjoyed had the contract been performed; or

(b) *nominal damages*, i.e. a small token award where there has been an infringement of a contractual right, but no actual loss has been suffered; or

(c) *exemplary damages*, i.e. the sum awarded is far greater than the pecuniary loss suffered by the plaintiff. It seems that exemplary damages are awarded only where a banker wrongfully dishonours a trader's cheque. Exemplary damages are not awarded for wrongful dismissal: *Addis* v. *Gramophone Co.* (1909).

6. Remoteness of loss and measure of damages

The rules governing remoteness and measure of damages are contained basically in *Hadley* v. *Baxendale* and the *Victoria Laundry* case. If, by application of the principles in these cases, there are any kinds, heads or types of loss which are not too remote, then the actual loss is recoverable. The problem of remoteness of loss is dealt with by the cases in terms of causation and foreseeability. The relevant passages of the judgments are set out below and should be read with care. In any claim for damages, if it can be established that any head of loss is not too remote, then the actual loss, so far as it can be calculated, is recoverable as damages. A plaintiff is not precluded from recovering damages simply because of the difficulty of ascertaining the loss: *Chaplin* v. *Hicks* (1911); *Jarvis* v. *Swan's Tours* (1973); and *Penvidic Contracting Co.* v. *International Nickel Co. of Canada* (1975). If the plaintiff has made an honest and genuine assessment of his loss and the defendant has not been able to show that the assessment is inflated or otherwise wrong, the court may award the amount claimed.

7. The rule(s) in *Hadley* v. *Baxendale*

The foundations of the modern approach to the related problems of causation of loss and remoteness of loss, were laid in *Hadley* v. *Baxendale* (1854). In that case, Baron Alderson said, 'Where two parties have made a contract which one of them has broken, the damages which the other party ought to receive in respect of such breach of contract should be such as may fairly and reasonably be considered either

(a) arising naturally, i.e. according to the usual course of things, from such breach of contract itself, or
(b) such as may reasonably be supposed to have been in the contemplation of both parties, at the time they made the contract, as the probable result of the breach of it.'

The 'either' and the 'or' produce, in effect, two distinct rules.

Damages awarded under the first rule are sometimes called general damages while those under the second rule are called special damages: *see* particularly *President of India* v. *La Pintada Compania* (1984) HL.

> *Hadley* v. *Baxendale* (1854): The plaintiffs were millers in Gloucester and the defendants were common carriers of goods. The crankshaft of the plaintiff's steam-engine was broken with the result that work in their mill had come to a

halt. They had ordered a new shaft from an engineer in
Greenwich and arranged with the defendants to carry the
broken shaft from Gloucester to Greenwich to be used by
the engineer as a model for the new shaft which had been
ordered. The defendants did not know that the plaintiffs
had no spare shaft and that the mill could not operate until
the new shaft was installed. The defendants delayed the
delivery of the broken shaft to the engineer for several
days, with the result that the plaintiffs were prevented from
working their steam-mills and grinding corn, and were
unable to supply their customers with flour during that
period. The plaintiffs claimed damages from the defendants.

On the question of measure of damages, HELD by the
Court of Exchequer: Where two parties have made a
contract which one of them has broken the damages which
the other party ought to receive in respect of such breach of
contract should be such as may fairly and reasonably be
considered as either arising naturally, i.e. according to the
usual course of things, from such breach of contract itself,
or such as may reasonably be supposed to have been in the
contemplation of both parties at the time they made the
contract as the probable result of the breach of it.

If special circumstances under which the contract was
actually made were communicated by the plaintiffs to the
defendants, and thus known to both parties, the damages
resulting from the breach of such a contract which they
would reasonably contemplate would be the amount of
injury which would ordinarily follow from a breach of
contract under the special circumstances so known and
communicated. But, on the other hand, if these special
circumstances were wholly unknown to the party breaking
the contract, he, at the most, could only be supposed to have
had in his contemplation the amount of injury which would
arise generally, and in the great multitude of cases not
affected by any special circumstances, from such a breach of
contract. For, had the special circumstances been known,
the parties might have specially provided for the breach of
contract by special terms as to the damages in that case; and
of this advantage it would be very unjust to deprive them.

In the present case, the only circumstances here

communicated by the plaintiffs to the defendants at the
time the contract was made were that the article to be
carried was the broken shaft of a mill and that the plaintiffs
were millers of that mill. Accordingly, the loss of profits
could not easily be considered such a breach of contract as
could have been fairly and reasonably contemplated by both
parties when they made the contract. Such a loss would
neither have flowed naturally from the breach in the great
multitude of such cases occurring under ordinary
circumstances, nor were the special circumstances, which
perhaps, would have made it a reasonable and natural
consequence of such breach of contract, communicated to
or known by the defendants.

8. A restatement

The rule in *Hadley* v. *Baxendale*, refined in the light of later
authorities, was restated in *Victoria Laundry* v. *Newman Industries*
(1949). In that case there was a single judgment which contained
a summary of the law relating to causation and remoteness of loss.

Victoria Laundry v. *Newman Industries* (1949): The plaintiffs,
who were launderers and dyers, decided to extend their
business, and with this end in view, purchased a large boiler
from the defendants. The defendants knew at the time of
the contract that the plaintiffs were laundrymen and dyers
and that they required the boiler for the purposes of their
business. They also were aware that the plaintiffs wanted
the boiler for immediate use. But the defendants did not
know at the time the contract was made exactly how the
plaintiffs planned to use the boiler in their business. They
did not know whether (as the fact was) it was to function as
a substitute for a smaller boiler already in operation, or as a
replacement of an existing boiler of equal capacity, or as an
extra unit to be operated in addition to any boilers already
in use.

The defendants, in breach of contract, delayed delivery of
the boiler for five months. The plaintiffs brought this action
for damages. The defendants disputed that the plaintiffs
were entitled to damages for the loss of profits they would
have earned if the boiler had been delivered on time. The

plaintiffs contended that they could have taken on a large number of new customers in the course of their laundry business and that they could and would have accepted a number of highly lucrative dyeing contracts for the Ministry of Supply. Streathfield J awarded £110 damages under certain minor heads but no damages in respect of loss of profits on the grounds that this was too remote. The plaintiffs appealed. HELD by the Court of Appeal: There were ample means of knowledge on the part of the defendants that business loss of some sort would be likely to result to the plaintiffs from the defendants' default in performing their contract; the appeal should, therefore, be allowed and the issue referred to an official referee as to what damage, if any, is recoverable in addition to the £110 awarded by the trial judge.

The importance of *Victoria Laundry* v. *Newman Industries* is that it gave to the Court of Appeal the opportunity to review and restate the principles governing measure of damages. After reviewing the authorities, Asquith LJ, who read the judgment of the court, said: 'What propositions applicable to the present case emerge from the authorities as a whole, including those analyzed above? We think they include the following:

(a) It is well settled that the governing purpose of damages is to put the party whose rights have been violated in the same position, so far as money can do so, as if his rights had been observed. This purpose, if relentlessly pursued, would provide him with a complete indemnity for all loss *de facto* resulting from a particular breach, however improbable, however unpredictable.

This, in contract at least, is recognized as too harsh a rule. Hence:

(b) In cases of breach of contract the aggrieved party is only entitled to recover such part of the loss actually resulting as was at the time of the contract reasonably foreseeable as liable to result from the breach.

(c) What was at that time reasonably foreseeable depends on the knowledge then possessed by the parties, or, at all events, by the party who later commits the breach.

(d) For this purpose knowledge "possessed" is of two kinds — one imputed, the other actual. Everyone, as a reasonable person, is taken to know the "ordinary course of things" and consequently what loss is liable to result from a breach of that ordinary course. This is the subject matter of the "first rule" in *Hadley* v. *Baxendale*, but to this knowledge, which the contract-breaker is assumed to possess whether he actually possesses it or not, there may have to be added in a particular case knowledge which he actually possesses of special circumstances outside the "ordinary course of things" of such a kind that a breach in those special circumstances would be liable to cause more loss. Such a case attracts the operation of the "second rule" so as to make the additional loss also recoverable.

(e) In order to make the contract-breaker liable under either rule it is not necessary that he should actually have asked himself what loss is liable to result from a breach. As has often been pointed out, parties at the time of contracting contemplate, not the breach of the contract but its performance. It suffices that, if he had considered the question, he would as a reasonable man have concluded that the loss in question was liable to result.

(f) Nor, finally, to make a particular loss recoverable, need it be proved that on a given state of knowledge the defendant could, as a reasonable man, foresee that a breach must necessarily result in that loss. It is enough if he could foresee it was likely so to result.'

The following cases are examples of the application of these principles. *See* also *Maredelanto Compania Naviera SA* v. *Bergbau-Handel GmbH* (1970).

Heskell v. *Continental Express* (1950): H had contracted to sell goods to X, an importer in Persia. There was a breach of this contract by H, owing to failure of the carriers, CE, to deliver the goods. Accordingly, H paid £1,319 damages to X, the amount being the assessment of X's loss of profits. H now sought to recover damages from CE. HELD: The measure of damages was £175, being the loss of profit on a sub-sale at the wholesale level of trade. Knowledge of the abnormally high retail prices obtaining temporarily in Persia could not be imputed to the carrier, CE.

Diamond v. *Campbell-Jones* (1961): C-J contracted to sell certain land, well-known to be ripe for development, to D, a property dealer. C-J wrongfully repudiated the contract and

D claimed damages. HELD: The measure of damages was the difference between the market value of the property at the date of the breach and the contract price. The profit which D could have made by developing the property was too remote a loss, because knowledge that D intended to use the property in a particular manner could not be imputed to C-J.

Cullinane v. *British Rema* (1953): The defendants sold a clay pulverizing and drying machine for £6,578. The defendants warranted that the machine would be capable of producing dry clay powder at the rate of six tons an hour. The machine supplied by the defendants was in accordance with contract specification but it could produce only two tons an hour and was, therefore, commercially useless to the plaintiff. The plaintiff claimed damages as follows: **(a)** the loss of capital, **(b)** interest on gross capital expenditure, and **(c)** loss of profit. HELD by the Court of Appeal: Where a machine was in accordance with contract specification, but unable to perform as warranted to perform, the buyer might adopt one of two courses. He might recover the capital cost incurred, less any amount obtained by disposing of the material he had got. Alternatively, he might claim recovery of the profit he had lost because of the failure of the machine to reach its warranted performance. The plaintiff was not able to recover both loss of capital and loss of profit.

For a recent application of the principle in the *Cullinane* case, see *CCC Films Ltd* v. *Impact Quadrant Films Ltd* (1984).

9.   A further refinement of the principles

In 1967 the House of Lords had occasion to consider the principles enunciated in *Hadley* v. *Baxendale* and *Victoria Laundry* v. *Newman Industries*, when the appeal was heard in the case of the *Heron II* (1967). In that case, Lord Upjohn said: 'Asquith LJ in the *Victoria Laundry* case used the words "likely result" and he treated that as synonymous with a serious possibility or a real danger. He went on to equate that with the expression "on the cards", but like all your lordships I deprecate the use of that phrase, which is far too imprecise and to my mind is capable of denoting a most improbable or unlikely event, such as winning a prize on a premium bond on any given drawing. It is clear that on the one hand the test of foreseeability as laid down in the case of tort is not the test for breach of contract; nor on the other hand must the loser establish that the loss was a near certainty or an odds-on probability. I am content to adopt as the test a "real danger" or a "serious possibility". There may be a shade of difference between these two phrases, but the assessment of damages is not an exact science and what to one judge or jury will appear a real danger may appear to another judge or jury to be a serious possibility. I do not think that the application of that test would have led to a different result in *Hadley* v. *Baxendale*. I cannot see why [the carrier] in the absence of express mention should have contemplated as a real danger or serious possibility that work at the factory would be brought to a halt while the shaft was away.'

The Heron II; Koufos v. *Czarnikow* (1967) HL: The respondents chartered the appellant's vessel, *Heron II*, to sail to Constanza, and there to load a cargo of sugar and to carry this to Basrah or to Jeddah at the charterer's option. The option was not exercised and the vessel arrived at Basrah with a delay of nine days due to deviations made in breach of contract. The respondents had intended to sell the sugar promptly after arrival at Basrah but the appellant did not know this, although he was aware that there existed a sugar market at Basrah. Shortly before the sugar was sold at Basrah, the market price fell partly by reason of the arrival of another cargo of sugar. If the appellant's vessel had not been in delay by nine days, the sugar would have fetched £32 10s per ton. The price realized on the market was £31 2s 9d per ton. The respondent charterers brought this action to recover the difference as damages for breach of contract.

The appellant shipowner, while admitting liability to pay interest for nine days on the value of the sugar, denied that the fall in market value should be taken into account in assessing damages. It was held by the Court of Appeal that the loss due to the fall in market price was not too remote and could be recovered as damages. The shipowner appealed to the House of Lords. HELD by the House of

Lords: The case fell within the first branch of the rule in *Hadley* v. *Baxendale* and that the difference was recoverable as damages for breach of contract. Per Lord Morris: 'The present case is one in which no special information was given to the carrier as to what the charterers intended to do with the goods after they arrived at Basrah. In those circumstances in deciding what damages would fairly and reasonably be regarded as arising, if the delivery of the goods was delayed, I think that the reasonable contemplation of a reasonable shipowner at the time of making the charter-party must be considered. I think that such a shipowner must reasonably have contemplated that, if he delivered the sugar at Basrah some nine or ten days later than he could and should have delivered it, then a loss by reason of a fall in the market price for sugar at Basrah was one that was liable to result or at least was not unlikely to result. This results from the facts of this case. It is a question of what the parties contemplated. Even without notice of special circumstances or special considerations there may be situations where it is plain that there was a common contemplation.'

10. Income tax

Income tax is not so remote that it should not be disregarded in assessing damages for loss of earnings in personal injuries cases (negligence) and in cases of wrongful dismissal (breach of contract): *British Transport Commission* v. *Gourley* (1955) HL. In *Gourley*'s case, Lord Reid said: 'The general principle on which damages are assessed is not in doubt. A successful plaintiff is entitled to have awarded to him such a sum as will, so far as possible, make good to him the financial loss which he has suffered, and will probably suffer, as a result of the wrong done to him for which the defendant is responsible.'

Later in his speech, Lord Reid continued: 'It has sometimes been said that tax liability should not be taken into account because it is *res inter alios*. That appears to me to be the wrong approach. Let me take the case of a professional man who is injured so that he can no longer earn an income. Before his accident he earned fees and paid rent and rates for his office, the salaries of clerks, the expenses of running a car and other outgoings, and he would have continued to do so if he had not been injured. Apart from one matter to which I shall refer later, I cannot see why these expenses are any less *res inter alios* than his payments of income tax in respect of his net earnings. Indeed, he could not avoid liability to pay tax, but he might have been able to diminish his outgoings if he had chosen to spend more time and effort on his work, or in travelling in the course of his work. Yet no one would suggest that it is improper to take into account expenditure genuinely and reasonably incurred, or that the plaintiff's damages should be assessed on the fees which he would have continued to receive without regard to the outgoings which he would have continued to incur.' *See* also *Shove* v. *Downs Surgical* (1984).

11. Damages for delayed payment

Where a contracting party fails to make payment on the due date according to the contract there is clearly a breach of contract. In times of inflation, when payment is eventually made, the value of the contract amount is less than it would have been at the due date. The loss of value of money is due to inflation. The question has arisen in some recent cases whether, in a period of inflation, this loss of value as a result of delayed payment is within the accepted principles of remoteness. If it is, then such loss of value can be claimed as damages. The position is not clear. For long the position was governed by the House of Lords decision in *London, Chatham & Dover Railway Co.* v. *South Eastern Railway Co.* (1893), in which it was laid down that, in the event of delayed payment, no interest is recoverable except where provided by agreement or by statute. But in *Techno-Impex* v. *Gebr van Weelde Scheepvaarkantoor BV* (1981), where there had been a delay in the payment of demurrage (a species of liquidated damages in shipping contracts), a majority of the Court of Appeal was able to distinguish the facts from those in the *London, Chatham & Dover Railway* case and decide that, on principle, 'arbitrators should be allowed to award damages for non-payment of money in those cases where such damage was within the reasonable contemplation of the parties under the *Hadley* v. *Baxendale* rule and that such damage could be assessed by taking a reasonable rate of interest'. In *Wadsworth* v. *Lydell* (1981) there was a failure to pay the sum of £10,000 under a contract in which time of payment was expressed to be of the essence. The plaintiff claimed, *inter alia*, the interest incurred as a result of the delay in payment. Brightman LJ said: 'The defendant knew or ought to have known (at the time of contracting) that if the £10,000 was not paid to him the plaintiff would need to borrow an equivalent amount or would have to pay interest to his vendor or would need to secure financial accommodation in some other way. The plaintiff's loss is in my opinion such that it may reasonably be supposed that it would have been in the contemplation of the parties as a serious possibility had their attention been directed to the consequences of a breach of contract.'

The Court of Appeal, finding in favour of the plaintiff, held that the circumstances were such that there was a special loss as a consequence of the non-payment of money, and the loss was foreseeable at the time of the contract and that loss was recoverable as special damages.

The latest development in the law governing the recovery of interest for the late payment of a debt is the decision of the House of Lords in *President of India* v. *La Pintada Compania* (1984). Because of the Court of Appeal decision in the *Techno-Impex* case, the appellants were permitted to follow the 'leapfrog' procedure direct to the House of Lords. The main question for decision was whether, in a voyage of charter, the owners were entitled to an award of interest because of the late payment of freight and demurrage. The House of Lords, in effect, overruled *Techno-Impex* and applied *London, Chatham and Dover Railway Co.* v. *South Eastern Railway Co.* It was held that a plaintiff could not recover general damages in respect of interest if the debt was paid late but before the commencement of proceedings for its recovery. The reasoning of the House of Lords was:

(a) that to allow the recovery of such interest would create anomalies and conflict with the statutory rules under s. 35A of the Supreme Court Act 1981; and

(b) it would be a usurpation of the legislative function to provide a remedy which Parliament had not seen fit to provide when enacting s. 35A.

The House of Lords took a completely different view of special damages, approving *Wadsworth* v. *Lydell*. A plaintiff is entitled to recover any special damage suffered as a result of late payment of a debt, i.e. where it known to both parties at the time of contracting that late payment will result in the plaintiffs having to pay interest on an overdraft.

The essential rule in regard to statutory interest is contained in s. 35A(1) of the Supreme Court Act 1981: '. . . in proceedings before the High Court for the recovery of a debt or damages there may be included in any sum for which judgment is given simple interest, at such rate as the court thinks fit or as rules of court may provide, on all or any part of the debt or damages in respect of which judgment is given, or payment is made before judgment, for all or any part of the period between the date when the cause of action arose and

(a) in the case of any sum paid before judgment, the date of the payment; and
(b) in the case of the sum for which judgment is given, the date of the judgment.'

12. Damages for mental distress

The nineteenth-century authorities indicate that damages will not be awarded for mental distress. These authorities now appear to be outdated in the light of the decision of the Court of Appeal in *Jarvis* v. *Swan Tours* (1972). In this case, Lord Denning MR said: 'In a proper case damages for mental distress can be recovered in contract, just as damages for shock can be recovered in tort. One such case is a contract for a holiday, or any other contract to provide entertainment and enjoyment. If the contracting party breaks his contract, damages can be given for the disappointment, the distress, the upset and frustration caused by the breach. I know that it is difficult to assess in terms of money, but it is no more difficult than the assessment which the courts have to make every day in personal injury for loss of amenities.'

> *Jarvis* v. *Swan Tours* (1972): The plaintiff booked a winter sports holiday described in a brochure issued by the defendants. During his stay at the holiday resort, the plaintiff found that the holiday provided was very much inferior to that described in the brochure. The plaintiff brought this action for damages for breach of contract. At first instance, the judge took as the measure of damages the difference between what the plaintiff had paid for the holiday (£63.45) and what he actually got, and on this

footing awarded damages of £31.72. The plaintiff appealed.
HELD by the Court of Appeal: This was a proper case in
which damages for mental stress could be awarded. The
measure of damages was the sum required to compensate
the plaintiff for the loss of entertainment and enjoyment
which he had been promised by the defendants and did not
get. In arriving at this sum, his vexation and
disappointment could not be taken into account. Damages
increased to £125.

In *Thake* v. *Maurice* (1986) a surgeon was in breach of duty of
care owed to the plaintiffs who were a husband and wife. The
surgeon had failed to give a warning that there was a slight risk
that the husband might become fertile again after a vasectomy
operation. As a result, the wife suffered an unwanted pregnancy.
The Court of Appeal awarded damages for prenatal distress, pain
and suffering to both plaintiffs and damages for the pain and
suffering of the birth to the wife. This latter was not cancelled out
by the relief and joy felt after the birth of a healthy baby.

Damages for anguish and vexation are not recoverable where
they arise out of a purely commercial contract: *Hayes* v. *Dodd (James
and Charles)* (1990) CA. Presumably, where a commercial contract
contains an element of unique personal importance damages may
be awarded for disappointment or mental distress. An example
would be the breach of the contract by a hotel to provide a wedding
reception for an only daughter. Damages for breach of a normal
contract or survey are recoverable only for distress caused by
physical consequences of the breach. Damages are not recoverable
for mental distress which was not caused by physical discomfort or
inconvenience.

13. The duty to mitigate the loss

Where one party has suffered loss resulting from the other
party's breach of contract, the injured party should take
reasonable steps to minimize the effect of the breach. Any failure
to mitigate the loss will be taken into account by the court in its
assessment of damages, and the injured party will be penalized to
that extent.

The principle of mitigation was explained by Viscount
Haldane LC in *British Westinghouse Electric and Manufacturing Co.*

v. *Underground Electric Rail Co.* (1912) as follows: 'I think that there are certain broad principles which are quite well settled. The first is that, as far as possible, he who has proved a breach of a bargain to supply what he contracted to get is to be placed as far as money can do it, in as good a situation as if the contract had been performed. The fundamental basis is thus compensation for pecuniary loss naturally flowing from the breach; but this first principle is qualified by a second, which imposes on a plaintiff the duty of taking all reasonable steps to mitigate the loss consequent on the breach, and debars him from claiming in respect of any part of the damage which is due to his neglect to take such steps. In the words of James LJ in *Dunkirk Colliery Co. v. Lever* (1878): "The person who has broken the contract is not to be exposed to additional cost by reason of the plaintiffs not having done what they ought to have done as reasonable men, and the plaintiffs not being under any obligation to do anything otherwise than in the ordinary course of business." As James LJ indicates, this second principle does not impose on the plaintiff an obligation to take any step which a reasonable and prudent man would not ordinarily take in the course of his business. But when, in the course of his business, he has taken action arising out of the transaction, which action has diminished his loss, the effect in actual diminution of the loss which he has suffered may be taken into account, even though there was no duty on him to act.'

The relationship between measure of damages and mitigation is often very close. As Oliver J explained in *Radford* v. *De Froberville* (1977): 'The measure of damages can be, very frequently, arrived at only by postulating and answering the question, what can this particular plaintiff reasonably do to alleviate his loss and what would be the cost to him of doing so at the time when he could reasonably be expected to do it?' In that case there was a breach of covenant by the defendant to build a dividing wall between adjacent plots of land. It was held that the plaintiff could not be reasonably expected to go to the expense of building the wall before the issue was decided by the court. Consequently, damages were awarded based on prices obtaining at the date of judgment.

The duty to mitigate does not preclude a party from going to the expense of performing his side of the contract after the other party has wrongfully repudiated the contract: *White & Carter* v. *McGregor* (1961).

Where an employee is wrongfully dismissed without the statutory notice to which he is entitled, he is under a duty to mitigate his loss and, accordingly, unemployment benefit will be taken into account in assessing damages. However, a plaintiff is only required to account by way of mitigation of a net gain which he would not have received but for the breach of contract. In *Westwood* v. *Secretary of State for Employment* (1984) it was decided by the House of Lords that the net gain to a wrongfully dismissed employee in benefits received was not the actual benefit he received during the 12 weeks' statutory notice period but the lesser sum he received as supplementary benefit after the premature expiration of the unemployment benefit and earnings-related supplement period caused by the dismissal.

14. Measure of damages in sale of goods

Where the buyer refuses to accept, or the seller refuses to deliver the goods under a contract of sale, the measure of damages is prima facie the difference between the contract price and the market price of the goods at the time when they ought to have been accepted or delivered: Sale of Goods Act 1979, ss. 50 and 51.

15. Contributory negligence

In an action for damages for negligences it was a complete defence at common law for the defendant to prove that there was contributory negligence on the part of the plaintiff. The Law Reform (Contributory Negligence) Act 1945 provided that contributory negligence would no longer afford a complete defence but would rather have the effect of reducing damages to the extent of the contributory negligence.

The relevant provisions of the 1945 Act are as follows. By s. 1(1), 'Where any person suffers damage as the result partly of his own fault and partly as the result of the fault of any other person or persons, a claim in respect of that damage shall not be defeated by reason of the fault of the person suffering the damage, but the damages recoverable in respect thereof shall be reduced to such extent as the court thinks just and equitable having regard to the claimant's share in the responsibility for the damage: Provided that:

(a) this subsection shall not operate to defeat any defence arising under a contract;

(b) where any contract or enactment providing for the limitation of liability is applicable to the claim, the amount of damages recoverable by the claimant by virtue of this subsection shall not exceed the maximum limit so applicable . . . .'

By s. 4, 'The following expressions have the meanings hereby respectively assigned to them, that is to say . . . "fault" means negligence, breach of statutory duty or other act or omission which gives rise to a liability in tort or would, apart from this Act, give rise to the defence of contributory negligence . . .'

In *Forsikrings Vesta* v. *Butcher* (1986) Hobhouse J explained that the question whether the 1945 Act applies to claims brought in contract can arise in a number of classes of case. The judge identified the following three categories:

(a) Where the defendant's liability arises from some contractual provision which does not depend on negligence on the part of the defendant.

(b) Where the defendant's liability arises from a contractual obligation which is expressed in terms of taking care (or its equivalent) but does not correspond to a common law duty to take care which would exist in the given case independently of contract.

(c) Where the defendant's liability in contract is the same as his liability in contract is the same as his liability in the tort of negligence independently of the existence of any contract.

By way of further explanation of the three categories Hobhouse J said that the role of a contract is, by agreement, voluntarily to introduce into the relationship between the parties rights and liabilities, immunities or obligations, which would not exist in the absence of that contract. What legal obligations and immunities are thus introduced and to what extent, if at all, the legal incidents of the common law relationship are displaced, redefined or supplemented is a matter of the construction of the contract together with any terms properly to be implied or inferred. If the contract does not on its true construction disclose an intention to redefine or vary in any of these ways the legal incidents of the common law relationship that exists, those incidents remain. Apportionment of blame, and therefore of liability, has since 1945 been one of these incidents.

Liquidated damages

16. Pre-assessment of loss

Where contracting parties make a genuine pre-assessment of the loss that would flow from any particular breach, and stipulate accordingly in their contract that this sum shall be payable in the event of a breach, the sum payable is *liquidated damages*.

Where the sum inserted in the clause is intended as a punishment on the contract-breaker and is not connected with the amount of loss which could be contemplated by the parties at the time of contracting, the sum is a penalty. Liquidated damages clauses and penalty clauses must be distinguished carefully.

17. Effect of liquidated damages and penalties compared

(a) A liquidated damages clause is binding on the parties. In the event of a breach, the sum fixed and no more and no less can be claimed. No action for unliquidated damages is allowed.

(b) A penalty clause is void. In the event of a breach, the injured party may bring an action for unliquidated damages. The penalty clause is disregarded.

18. Penalty or liquidated damages?

It occasionally happens that contracting parties are in dispute as to whether a sum stipulated is a penalty or liquidated damages. In these circumstances it is the duty of the court to decide the issue in the light of the rules given by Lord Dunedin in *Dunlop Pneumatic Tyre Co.* v. *New Garage and Motor Co.* (1914), a House of Lords case. The rules consist of the following propositions:

(a) The use by the parties of the words 'penalty' or 'liquidated damages' is not conclusive.

(b) The essence of a penalty is a payment stipulated as *in terrorem* of the offending party: the essence of liquidated damages is genuine pre-estimate of loss.

(c) The issue is one of construction of each particular contract, judged at the time of making the contract and not at the time of the breach. In construing the contract, the following tests may be used:

(*i*) If the sum stipulated is extravagant or unconscionable in amount compared with the greatest loss which could conceivably be proved to have followed from the breach, it is a penalty.

(*ii*) If the breach consists only of the non-payment of money, and the sum stipulated is greater, it is a penalty.

(*iii*) Where a single lump sum is payable on the occurrence of one or more of several events, some of which may occasion serious and others but trifling loss, there is a *presumption* that it is a penalty.

(*iv*) It is no obstacle to the sum stipulated being a genuine pre-estimate of loss that the consequences of the breach are such as to make precise pre-estimation almost an impossibility.

In construing the contract, the court will take into account all the circumstances at the time the contract was made. For example, where the hirer of a juke box under a hire-purchase contract terminated the agreement and returned the juke box a reasonable sum stipulated to be payable by way of depreciation was held to be liquidated damages: *Phonographic Equipment* v. *Muslu* (1961). But where a depreciation clause in a hire-purchase contract of a motor car bore no relation to the actual depreciation in value of the car, but was intended only to ensure a certain financial return to the owner, the clause was held to be a penalty clause: *Bridge* v. *Campbell Discount Co.* (1962).

Dunlop Pneumatic Tyre Co. v. *New Garage and Motor Co.* (1914) HL: Dunlop, through an agent, entered into a contract with New Garage Co., by which they supplied them with their goods, consisting mainly of motor-car tyres, covers and tubes. By this contract, New Garage Co. undertook not to do a number of things, including the following: not to tamper with the manufacturer's marks; not to sell to any customer at prices less than the current list prices; not to supply to persons whose supplies Dunlop had decided to suspend; not to exhibit or to export without Dunlop's assent. The agreement contained the following clause: 'We agree to pay to the Dunlop company the sum of

£5 for each and every tyre, cover or tube sold or offered in breach of this agreement, as and by way of liquidated damages and not as a penalty.' The New Garage Co. sold covers and tubes at prices below the list prices and Dunlop brought this action for liquidated damages. On the question whether the £5 stipulated in the agreement was penalty or liquidated damages, HELD by the House of Lords: The stipulation was one for liquidated damages and the New Garage Co. was liable to pay the sum specified in respect of each and every breach of the contract.

It was held by the Court of Appeal that an agreement was a penalty where an insurance agent agreed to repay to his employer all commission earned if he should be dismissed: *Liberty Life Assurance* v. *Sheikh* (1985).

This decision should be compared with *Export Credit Guarantee Department* v. *Universal Oil* (1983) in which the House of Lords considered a clause requiring the defendants to reimburse the ECGD for any sums paid by them under contracts of guarantee in the event of their default. It was held that as the clause required the defendants to reimburse the ECGD for actual loss suffered, it was not a penalty.

It was held by the Court of Appeal in *Ariston SRL* v. *Charly Records* (1990) that a sum payable in the event of specified contract breaches was a penalty if it was payable on minor breaches as well as serious breaches.

A clause which provides for the repayment of capital in the event of the borrower's default in repayment of interest is not a penalty: *Angelic Star* (1988).

Quantum meruit as a remedy for breach

19. The *quantum meruit* claim

Where a plaintiff sues to recover an *unliquidated* sum by way of payment for services rendered, he is said to claim on a *quantum meruit* (as much as he has earned). The distinction between a *quantum meruit* claim and a claim for damages is that the former is a claim for reasonable remuneration, while the latter is a claim for compensation for a loss. Both are claims for an unliquidated sum.

It is usually a matter of procedural tactics whether a plaintiff claims on a *quantum meruit* in preference to a claim for damages.

20. Circumstances where a *quantum meruit* is appropriate

(a) Where there is an express or implied contract to render services, but no agreement as to remuneration, reasonable remuneration is payable. The court decides what is reasonable. The reasonable remuneration is the *quantum meruit*.

> *Upton RDC* v. *Powell* (1942): There was an implied contract between P and the Upton Fire Brigade for the services of the brigade. HELD by the Court of Appeal: Reasonable remuneration was payable by P for the services he had received.

(b) Where, from the circumstances of the case and the conduct of the parties, a new contract is implied, taking the place of their original contract, an action on a *quantum meruit* is available to a party who has performed his obligations under the fresh implied contract.

> *Steven & Co.* v. *Bromley & Son* (1919): There was a contract between S, a shipowner, and B, a charterer, for the carriage of a certain consignment of steel, at an agreed rate of freight. The goods actually delivered to S for shipment consisted partly of steel and partly of general merchandise, for which the freight rates were higher than for steel. S accepted the goods entirely and they were stowed on the ship. S claimed freight in excess of that agreed under the contract. HELD: A new contract could be implied from the facts, and the higher freight could be claimed as reasonable remuneration, i.e. on a *quantum meruit*.

But where no new contract can be implied, the plaintiff cannot succeed in a claim on a *quantum meruit*: *see Sumpter* v. *Hedges* (1898), 16:**3**.

(c) Where a contracting party has elected to treat the contract as discharged by the breach by the other party, he may bring an action on a *quantum meruit*. Similarly, where one party prevents the other party from performing his obligations under a contract, that other party may sue on a *quantum meruit*.

De Bernady v. *Harding* (1853): A principal wrongfully revoked his agent's authority before the agent had completed his duties. HELD: The agent could recover on a *quantum meruit* for the work that he had done and the expenses he had incurred in the course of his duties.

See also *Planché* v. *Colburn* (1831).

Note

(a), **(b)** and **(c)** above are examples of *quantum meruit* as a remedy for breach of contract. The remedy may also be available in some cases of quasi contract.

Recovery of a reasonable price for goods

21. The price of goods

Where, under a contract of sale, the buyer wrongfully neglects or refuses to pay for the goods according to the terms of the contract, the seller may maintain an action against him for the price of the goods: Sale of Goods Act 1979, s. 49. Where the price is ascertainable in a manner provided in s. 8 of the Act, the appropriate claim is a liquidated demand: the remedy is the award of the liquidated sum. But where the price is not determined in accordance with s. 8, the buyer must pay a *reasonable price*. What is a reasonable price is a question of fact dependent on the circumstances of each particular case: s. 8.

22. The action for a reasonable price

The action for a reasonable price for goods is a claim for an unliquidated sum. The remedy is the award of whatever sum the court (or the jury, if there is one) considers reasonable in the circumstances.

23. *Quantum valebant*

Before 1894, when the Sale of Goods Act 1893 came into operation, an action for the reasonable price of goods under a contract of sale took the form of a claim of *quantum valebant* (as much as they are worth). This common law action is comparable to the *quantum meruit* in the case of services rendered. A claim on a *quantum valebant* may still be available today in cases where there has been no breach of contract. Such a claim would arise *quasi ex contractu*.

Specific performance

24. An equitable remedy

A decree of specific performance is issued by the court to the defendant, requiring him to carry out his undertaking exactly according to the terms of the contract. Specific performance is an equitable remedy and is available only where there is no adequate remedy at common law or under a statute. Generally, this means that specific performance is available only where the payment of a sum of money would not be an adequate remedy. Specific performance is, therefore, an appropriate remedy in cases of breach of a contract for the sale or lease of land, or of breach of contract for the sale of something which is not available on the market, e.g. a rare book.

25. A discretionary remedy

The granting or withholding of a decree of specific performance is in the discretion of the court. The discretion is, however, exercised on certain well-established principles:

(a) Specific performance will never be granted where damages or a liquidated demand is appropriate and adequate.

(b) The court will take into account the conduct of the plaintiff, for he who comes to equity must come with clean hands.

(c) The action must be brought with reasonable promptness, for delay defeats the equities. Undue delay sufficient to cause the court to withhold an equitable remedy is known as laches.

(d) Specific performance will not be awarded where it would cause undue hardship on the defendant.

(e) A promise given for no consideration is not specifically enforceable, even if made under seal.

(f) Specific performance will not be awarded for breach of a contract of personal services.

(g) Specific performance will not be awarded for breach of an obligation to perform a series of acts which would need the constant supervision of the court. Thus building contracts are specifically enforceable only in certain special circumstances.

(h) Specific performance will not be awarded for breach of a contract wanting in mutuality, i.e. a contract which is not binding on both parties. Thus where a contract is voidable at the option of one party, he will not get specific performance against the other. This rule is of particular importance in connection with infants' voidable contracts.

The Privy Council has recently stated that in regard to specific performance the court must first consider whether there has been any want of good faith, honesty or righteous dealings on the part of the applicant and then consider whether to exercise the discretion to grant the remedy in all the circumstances of the case, which may include any misconduct on the part of the defendant: *Sang Lee Investment Co.* v. *Wing Kwai Investment Co.* (1983) PC.

Injunction

26. Breach of a negative term

The court has a discretionary power to grant an injunction to restrain the breach of a negative term of a contract even though the positive part of the contract is not specifically enforceable, e.g. in the case of a contract of personal service.

Lumley v. *Wagner* (1852): Joanna Wagner entered into a written contract with the plaintiff to sing in operas to be performed in his theatre during a period of three months. As part of this contract, Mademoiselle Wagner undertook 'not to use her talents at any other theatre, nor in any concert or re-union, public or private, without the written authorization of Mr Lumley'. In breach of her agreement, Mademoiselle Wagner engaged herself to sing at another theatre. The plaintiff brought this action for an injunction to restrain the breach of this negative term. HELD: The court had jurisdiction to grant an injunction to restrain the defendant from performing at any theatre other than the defendant's; it is no objection to the exercise of this jurisdiction that the plaintiff may have a right to recover damages at common law.

The rationale of the jurisdiction to grant an injunction to restrain a breach of contract was explained by Lord St Leonards LC in *Lumley* v. *Wagner*: 'Wherever this court has not proper jurisdiction to enforce specific performance, it operates to bind men's consciences, so far as they can be bound, to a true and literal performance of their agreements; and it will not suffer them to depart from their contracts at their pleasure, leaving the party with whom they have contracted to the mere chance of any damages which a jury may give. The exercise of this jurisdiction has, I believe, had a wholesome tendency towards the maintenance of that good faith which exists in this country to a much greater degree perhaps than in any other; and although the jurisdiction is not to be extended, yet a judge would desert his duty who did not act up to what his predecessors have handed down as the rule for his guidance in the administration of such an equity.'

In *Evening Standard* v. *Henderson* (1986) a newspaper company was granted an interlocutory injunction to restrain an employee production manager from working for a rival newspaper during his contractual notice period as long as the company continued to provide him with remuneration and other contractual benefits without insisting that he perform any services for it.

27. The equitable nature of the remedy

Where a contract of personal service contains a negative term, the enforcement of which would amount either to a decree of specific performance of the positive part of the contract or to a decree under which the defendant would have to choose between complying with the positive terms or remaining idle, the court will not grant an injunction.

Ehrman v. *Bartholomew* (1898): An employee contracted to serve his employer for ten years and during that period not to engage in any other business. The employee left his employment in breach of the positive term and obtained other employment in breach of the negative term. HELD: An injunction would not be granted to restrain the breach of the negative term because, in the circumstances of the case, it would inflict undue hardship on the defendant (i.e. an injunction would force the defendant to choose between starvation or returning to his former employer).

Since an injunction is a discretionary remedy, the court may limit it to what the court considers reasonable in all the circumstances of the case. For example, where a negative term forbad the defendant to engage in 'any trade, business, or calling, either relating to goods of any description sold or manufactured by the [plaintiff] or in any other business whatsoever' the court severed the negative term. An injunction was granted, not to restrain the defendant from engaging in 'any other business whatsoever', but framed so as to give the plaintiff a reasonable protection and no more: *William Robinson & Co.* v. *Heuer* (1898).

Warner Bros. Pictures Inc. v. *Nelson* (1937): The defendant, a prominent film actress, entered into a contract with the plaintiffs by which she undertook not to render any services for or in any other photographic or stage or motion-picture production or business of any other person or engage in any other occupation during the term of employment without the written consent of the plaintiff. The defendant, in breach of this agreement, made arrangements to work for another film company. The plaintiffs brought this action for an injunction. HELD: **(a)** The case was one in which it would be proper to grant an injunction unless to do so would be tantamount to specific performance or to remain idle; **(b)** it would be impossible, therefore, to grant an injunction covering all the negative covenants in the contract; **(c)** injunction granted in restricted terms, namely in terms forbidding the defendant, without the consent of the plaintiffs, to render any services for or in any motion-picture or stage production for anyone other than the plaintiffs; **(d)** the injunction to remain in force during the continuance of the contract or for three years, whichever is the shorter.

Progress test 17

1. Explain the nature of damages in relation to Lord Diplock's analysis of primary and secondary obligations.

2. What is an anticipatory breach of contract?

3. What are:

    (a) substantial damages;
    (b) nominal damages; and
    (c) exemplary damages?

4. What is the connection between 'remoteness of loss' and 'measure of damages'?

5. Explain how the rule in *Hadley* v. *Baxendale* was refined and restated in *Victoria Laundry* v. *Newman*.

6. Are damages payable in respect of breach by way of delayed payment?

7. 'Where one party is in breach of contract, there is a duty on the other to mitigate the loss occasioned by the breach.' Explain this statement with reference to cases.

8. What is a penalty clause? How does a penalty clause differ from liquidated damages?

9. Distinguish between a *quantum meruit* claim and a claim for damages. In what circumstances is a *quantum meruit* claim appropriate?

10. In what circumstances does an unpaid seller bring an action for *reasonable price* for goods?

11. Compare *quantum meruit* with *quantum valebant*.

12. What is specific performance? Explain the principles on which the court awards or withholds the remedy.

13. In what circumstances is an injunction the appropriate remedy for breach of contract?

14. A enters a contract with B, a portrait painter, to have his portrait painted for £250. After the first sitting, B tells A that he does not wish to complete the painting, and that he (A) need not bother to attend further sittings. Nevertheless A persists in his attempts to get B to finish the painting, until the day B is killed in a motor accident. Consider the legal position.

15. A large education authority invited tenders for the supply of school furniture as and when required. The tender submitted by C, a furniture manufacturer, was accepted. The first order from the authority was for 200 desks to be delivered during August. Owing to a breach of contract on the part of C's timber suppliers, D, it was not possible for C to deliver the desks, but C received a letter from the authority informing him that no further orders would be placed with him, since he could not be relied upon to deliver promptly. C now intends to bring an action against D for breach of contract. Consider the factors the court will take into account when assessing damages.

16. E, a jam manufacturer, orders a consignment of strawberries from a grower, F. The price agreed on by the parties is £460. F sends the consignment to E according to the contract, but E refuses to accept delivery, and the strawberries are returned to F. The carrier's charges for this consignment amount to £8, which F pays. F sells the strawberries to another buyer for £420. If F brings an action against E for breach of contract, how much do you think he is likely to recover by way of damages?

17. G enters a written agreement with H under which G promises to deliver certain goods to H on a specified date. The contract contains a term providing that liquidated damages of £60 will be payable by G to H in the event of any of the following breaches:

    (a) if the goods are not of the stipulated quality;
    (b) if the goods are not delivered on the contract date;
    (c) if less than the stipulated quantity is delivered.

G delivers the goods of the right quality, and the right quantity, but one day after the stipulated date. H accepts the goods. H now intends to bring an action against G for breach of contract. Advise him as to whether he can claim £60 as liquidated damages. Assume that the breach caused H no actual loss.

18. There is an agreement between J and K, a house painter, by which K undertakes to paint the interior of J's house. The parties made no mention of remuneration during their negotiations. K completes the job satisfactorily, and then sends a bill to J. J refuses to pay, saying the K's charges are unreasonable. Advise K.

19. L, a shipowner, enters a contract with M for the carriage of a certain consignment of sheet steel, at an agreed rate of freight. The goods actually delivered to L for shipment consist partly of sheet steel, and partly of general merchandise, for which higher freight rates obtain. L accepted the goods entirely and they were stowed on his ship. Advise L as to whether he can claim from M the higher rate of freight.

20. N has agreed to sell O a rare postage stamp for £500. N subsequently discovers that P is prepared to pay £750 for the stamp. If N neglects to deliver the stamp to O, what remedy would you advise O to seek?

21. Q, an actor, has entered a contract with a television company to appear in a series of television plays, to take place weekly over a period of one year. The contract provides that Q shall not, during the contract period, engage in any other work without the consent of the television company. Q has now entered another contract, this time with a film company, under which he is to act in a film to be made during the television contract period. The television company seek your advice as to whether Q can be restrained from acting for the film company. Advise.

Appendix 1
Examination technique

Revision

1. Introduction

All students have their own methods of revising and you will certainly have yours. It is likely, however, that you will benefit by spending a few minutes reading this short guide to revision.

Your revision should have three main aims:

(a) complete understanding of the subject;
(b) retention and recall of the subject;
(c) the ability to explain and apply the subject.

Understanding is the key to both the learning and use of a subject. Thus it is understanding which is crucial to examination success and your revision should be designed above all to reinforce understanding. No matter how much a subject may interest you when you actually study it, learning it for an examination can at best be tedious and at worst boring. You must try to lessen this effect.

2. Revision programme

Tedium in revision is caused mainly by reading the same original notes over and over again . This is also unproductive. It is far better to adopt a *positive revision* programme, one which uses your time profitably and enables you to teach yourself. Your Handbook is the perfect basis for such a programme.

Revision should be done a chapter at a time. Try adopting the following sequence.

(a) *Re-read* the chapter thoroughly.

(b) *Make revision notes.* These can consist of no more than the headings in the text with a very brief note about important principles. Take each note in turn and try to recall and explain the subject matter. If you can, proceed to the next; if you cannot, look in your Handbook. By doing this, you will revise, test your knowledge and spend your time profitably by concentrating your revision on those aspects of the subject with which you are least familiar. In addition, you will have an excellent last-minute revision aid.

(c) Construct a chart for each topic using the headings in your Handbook. Many people respond well to diagrammatic explanations and summaries which provide an extremely quick and efficient means of revision. You need to think how best to construct them and in doing so you teach yourself and better understand the subject.

Two tips: do not try to include too much on each diagram; and do not try to economize on paper. The impact and usefulness of a diagram depends very much on its visual simplicity. The same applies to revision notes.

(d) Prepare concise explanations of key principles that you are likely to need so that during the examination you do not have to think about how to explain something which you probably know well but cannot easily put into words there and then.

(e) Answer the progress tests again. You should find a significant improvement in the number of questions that you can answer immediately. This exercise will primarily test your ability to recall and explain facts.

(f) Plan answers to the specimen examination questions in the Handbook and any others set by the relevant examining body. Planning answers is often a more useful exercise than actually writing the answer out in full. In planning you have in effect answered the question and writing it out is a largely mechanical exercise. If, however, you feel that you need the practice in essay writing, answer some fully.

Read the notes on answering questions (*see* **3** below) before planning any answers.

The examination

3. General examination technique

(a) Read the examination instructions carefully.

(b) Read through the questions and provisionally mark which ones to answer. Take care over your choice. An apparently simple question might have a hidden twist — do not get caught out. Similarly, never decide to answer a question which is in two or more parts on the strength of the first part alone. Make sure that you can answer *all* parts.

(c) Make sure you have selected the right number of questions — you get no extra marks for answering more!

(d) Remember that the first 50 per cent of the marks for any question is the easier to earn. Unless you are working in complete ignorance, you will always earn more marks per minute while answering a new question than while continuing to answer one that is more than half done. So you can earn many more marks by half-completing two answers than by completing either one individually.

(e) Concentrate on displaying your knowledge. There is almost always one question that you are not happy about but nevertheless need to attempt. In answer to such a question put down all you *do* know, and then devote the unused time to improving some other answer. Certainly you will not get full marks by doing this, but nor will you fill your page with nonsense. By spending the saved time on another answer you will at least be gaining the odd mark or so.

(f) Plan all your answers — this is absolutely vital.

(g) If time is running out put down your answer in the form of notes, making sure that every part of the question has some answer — no matter how short — that summarizes the key elements. Don't worry about shortage of time: it is more often a sign of knowing too much than too little.

(h) Check through your answers. A few minutes doing this can eliminate many minor errors and give a final 'polish' to your answers.

4. Techniques for law examinations

When preparing for an elementary law examination you must train yourself to answer two kinds of examination question:

(a) *Textbook questions*, i.e. requiring the exposition or discussion of a particular topic.

(b) *Problems*, i.e. requiring the application of legal principles to a given situation.

You are advised always to obtain copies of past examination papers from your own particular examination authority. Reference to appropriate past questions should be made after reading each chapter of text. Ideally, some questions should be answered in writing so as to acquire practice before taking the examination.

5. Textbook questions

These are designed to test your knowledge and understanding of the subject. Such questions require the statement, criticism or discussion of principles. Here are some points for guidance:

(a) *Read the question very carefully*. In any examination, there are always students who fail to do this. Underline any parts of question which seem to you to be significant. Notice particularly what you are told to do and bear it in mind while you work on that question.

(b) *Make an outline plan of your answer*. In order to do this, you must try to see exactly what the examiner wants. If the question is widely drawn, you will need a widely drawn plan. If the question is narrowly drawn, you will need a narrowly drawn plan. Make sure that the aim and scope of your plan exactly satisfy the question. It is at this stage that you must discard irrelevancies. It is at this stage that you must settle what goes into the answer. Your outline plan will probably consist of four or five key sentences arranged in logical sequence. (Each of these key sentences will probably develop into a paragraph of your final answer). Jot down the names of cases and statutes you wish to cite.

(c) *Write an answer based on the plan*. Stick to the plan and try to set out the answer in an attractive way. Let the plan 'show through' the answer so that your work has an obvious shape to it. If you think that subheadings will help to underline the form of your answer, then use them.

(d) *Express yourself with clarity and precision*. Your style of writing is personal, but in law examinations it is usually best to aim at simplicity. Never use a long sentence when a shorter one will do.

Never use a long sentence when the ideas contained in it can be more simply expressed in two or three short sentences. Keep close to the line of argument in your outline plan. Above all, do not 'waffle': the examiner will always recognize this for what it is, and it will gain you no marks.

6. Problems

These are designed to discover whether you can

(a) recognize the legal principles which are applicable to any given situation, and

(b) apply these principles.

Here are some points for guidance:

(a) *Read the problem very carefully.* Be sure that you have considered all the facts stated. Do not bother how these facts could be proved: just accept them as facts. Notice what the instructions are. You may be required, for example, to advise X, or to comment on the legal position, or to say whether you think A and B are contractually bound. In your answer, you should carry out these instructions exactly.

(b) *Decide what principles should be applied.*

(c) *Make an outline plan of your answer.* The plan should consist of the principles briefly stated. The sequence should be such as to allow you to bring out the relationship between these principles, e.g. where you need to apply a rule which is an exception to the general rule, state the general rule and follow it with the exception; also, where two conflicting rules seem to apply, state both rules. Jot down the names of cases to be cited. Complete your plan by making a brief note of the result when relevant principles are applied to the case in question.

(d) *Write an answer based on the plan.* Aim at a *concise* statement of the rules applicable to the problem. Give an authority for each rule stated. The name of a case is usually sufficient. Do not launch out on a long rigmarole about the facts of cited cases. The examiner is looking for an ability to solve legal problems, he is not trying to test your memory. When your brief statement of the law is complete, come immediately to the solution of the problem. It may be necessary to compare the facts in the problem with the facts of decided cases. Mention only those facts which are relevant to the point under discussion. Do not succumb to the temptation to display the detailed knowledge you have of all the relevant details. The examiner is interested to know whether you are able to identify and isolate the facts which are of legal significance. These are the only facts with which you should concern yourself. Where the answer to the problem depends upon a fact which has been deliberately omitted, you should say so. In this event, you will have to supply the alternative facts yourself, and model the rest of the answer accordingly. This may mean that the final solution of the problem will branch out into two limbs as alternatives.

Appendix 2
Unfair Contract Terms Act 1977

Part 1

Amendment of law for England and Wales and Northern Ireland

Introductory

1. (1) For the purposes of this Part of this Act, 'negligence' means the breach:

(a) of any obligation, arising from the express or implied terms of a contract, to take reasonable care or exercise reasonable skill in the performance of the contract;

(b) of any common law duty to take reasonable care or exercise reasonable skill (but not any stricter duty);

(c) of the common duty of care imposed by the Occupiers' Liability Act 1957 or the Occupiers' Liability Act (Northern Ireland) 1957.

(2) This part of this Act is subject to Part III; and in relation to contracts, the operation of ss.2 to 4 and 7 is subject to the exceptions made by Schedule 1.

(3) In the case of both contract and tort, ss.2 to 7 apply (except when the contract is stated in s. 6(4)) only to business liability, that is liability for breach of obligations or duties arising:

(a) from things done or to be done by a person in the course of a business (whether his own business or another's); or

(b) from the occupation of premises used for business purposes of the occupier;

and references to liability are to be read accordingly.

(4) In relation to any breach of duty or obligation, it is immaterial for any purpose of this Part of this Act whether the breach was inadvertent or intentional, or whether liability for it arises directly or vicariously.

Avoidance of liability for negligence, breach of contract, etc.

2. (1) A person cannot by reference to any contract term or to a notice given to persons generally or to particular persons exclude or restrict his liability for death or personal injury resulting from negligence.

(2) In the case of other loss or damage, a person cannot so exclude or restrict his liability for negligence except so far as the term or notice satisfies the requirement of reasonableness.

(3) Where a contract term or notice purports to exclude or restrict liability for negligence a person's agreement to or awareness of it is not of itself to be taken as indicating his voluntary acceptance of any risk.

3. (1) This section applies as between contracting parties where one of them deals as consumer or on the other's written standard terms of business.

(2) As against that party, the other cannot by reference to any contract term:

(a) when himself in breach of contract, exclude or restrict any liability of his in respect of the breach; or
(b) claim to be entitled:
   (*i*) to render a contractual performance substantially different from that which was reasonable expected of him, or
   (*ii*) in respect of the whole or any part of his contractual obligation, to render no performance at all;

except in so far as (in any of the cases mentioned above in this subsection) the contract term satisfies the requirement of reasonableness.

4.   (1) A person dealing as consumer cannot by reference to any contract term be made to indemnify another person (whether a party to the contract or not) in respect of liability that may be incurred by the other for negligence or breach of contract, except in so far as the contract term satisfies the requirement of reasonableness.

(2) This section applies whether the liability in question:

(a) is directly that of the person to be indemnified or is incurred by him vicariously;

(b) is to the person dealing as consumer or to someone else.

Liability arising from sale or supply of goods

5.   (1) In the case of goods of a type ordinarily supplied for private use or consumption, where loss or damage:

(a) arises from the goods proving to be defective while in consumer use; and

(b) results from the negligence of a person concerned in the manufacture or distribution of the goods;

liability for the loss or damage cannot be excluded or restricted by reference to any contract term or notice contained in or operating by reference to a guarantee of the goods.

(2) For these purposes:

(a)   goods are to be regarded as 'in consumer use' when a person is using them, or has them in his possession for use, otherwise than exclusively for the purposes of a business; and

(b)   anything in writing is a guarantee if it contains or purports to contain some promise or assurance (however worded or presented) that defects will be made good by complete or partial replacement, or by repair, monetary compensation or otherwise.

(3) This section does not apply as between the parties to contract under or in pursuance of which possession or ownership of the goods passed.

6. (1) Liability for breach of the obligations arising from:

(a) section 12 of the Sale of Goods Act 1893 (seller's implied undertakings as to title, etc.);
(b) section 8 of the Supply of Goods (Implied Terms) Act 1973 (the corresponding thing in relation to hire-purchase);

cannot be excluded or restricted by reference to any contract term.

(2) As against a person dealing as consumer, ability for breach of the obligations arising from:

(a) sections 13, 14 or 15 of the 1893 Act (seller's implied undertakings as to conformity of goods with description or sample, or as to their quality or fitness for a particular purpose);
(b) sections 9, 10 or 11 of the 1973 Act (the corresponding things in relation to hire-purchase);

cannot be excluded or restricted by reference to any contract term.

(3) As against a person dealing otherwise than as consumer, the liability specified in subsection (2) above can be excluded or restricted by reference to contract term, but only in so far as the term satisfies the requirement of reasonableness.

(4) The liabilities referred to in this section are not only the business liabilities defined by s.1(3), but include those arising under any contract of sale of goods or hire-purchase agreement.

7. (1) Where the possession or ownership of goods passes under or in pursuance of a contract not governed by the law of sale of goods or hire purchase, subsections (2) to (4) below apply as regards the effect (if any) to be given to contract terms excluding or restricting liability for breach of obligation arising by implication of law from the nature of the contract.

(2) As against a person dealing as consumer, liability in respect of the goods' correspondence with description or sample, or their quality or fitness for any particular purpose, cannot be excluded or restricted by reference to any such term.

(3) As against a person dealing other than as consumer, that liability can be excluded or restricted by reference to such a term, but only in so far as the term satisfies the requirement of reasonableness.

(4) Liability in respect of:

(a) the right to transfer ownership of the goods, or give possession; or

(b) the assurance of quiet possession to a person taking goods in pursuance of the contract;

cannot be excluded or restricted by reference to any such term except in so far as the term satisfies the requirement of reasonableness.

(5) This section does not apply in the case of goods passing on a redemption of trading stamps within the Trading Stamps Act 1964 or the Trading Stamps Act (Northern Ireland) 1965.

Other provisions about contracts

8. (1) In the Misrepresentation Act 1967, the following is substituted for s.3:

'Avoidance of provision excluding liability for misrepresentation.

3. If a contract contains a term which would exclude or restrict:

(a) any liability to which party to a contract may be subject by reason of any misrepresentation made by him before the contract was made; or

(b) any remedy available to another party to the contract by reason of such a misrepresentation;

that term shall be of no effect except in so far as it satisfies the requirement of reasonableness as stated in s.11(1) of the Unfair Contract Terms Act 1977; and it is for those claiming that the term satisfies that requirement to show that it does.'

(2) The same section is substituted for s.3 of the Misrepresentation Act (Northern Ireland) 1967.

9. (1) Where for reliance upon it a contract term has to satisfy the requirement of reasonableness, it may be found to do so and be given effect accordingly notwithstanding that the contract has been terminated either by breach or by a party electing to treat it as repudiated.

(2) Where on breach the contract is nevertheless affirmed by

a party entitled to treat it as repudiated, this does not of itself exclude the requirement of reasonableness in relation to any contract term.

10. A person is not bound by any contract term prejudicing or taking away rights of his which arise under, or in connection with the performance of, another contract, so far as those rights extend to the enforcement of another's liability which this Part of this Act prevents that other from excluding or restricting.

11. (1) In relation to a contract term, the requirement of reasonableness for the purposes of this Part of this Act, s.3 of the Misrepresentation Act 1967 and s.3 of the Misrepresentation Act (Northern Ireland) 1967 is that the term shall have been a fair and reasonable one to be included having regard to the circumstances which were, or ought reasonably to have been, known to or in the contemplation of the parties when the contract was made.

(2) In determining for the purposes of ss.6 or 7 above whether a contract term satisfies the requirement of reasonableness, regard shall be had in particular to the matters specified in Schedule 2 to this Act; but this subsection does not prevent the court or arbitrator from holding, in accordance with any rule of law, that term which purports to exclude or restrict any relevant liability is not a term of the contract.

(3) In relation to a notice (not being a notice having contractual effect), the requirement of reasonableness under this Act is that it should be fair and reasonable to allow reliance on it, having regard to all the circumstances obtaining when the liability arose or (but for the notice) would have arisen.

(4) Where by reference to a contract term or notice a person seeks to restrict liability to specified sum of money, and the question arises (under this or any other Act) whether the term or notice satisfies the requirement of reasonableness, regard shall be had in particular (but without prejudice to subsection (2) above in the case of contract terms) to:

(a) the resources which he could expect to be available to him for the purpose of meeting the liability should it arise; and

(b) how far it was open to him to cover himself by insurance.

(5) It is for those claiming that a contract term or notice satisfies the requirement of reasonableness to show that it does.

12. (1) A party to a contract 'deals as consumer' in relation to another party if:

(a) he neither makes the contract in the course of a business nor holds himself out as doing so; and
(b) the other party does make the contract in the course of a business; and
(c) in the case of contract governed by the law of sale of goods or hire-purchase, or by s.7 of this Act, the goods passing under or in pursuance of the contract are of a type ordinarily supplied for private use or consumption.

(2) But on a sale by auction or by competitive tender the buyer is not in any circumstances to be regarded as dealing as consumer.

(3) Subject to this, it is for those claiming that a party does not deal as consumer to show that he does not.

13. (1) To the extent that this Part of this Act prevents the exclusion or restriction of any liability it also prevents:

(a) making the liability or its enforcement subject to restrictive or onerous conditions;
(b) excluding or restricting any right or remedy in respect of the liability, or subjecting a person to any prejudice in consequence of his pursuing any such right or remedy;
(c) excluding or restricting rules of evidence or procedure; and (to that extent) ss.2 and 5 to 7 also prevent excluding or restricting liability by reference to terms and notices which exclude or restrict the relevant obligation or duty.

(2) But an agreement in writing to submit present or future differences to arbitration is not to be treated under this Part of this Act as excluding or restricting any liability.

14. In this Part of this Act:

'business' includes a profession and the activities of any government department or local or public authority;

'goods' has the same meaning as in the Sale of Goods Act 1893;

'hire-purchase agreement' has the same meaning as in the Consumer Credit Act 1974;

'negligence' has the meaning given by s.1(1);

'notice' includes an announcement, whether or not in writing, and any other communication or pretended communication; and

'personal injury' includes any disease and any impairment of physical or mental condition.

Schedule 1

Scope of sections 2 to 4 and 7

1. Sections 2 to 4 of this Act do not extend to:

(a) any contract of insurance (including a contract to pay an annuity on human life);

(b) any contract so far as it relates to the creation or transfer of an interest inland, or to the termination of such an interest, whether by extinction, merger, surrender, forfeiture or otherwise;

(c) any contract so far as it relates to the creation or transfer of a right or interest in any patent, trade mark, copyright, registered design, technical or commercial information of any such right or interest;

(d) any contract so far as it relates:

(i) to the formation or dissolution of a company (which means any body corporate or unincorporated association and includes a partnership), or

(ii) to its constitution or the rights or obligations of its corporators or members;

(e) any contract so far as it relates to the creation or transfer of securities or of any right or interest in securities.

2. Section 2(1) extends to:

(a) any contract of marine salvage or towage;

(b) any charter-party of ship or hovercraft; and

(c) any contract for the carriage of goods by ship or hovercraft;

but subject to this ss.2 to 4 and 7 do not extend to any such contract except in favour of a person dealing as consumer.

3. Where goods are carried by ship or hovercraft in pursuance of contract which either:

(a) specifies that as the means of carriage over part of the journey to be covered, or
(b) makes no provision as to the means of carriage and does not exclude that means,

then ss.2(2), 3 and 4 do not, except in favour of a person dealing as consumer, extend to the contract as it operates for and in relation to the carriage of the goods by that means.

4. Section 2(1) and (2) do not extend to a contract of employment, except in favour of the employee.

5. Section 2(1) does not affect the validity of any discharge and indemnity given by a person, on or in connection with an award to him of compensation for pneumoconiosis attributable to employment in the coal industry, in respect of any further claim arising from his contracting that disease.

Schedule 2

'Guidelines' for application of reasonableness test

The matters to which regard is to be had in particular for the purposes of ss.6(3), 7(3) and (4), 20 and 21 are any of the following which appear to be relevant:

(a) the strength of the bargaining positions of the parties relative to each other, taking into account (among other things) alternative means by which the customers requirements could have been met;
(b) whether the customer received an inducement to agree to the term, or in accepting it had an opportunity of entering into a similar contract with other persons, but without having to accept a similar term;
(c) whether the customer knew or ought reasonably to have

known of the existence and extent of the term (having regard, among other things, to any custom of the trade and any previous course of dealing between the parties);
(d) where the term excludes or restricts any relevant liability if some condition is not complied with, whether it was reasonable at the time of the contract to expect that compliance with that condition would be practicable;
(e) whether the goods were manufactured, processed or adapted to the special order of the customer.

Amendments to the Unfair Contract Terms Act 1977

1. The Sale of Goods Act 1979
Schedule 3, paras. 19–22, provides that:

19. In section 6 of the Unfair Contract Terms Act 1977 —

(a) in subsection (1) (*a*) for 'section 12 of the Sale of Goods Act 1893' substitute 'section 12 of the Sale of Goods Act 1979';
(b) in subsection (2) (*a*) for 'section 13, 14 or 15 of the 1893 Act' substitute 'section 13, 14 or 15 of the 1979 Act'.

20. In Section 14 of the Unfair Contract Terms Act 1977, in the definition of 'goods', for 'the Sale of Goods Act 1893' substitute 'the Sale of Goods Act 1979'.

21. In section 20(1)(*a*) and (2)(*a*) of the Unfair Contract Terms Act 1977 for '1893' substitute (in each case) '1979'.

22. In section 25(1) of the Unfair Contract Terms Act 1977, in the definition of 'goods', for 'the Sale of Goods Act 1893' substitute 'the Sale of Goods Act 1979'.

2. The Supply of Goods and Services Act 1982
Section 17(2) provides that:

'(2) The following subsection shall be inserted after section 7(3) of the 1977 Act:
"(3A) Liability for breach of the obligations arising under section 2 of the Supply of Goods and Services Act 1982 (implied

terms about title etc. in certain contracts for the transfer of the property in goods) cannot be excluded or restricted by reference to any such term."

(3) In consequence of subsection (2) above, in section 7(4) of the 1977 Act, after "cannot" there shall be inserted "(in a case to which subsection (3A) above does not apply".'

3. The Occupiers' Liability Act 1984
Section 2 provides that:

'At the end of section 1(3) of the Unfair Contract Terms Act 1977 (which defines the liability, called "business liability", the exclusion or restriction of which is controlled by virtue of that Act) there is added —

"but liability of an occupier of premises for breach of an obligation or duty towards a person obtaining access to the premises for recreational or educational purposes, being liability for loss or damage suffered by reason of the dangerous state of the premises, is not a business liability of the occupier unless granting that person such access for the purposes concerned falls within the business purposes of the occupier".'

Appendix 3
Matters affecting the validity of a contract: summary

1. Vitiating factors

The validity of a contract may be impaired in any of the following circumstances:

(a) Where the element of agreement is impaired by:
- (*i*) *mistake*, i.e. where one party, or both parties, entered the contract under a misapprehension; or,
- (*ii*) *misrepresentation*, i.e. where one party was induced to enter the agreement partly by a false representation of the other party, the false representation not being a term of the contract; or,
- (*iii*) *duress or undue influence*, i.e. direct or subtle coercion brought to bear on a contracting party.

(b) Where one or more of the contracting parties has not full contractual capacity.

(c) Where the contract is illegal.

(d) Where the contract is partly or wholly void under a statute.

(e) Where a contract is partly or wholly void at common law as being against public policy.

(f) Where the contract is of a class requiring formalities, and these are absent.

2. The impaired contract

Where any vitiating factor is present in a contract, the legal consequences will vary according to the circumstances. The problems involved are considered in Chapters 7–13. It will be seen that a contract may be:

(a) *Void*, i.e. an absolute nullity.

(b) *Voidable*, i.e. a contract which gives rise to legal consequences, but may be set aside, or rescinded.

(c) *Illegal*, i.e. one upon which no action may be taken except in very special circumstances.

(d) *Unenforceable*, i.e. a good contract, but one upon which a plaintiff may not bring an action at law because of the absence of written evidence where this is required, or because of some defect in the contractual capacity of the defendant.

Index